# THE PARROTS OF SOUTH AMERICA

# THE PARROTS OF SOUTH AMERICA

ROSEMARY LOW

JOHN GIFFORD LTD.
*LONDON*

*First published in Great Britain 1972*
*by John Gifford Ltd, 125 Charing Cross Road,*
*London WC2H 0EB*

ISBN 07071 0063 1

*Printed in Great Britain by Bristol Typesetting Co. Ltd*
*Barton Manor - St Philips Bristol*
*Colour printed by Hope Printers, London*
*Books bound by James Burn, Esher*

For Bob, George and Thomas

## ACKNOWLEDGEMENTS

I AM indebted to George A. Smith and T. R. M. Brosset for their kindness and assistance. Both provided valuable sources of published information; G. A. Smith also read the manuscript and offered much helpful advice.

The photographs which illustrate the book are the work of R. H. Grantham (1, 2, 3, 5, 11, 14, 16, 17, 18, 19, 21, 25, 29, 30, 31, 32, 33, 36, 37, 40, 41, 42, and cover) and T. R. M. Brosset (4, 6, 7, 8, 9, 10, 12, 13, 15, 20, 22, 23, 24, 27, 28, 34, 35, 38, 39). Again I am indebted to them for their endless patience in producing photographs of such a high standard.

I should also like to thank the many aviculturists who provided information at my request; the Avicultural Society and the Foreign Bird League for granting permission to quote from their publications, and the British Museum (Natural History) for the use of its skin collection for study purposes.

## CONTENTS

# INTRODUCTION

KEEPING parrot-like birds has a fascination which is difficult to explain; it is not of the same kind as keeping other birds. A fairly new recruit to its ranks made what I considered a rather accurate observation when he described it as 'a strange kind of madness'!

In the past, and even now, most of the parrots kept for breeding have been Australian species, mainly because they are comparatively free breeders and will bring some return – often a good one – on the original outlay. During recent years, however, more and more aviculturists have discovered that the parrots from South and Central America, the neo-tropical species, are equally worthy of attention and that, given the right conditions, they will rear young. But not enough attempts have been made to breed from these birds.

Time may be running out. Many countries throughout the world have introduced legislation to prohibit the export of their native birds. In some countries importation is also forbidden – and that may soon be the situation in Britain. It could happen, not so far in the future, that the only birds available to aviculturists will be aviary-bred ones.

The future of many Australian psittacines in aviaries is assured; that of nearly all neo-tropical parrots is not. The latter are, in my opinion, the most interesting subjects and deserve a much larger following. Many show great character and intelligence; their disposition is quite different from, and much more confiding than, that of the popular Australian parrakeets, whose aloofness prevents any real contact.

Others, like myself, having discovered the parrots of South and Central America to be completely captivating, will also find that they have been rather neglected in avicultural literature. This book has therefore been written hoping that it will provide a useful guide to their management and identification. Every species is described.

Central and South America is geographically so vast and ecologically so varied that the scientific study of its birds is far from complete. Some which are now given specific status, will with further knowledge and collection of intermediate specimens, almost certainly prove to be not distinct but rather geographical races or sub-species. Where I differ from the majority of authors in believing 'species' to be nothing more than sub-species I have placed in brackets the specific name which I believe should be attributed to the species.

America has a greater number of parrot species (using Peters' classification, 144, as opposed to 189 for the rest of the world) than any other continent, although the birds do not show such a diversity of form as do those from Australia, for example. The majority are found in the northern part of South America but they actually range from south-eastern Arizona in the USA, where the Thick-billed Parrot occasionally appears in the pine forests, to Tierra Fuego, in the southernmost part of South America, where the Magellan Conure is found.

For easier reference four sub-headings are used under each species. *Descriptions* were made from life or from skins in the British Museum; in some instances it was necessary to refer to the literature. Where all sources of reference were lacking the heading has been omitted.

It should be borne in mind that in many species, especially those with a wide distribution, there is considerable individual variation in the plumage – most noticeably in *Amazona* and *Pionus* parrots.

Details of mutations are given under this heading.

*Distribution.* The range covered by any species is not precisely defined because of lack of knowledge. Peters' *Check List of Birds of the World* has formed the basis of this section, with additional material from more modern sources such as de Schauensee's *The Species of Birds of South America.*

*Remarks.* This heading includes general observations, such as availability of species. In the case of rarely imported ones, I have mentioned where individuals can be seen.

*Breeding Records.* Where this heading has been omitted no published records could be found. Inevitably, many species in addition to those listed must have been bred, either by those who have no interest in recording their successes or who are perhaps unaware of the existence of specialist societies.

The numbers in brackets throughout the text, following the names of authors, relate to the publications numbered in the bibliography.

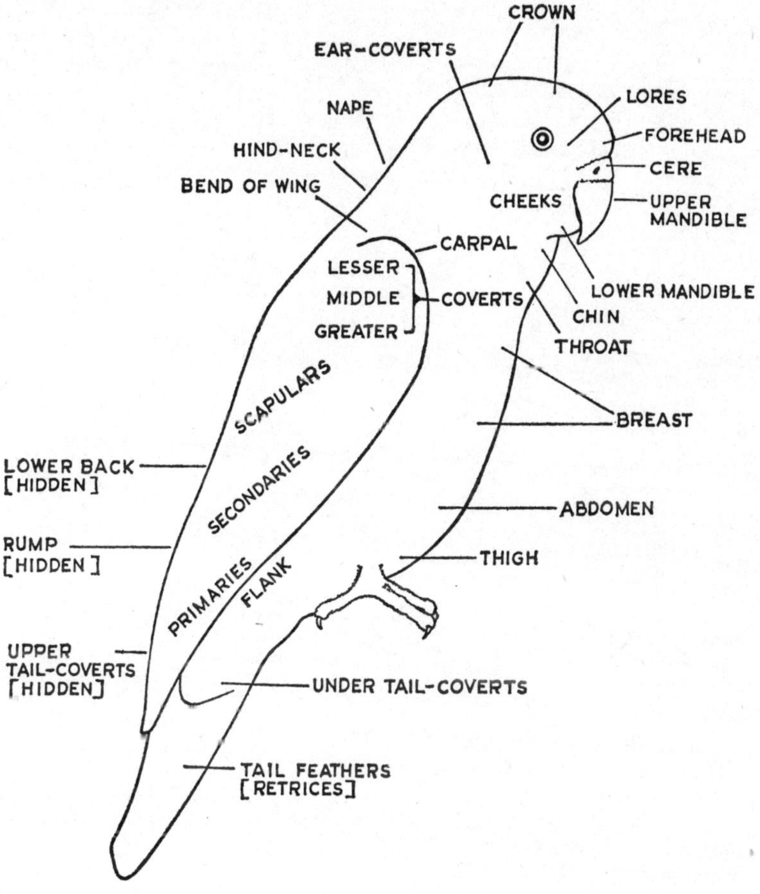


TOPOGRAPHY OF A PARROT

CHAPTER I

# PURCHASE AND ACCOMMODATION

BUYING a parrot, especially a newly-imported one, is something which requires a certain amount of experience. The intending purchaser of a first parrot should enlist the aid of someone with a knowledge of these birds. In this way the more obvious pitfalls will be avoided. This applies, in particular, to the prospective pet owner, since almost all those buying parrot-like birds for aviaries will have had some experience with smaller foreign birds.

Needless to say, only healthy, vigorous birds should be bought. Feather condition is almost immaterial in newly-imported parrots. Often the flight feathers, or even part of the tail, have been cut. The plumage looks dry and lacks the sheen and brightness of aviary-moulted specimens, which is only to be expected. After a moult the feathering will look quite different.

Health is most important of all; the bird must be bright-eyed and take an interest in what is going on around it. Those with a sleepy appearance, or which are hunched across the perch, should be avoided. Always look at the nostrils; they should be clear and dry, for a watery discharge can mean that the bird is seriously ill. The head feathers should be sleek, not ruffled and, when the parrot is resting with its head in its wing only one foot should be on the perch. Very young birds sometimes rest with both feet on the perch but it is unusual for a fit adult to do so. A sick bird invariably does. Alertness, however, is the key factor; a bird that is active and alert is a healthy one, but those that are *excessively* nervous should be avoided at all costs.

Examination of a parrot's droppings will reveal little; they may be brown or green, solid or fairly fluid, depending on the food provided. Droppings of a very watery nature indicate that something is seriously wrong, probably a kidney disorder. Soiled feathers surrounding the vent are an indication of enteritis. One should feel the breast bone of newly imported birds, especially Amazons. If this is very prominent the bird is under-nourished or, in extreme cases, wasting away and unlikely to survive long.

Always take note of the food that the parrot has been eating and, if possible, obtain some. Some parrots are reluctant to sample anything with which they are not familiar. A *Pionus* parrot of mine, while in the temporary care of a friend, at first refused to sample striped sunflower seed because I had offered it white sunflower only! Also notice the position of the food pots; some parrots would stubbornly starve rather than eat from an aviary feeding shelf. Newly acquired birds should therefore be given a container of food, placed at the end of the perch. Additional food can be put on the feeding shelf in the aviary or, for small species in cages, on the floor. Millet sprays will often encourage a nervous bird to feed.

I have often been asked by pet owners how to determine a parrot's age. Once adult plumage has been attained there is no way of doing this. Examination of the feet or beak will usually provide an indication of whether the bird is very young or very old. In very young parrots the colour of the eye is darker or less well defined than in adults and in those that have recently fledged the beak may also be a different colour.

Whether a new purchase is to be kept in a cage or is destined for an aviary I think it is advisable to keep it in a cage under close observation for a few days. One can then see exactly what and how much it is eating; also, if any disease is developing, this will not be passed on to existing stock.

I believe that the best time of day to place a bird in new surroundings is not during the early morning, as is usually recommended, but about midday. By this time it will have had a good feed and if it is too nervous to eat during its first day no harm will be done. On occasions a nervous bird may eat only a small amount for three or four days.

When a parrot-like bird is introduced to an aviary containing one or several other birds their reaction should be closely observed during the whole day. Should any trouble arise one is then at hand to intervene. Some birds which are kept in colonies have a very definite order among their ranks; this is known as the 'pecking order'. When a new bird is introduced it will be bullied and chased mercilessly to establish its position.

This is very noticeable in my colony of *Pyrrhura* conures, consisting mainly of Red-bellied and Pearly Conures. When I introduce a new bird I know that it will be chased until it drops exhausted to the ground, for the established members of the colony will try to prevent the newcomer from perching. I have never known any harm to be caused on introduction, but I always watch them very carefully.

In an experiment with Tovi Parrakeets, Dennis Power (30a) found that a newcomer to a flock is attacked because of its behaviour, i.e. it is passive and silent, being unfamiliar with its surroundings. If it behaved as though on familiar territory and was normally active it would not be attacked. Power tested the theory that prior association is necessary for peaceful relationships by disguising birds familiar and unfamiliar to the flock with paint. The orange chin spot was concealed with water paint blended to match the colour of the body feathers; thus the distinguishing feature of the species was removed. The bird was then released into the aviary to which it belonged, attracted no attention, and was soon reunited with its mate. On the following day the experiment was repeated using two birds from the flock and similar results were observed. In another experiment, a Tovi was given a bright yellow forehead so that it was almost identical with a Tui Parrakeet. Again, the flock accepted it, proving that once relationships are established within a flock and between mates the way a bird behaves seems to be more important than coloration with regard to individual recognition and acceptance.

Power also found that aggressive encounters between birds far apart in the pecking order were infrequent, apparently because subordinate birds learn to recognise and avoid more dominant individuals. Between flock members of more equal rank the order is maintained on the basis of which bird has won the majority of aggressive encounters with the other. Nesting pairs are socially superior to non-nesting birds and single birds are usually more successful in aggressive encounters if their mates are nearby. I have often noticed that a bird which would hesitate to attack another if it were on its own will do so without fear with the assistance of its partner.

*Accommodation* for birds is a subject which could be written about at great length, and one which has been covered in numerous books of a more general nature. Since few aviculturists take up parrot-like birds without experience of keeping smaller species I will not go into details of aviary construction and maintenance.

Those who specialise in psittacines require an entirely different layout from those who keep mixed collections, since, with rare exceptions, they must be housed one pair per aviary. This is essential if breeding is the aim. A design which is universally accepted is the range of aviaries with a covered corridor behind the shelter part of the aviary. It has many advantages. The birds can be fed from the corridor, eliminating the need to enter the aviary. In winter the birds can be fed and inspected from the comparative comfort of the corridor. It also acts as a safety passage if a bird escapes through the feeding door.

The back of the shelter, which is reached from the corridor, should have a removable frame for easy cleaning. In the front of the shelter, fairly high, the pop-hole (entrance hole) is placed, giving the occupants access to the flight. The floor of the shelter can be only 3ft from the ground if the space below is required for storage of food, cages, etc. Many small birds prefer a shelter of this type to one which extends to ground level. To encourage the birds to use the shelter for roosting, the perch inside must be higher than any perch in the aviary flight. A ledge built near the top of the shelter will prove irresistible to such birds as conures.

Yet another advantage of this type of design is that it is easily added to. As collections have a habit of expanding to a size far beyond that originally envisaged, this is an important point. The number of birds that make up a collection is of vital consideration with parrot-like birds, particularly the larger ones. The fewer kept, the greater the pleasure that each individual will give, because more time will be available for the attention of each one. It is far better to have a small collection which leaves one with a little time to spare than a large collection which is completely time consuming. If one has too many birds their care may cease to be a pleasure and simply become a chore.

An important consideration in aviary construction is the wire-netting or wire-mesh used. As most parrots have strong beaks the material used should be of the best quality that can be afforded. A strong gauge will last longer than a finer and less expensive one. It will be less easily destroyed, and will need renewing less often. This, in itself, is a good reason for using a strong gauge, for rewiring aviaries is a tedious job. Before netting or rectangular mesh is used it should be painted black or covered with bitumen, which will add several years to its life, and has the added advantage of enabling one to see the birds more clearly. Rectangular mesh is preferable to wire netting, as it is less easily destroyed. For large birds with strong beaks such as macaws, it is normally necessary to use chain link which is, unfortunately, very expensive.

Macaws and parrots never look more attractive than when at liberty but if their freedom is unintentional they are extremely difficult to recapture! Neglected or unsuitable wire-mesh can therefore prove very expensive. Another mistake which can prove costly is failure to double-wire the aviaries, which the inexperienced may believe to be an unnecessary expense. Parrot-like birds can inflict serious injuries – slit tongues, remove nails or even tear off another bird's mandible – through even the smallest mesh. Recently fledged youngsters are especially vulnerable, as they tend to spend much time clinging to the wire.

It is therefore wise to have two sections of wire-netting, approximately 2in apart, between each aviary. The end aviaries should be double-wired to deter cats. If the latter are troublesome, a false roof consisting of a wide mesh wire, 2in mesh, for example, will deter them from walking on the roof of the flights.

I find that parrots soon get used to the presence of cats which make no attempt to harm them; the large birds watch them carefully but are seldom alarmed by them. Cats in the vicinity of aviaries are an asset where mice are present. It is always difficult to use poison in aviaries, and great care must be taken to ensure that the birds do not have access to it. With very inquisitive and active species this often presents a problem. Spring traps are obviously out of the question for the same reason.

One of the most important points to consider is the material to be used on the floor of the flights. There are a number of alternatives and some thought should be given to the fact that some birds spend quite a lot of time on the ground, while others never descend to the aviary floor. The most usual floor coverings are grass, cement and shingle, or a combination of two of these. If the aviary is small and has to be entered by a door in the flight there is no point in laying turf on the floor, for this will soon be trodden down and only mud will remain. For birds which spend a lot of time on the ground grass is ideal but the area below the perch at both ends should be concreted or covered with shingle for easy cleaning.

The entire floor can be of concrete or shingle, if desired. Concrete has the advantage of being easily hosed down, provided that provision is made for drainage. Shingle has the advantage of natural drainage.

Planted aviaries are, of course, out of the question for housing parrots. Shrubs and trees are stripped as every new shoot appears. Natural perching should be used for the smaller or less destructive parrots, branches from fruit trees such as apple, pear and plum being ideal. The bark will immediately be stripped, a process which all parrots enjoy enormously.

The importance of regularly providing branches for gnawing cannot be over-emphasised. Ideally, they should be provided daily, but this is out of the question for any but the smallest collection. Overgrown lower mandibles are often a problem with newly-imported young birds and I have experienced this trouble with Red-capped Parrots, Caiques, Hawk-heads and a White-crowned Pionus. In such cases a constant supply of hard wood is essential. Permanent perching for destructive species such as macaws should be made from the hardest wood available; even broom handles can be useful.

CHAPTER 2

# FEEDING AND CARE

THERE are two ways of feeding a collection of parrots. One entails a minimum of trouble for the owner and provides a minimum of enjoyment and benefit for the birds, and the other involves rather more time and thought on the part of the owner and a maximum of enjoyment for the parrots.

Few birds show such obvious appreciation of a varied diet as do parrots. Food comes right at the top of their list of priorities, and I always feel very sorry for those that are provided with little more than seed and water. Mine watch my progress at feeding times to discover which tit-bits are on the menu. Every birds receives the seeds, fruit and greenfood daily that it prefers. Almost no two select precisely the same foods. In addition, such items as boiled potato, biscuit, hard crusts of bread, tinned fruit (some refuse fresh fruits) and cheese are given to those that like them. Certain birds receive half a millet spray daily. Many ignore peanuts, one selects them to form about 50 per cent of its diet. I believe in treating birds as individuals and allowing them, within reason, to eat what they want to eat.

The two most important points to bear in mind are that the diet should be nutritionally sound and as varied and interesting as possible. Most of the large parrots eat sunflower (white or striped) and peanuts, and ignore small seeds. Sunflower is rich in protein and oil. Unfortunately for those who may consider growing their own, the climate of Britain is not normally hot enough or dry enough to produce plump seeds.

Canary seed is one of the most valuable that can be provided. It is comparatively rich in protein, the kernel content being about 17 per cent. White millet is the most suitable of the loose millets for parrot-like species; the small panicum is usually ignored. Almost all of them relish spray millet, which is especially valuable while there are young in the nest – doubly so if it is soaked first.

The cereal seeds such as canary and millet are relatively deficient in the amino acid lycine; therefore some non-cereal seeds should be included in the diet, such as hemp, niger or maw. These contain from 35 per cent to 45 per cent oil and about 20 per cent to 25 per cent protein. Niger, a thin black shiny seed, is probably the most useful of these. Hemp is brownish in colour and about three times the size of white millet. The inside of the husk is greenish and the kernel has a pleasant, almost sweet, taste. Many parrot-like birds, even the larger ones which ignore other small seeds, are very fond of it. It is a nourishing and useful addition to the diet of breeding birds and those wintered outside. Unfortunately, it is also the most expensive of the seeds mentioned, with the exception of maw, which is seldom used for parrakeets.

A serious deficiency in all seeds is that of vitamins A and D. For birds which will eat only small amounts of greenfood and fruit it is absolutely essential to provide a vitamin supplement. A lack of vitamin A in the diet is often the cause of death in South American parrots, particularly fairly newly imported ones. The essential vitamins are so easily provided that all aviculturists should ensure that they are given regularly.

The method I use is to make a 'nectar' mixture, which is provided at least twice weekly. To every drinker of nectar for a pair of birds three or four drops of Abidec or the orange-flavoured Vitavel are added; any multi-vitamin preparation can be used. The nectar can consist of a proprietary brand or one's own recipe. I use two teaspoonfuls of honey and two of rose-hip syrup, dissolved in half a pint of water. There are endless variations on this theme; sometimes I add meat extract or a little Parrish's Chemical Food.

All parrots, not just those thought of as 'nectar feeders', will benefit from the inclusion of nectar in their diet. In the wild many small parrots, in addition to lories and lorikeets, feed on nectar. Those who have lories in their collections should offer any nectar left over to the other parrots. My lories receive nectar made from malt, condensed milk and honey. The left-overs go into the aviary containing the colony of *Pyrrhuras*. They never leave any!

Fruit is an extremely important item of the diet. Almost any kind of fruit can be offered, although grapes and apple are usually eaten more readily than others. Cherries are undoubtedly the favourite soft fruit. Pear, gooseberries, damsons, plums, oranges, tangerines, bananas and elderberries will be eaten by various species.

Many parrots are more interested in the pips than in the soft part of the fruit, which they tear apart and discard. Others will eat all the fruit, or may leave the pips. As fruit is one of the main items of expenditure, a considerable saving can be made if one bears in mind which part of the fruit is favoured by certain birds. It is a complete waste to give some birds half an apple, for example, if only the pips are eaten. Pomegranates, when in season, will be relished by these birds.

My *Pionus* parrots derive a great deal of enjoyment from shredding up the skin of citrus fruits such as grapefruit and tangerines, although if offered a piece of tangerine it is thrown down untasted. The same piece of fruit given to an Amazon of mine will cause her to hold back her head in obvious enjoyment while the juice runs down her throat. One should therefore experiment with various fruits as much as possible.

Some parrots are very reluctant to sample fruit or other foods which they have not eaten previously. If housed with other birds their reluctance is usually overcome by curiosity, but if kept on their own devious means of persuading them to eat fruit must be used. My cock Purple-bellied Parrot *(Triclaria malachitacea)* steadfastly refused to eat any form of fruit or greenfood until I noticed that he enjoyed stripping the shoots from the sucker from a plum tree that grew in his flight. I therefore attached grapes to the tips of the nibbled twigs. These were investigated almost immediately and the grapes removed and eaten – or rather the pips were. He usually throws the soft part of the fruit to the ground. After a while I placed the grapes in a food container and he was soon persuaded to eat cherries. This does demonstrate that, with a little thought, parrots can be encouraged to try new foods.

Some birds, the *Pyrrhura* conures, for example, are so curious about any new food that they will sample it immediately. Many are more cautious, and some will ignore all greenfood. The most universally-liked forms are seeding grasses, chickweed, young dandelion leaves, flowering dandelion heads, sowthistle and spinach beet. The latter is easily the most popular of the cultivated greenfoods and is the only one that many will eat. Cabbage is not very popular. While rearing young, some birds will feed spinach beet to the exclusion of all other greenfoods. It is easy to grow and will last throughout the winter, surviving under conditions – such as several inches of snow – that would kill other plants. The fleshy stalks are especially relished, so much so that no parrot keeper should be without a few rows of it.

It is important to ensure that all greenfood offered is clean, unfrosted and from an uncontaminated source. It should be washed well and not fed if discoloured or limp. Dirty or stale greenfood is thought to be one of the most common causes of enteritis. These days it is not safe to collect seeding weeds from farmland or grass verges because of the danger of poisoning from chemical sprays.

When no greenfood is available, soaked and sprouted seeds are a valuable substitute and a useful addition to the diet, especially while young are being reared. Seed for sprouting should be washed, then soaked overnight. In the morning it can be spread on trays and left in a warm damp place until the shoots are a quarter of an inch long. In warm weather, growth is much more rapid. Seed can also be fed after it has been soaked for about 36 hours. The water should be changed once and the seed thoroughly washed and strained before it is used. Excess moisture can be removed by placing the seed in a clean, dry cloth.

I find that parrots relish a clod of grass with roots and earth intact more than any other greenfood. The roots are eaten before the blades of grass, but first the earth is crumbled. Soil is a valuable source of trace metals such as manganese, iron, copper and zinc, in which a parrot's diet is often deficient.

The larger parrots usually ignore grit, so cuttlefish bone must be provided. While they are breeding large quantities are consumed. It is, of course, their chief source of calcium, which is essential for the formation of egg shells. If it is not available at all times the result may be soft-shelled eggs. Oyster-shell, limestone or mineral grit must be available for the smaller species and any of the larger ones that will eat it.

Boiled whole (not kibbled) maize is usually provided only for newly imported parrots. It is extremely valuable for these birds, but there is no reason why it should not be fed to established ones. Few of my birds refuse it, and it helps to vary the diet of those that show little interest in any seed but sunflower.

Newly imported birds require special attention. Soft foods must be provided, in addition to hard seed. Even if they are able to eat the latter they will benefit greatly from nourishing supplements such as baby food with honey or glucose added, sponge-cake and nectar or a mixture of Bemax and Farex, hard-boiled egg, etc. Such foods may be the means of saving the life of a poorly-nourished or very young bird. A little trouble taken with its feeding will pay large dividends. Adult birds and young ones eating hard seed may refuse soft foods but there is no reason why they should not form a permanent part of the diet if a bird shows a liking for them.

Needless to say, water must always be available and should be renewed daily. For those birds that bathe in their water dishes, a small hook-on plastic drinker or clear plastic tube drinker should also be provided to ensure that they are never without water.

Different kinds of seeds should always be given in separate dishes. This prevents wastage and allows one to see which seeds are preferred. Maize should be placed in a separate container and not mixed with other foods; its dampness will cause seed to turn mouldy. Fruit can be spiked on to nails knocked into the feeding shelf or placed in a container. Nectar should not be provided in tubes for parrots, as it may be ignored, but in hook-on drinkers which are best positioned at the end of a perch.

Little need be said about general care, which is just a question of commonsense. One word of warning should be given, however. Birds which receive a lot of fruit in their diet must be kept in aviaries which are cleaned regularly, especially during hot weather. If fruit or other food which is dropped on to the ground is allowed to become mouldy the spores from the mould will attack the birds' lungs and air sacs, causing aspergillosis. Its symptoms are wheezy, laboured breathing, with jerking tail (which may, of course, also be symptons of other diseases). There is no cure for aspergillosis. Cleanliness is therefore essential.

Most acclimatised parrot-like birds are exceptionally hardy and, *if correctly fed and housed,* will remain healthy indefinitely. It is newly imported birds that are most likely to fall ill, because the stress caused by their capture and importation and the foods to which they are not accustomed combine to lower their natural resistance to disease. Most birds have parasites that do not cause them any harm; should their resistance be lowered, however, then the natural balance is destroyed and the parasites gain the upper hand, killing their host.

A sick bird is a difficult subject to treat, for the simple reason that in most cases it is impossible to identify the cause of the trouble while the bird is alive; many ailments show the same symptoms. Diagnosis may prove difficult even if a post-mortem examination is carried out, especially if the body is not fresh. If that is the case only obvious causes such as a cerebral haemorrhage may be identified.

If a bird appears to be off-colour, even to a small degree, it should immediately be caught and placed in a temperature of about 85°F. I prefer a high temperature in a small room to a hospital cage, most of which are not designed for large parrots. However, the former may be out of the question, in which case a hospital cage will have to be used. A broad-spectrum antibiotic must then be provided; this can be obtained only on prescription from a veterinary surgeon. The prescribed amount must be added to the drinking water, with a vitamin supplement such as Abidec (unless this has already been incorporated in the antibiotic). Four days is the normal length of a course of treatment.

If the bird recovers the temperature must be gradually reduced until it coincides with that of the aviary to which the bird will be returned.

Broad-spectrum antibiotics will kill most germs and are particularly valuable for treating birds whose illness has not been diagnosed. For more specific ailments, such as abscesses, penicillin would be prescribed or, for a bowel disorder, streptomycin. All too often, however, the source of the trouble is unknown.

A four-day course of chloramphenicol for a *Pionus* parrot with chronic catarrh produced an unbelievably rapid recovery. The bird's streaming eyes and nostrils soon cleared. On the strength of this result I recommended the owner of a pet Grey Parrot, which had had catarrh for nearly five months and was in such poor condition that it kept to the cage floor, to obtain chloramphenicol from her veterinary surgeon. Other drugs had produced no improvement in the bird's condition, yet again the chloramphenicol cleared the trouble.

Antibiotics are a boon to the modern bird keeper, provided that they are used carefully. I regret to say that some dealers give newly imported birds only drinking water treated with antibiotics. Such a practice is to be deplored; the over-use of antibiotics is extremely dangerous since it kills good and bad bacteria, leaving the bird with no resistance to disease at all.

It should perhaps be mentioned that the virus disease psittacosis, which can be transferred to human beings, giving them flu-like symptoms, is no longer a danger to humans, since if diagnosed correctly it is easily cured with antibiotics. Psittacosis is not a disease confined to parrots, as it is sometimes thought; any bird may contract this disease, which is known as ornithosis in birds other than parrots.

If a sick parrot is treated immediately there is a good chance that it will recover and live for many years. Small birds such as finches seldom completely recover from an illness. Larger birds are easier to treat and they can even be injected but, this is not always advisable, as the shock to a parrot's nervous system following an injection may kill it. Vitamins are sometimes given by injection in extreme cases, but if all birds are regularly given vitamins in their nectar or drinking water such treatment is totally unnecessary.

Many diseases can be traced to a dietary deficiency. As already mentioned, a lack of vitamin A is a common cause of death in the parrots fom Central and South America, usually newly imported specimens. Multi-vitamin preparations contain a high level of vitamin A. A deficiency of vitamin B can cause curled toes and paralysis of the nervous centres. This vitamin is easily provided by sprinkling dried brewer's yeast or proprietary yeast for cage birds on the seed. Paralysis may also be caused by kidney damage, which is not evident until an autopsy is carried out. Watery – not just loose – droppings are an indication of a kidney disorder.

Lack of iodine in the diet is responsible for enlargement of the thyroid gland, which presses on the wind-pipe and causes respiratory trouble. Iodine nibbles or iodine (one drop of tincture of iodine diluted in half a gallon of water) will rectify iodine deficiency if it is given in time.

In all cases, however, prevention is obviously better than cure. A balanced diet will therefore ensure good health in a way that nothing else can.

*Keeping a pet.* When one of the larger parrots such as an Amazon or a macaw is kept as a pet it is better described as a member of the household. Anyone who can cope only with a pet that does not require too much attention or one obtained 'just for talking' can disregard the large and intelligent parrots. Hundreds of such birds are offered to zoos every year by people who find that they have bitten off more than they can chew. One of my acquaintances who made it known in the press that he required ex-pet Amazons for breeding was inundated with replies. Few who buy Amazons realise just how demanding they will become.

From non-fanciers I have come to expect such unenlightened questions as 'Do your parrots talk?' It is perhaps the parrot's greatest misfortune that it is a good mimic. If it did not have this ability it might be treated less like a toy, to be neglected or passed on to a new owner when its novelty wears off or when it fails to talk. How much more satisfaction would pet-owners derive from their parrots if they spent less time teaching them to talk and more time discovering what attractive and intelligent individuals they are.

Many parrots are capable of demonstrating their intelligence and of feeling and expressing emotion in a way that would surprise anyone unfamiliar with them. Not least of the emotions common to them is jealousy. Most are 'one-man' pets and not only do they frequently show an active dislike of other members of the family, particularly in a household consisting of only two persons, but they do not hesitate to demonstrate their dislike in a manner which does not exactly guarantee their popularity!

These birds can also become terribly jealous of other parrots. The ideal is one man, one parrot. Here, I confess, I do not practice what I preach and I therefore know that dividing one's affections is not the way to get the maximum enjoyment from each bird. A parrot's temperament can be completely ruined by jealousy. If the pet owner cannot resist the temptation of buying attractive parrots then my advice to him would be to build some aviaries and attempt to breed from a pair or two, rather than have several single birds about the house.

Most New World parrots are easy to tame if obtained young, unlike Grey Parrots, which are very cautious, and Australian species, notably the parrakeets, which do not make suitable pets, unless perhaps hand-reared.

Altogether, I doubt if there is a group of birds in the world more amenable to training. Their confidence is easily gained. Whatever size bird one requires a suitable species can be found, from the small *Brotogeris*, to the medium-sized *Pionus* and larger Amazons and giant macaws.

A cage for a medium-sized Amazon should be about 18in square and 27in high. For *Pionus* the minimum measurements should be 16in square and 24in high. Reasonably tame birds should be let out daily for exercise in the house. Some will spend most of the time just sitting on the top of the cage but others are more adventurous. If the flight feathers of one wing are cut the bird can be allowed to sit on top of its cage and climb around it while there is someone present in the house. Full-winged Amazons, given the freedom of a house, are delightful but mischievous pets, and can cause much damage to furniture, doors, picture rails, etc.

In many parrot cages the seed containers are far too small; these can be removed and replaced by large hook-on plastic containers. An additional perch placed diagonally above the one supplied by the cage manufacturer is invariably appreciated, usually more so than a swing, which can be removed if the bird shows no interest in it. Newspaper is the best floor covering, and should be changed daily. Parrots often tear up newspaper, but this does them no harm and keeps them occupied. The grid above the tray should always be removed, as parrots enjoy playing about on the cage floor.

When kept indoors these birds must be sprayed at least twice weekly, or their plumage will become dull and dry. I keep an old cage for this purpose, remove the tray and floor and stand it over a sink. As the parrot's own cage may be too large for this use, an old but small cage is a very useful item of equipment.

A parrot that is correctly cared for and given plenty of attention will live to a far greater age than any other pet – feathered or furred.

CHAPTER 3

# BREEDING

IN aviculture there is no sight more rewarding than that of newly fledged young. For the enthusiast who enjoys the challenge offered by a species which has seldom or even never previously been bred in confinement, there is tremendous scope where the neo-tropical parrots are concerned. In many cases new ground will be covered and here the aviculturist can be of real service in carefully recording successes and failures, as equally important information is to be gained from the latter.

Further, the aviculturist can play a valuable role not only in producing young but also in building up a strain of a certain species. At the time of going to press there were no restrictions on the importation of parrots and other foreign birds into Britain, but it seemed likely that this state of affairs would be altered in the near future. The importance of breeding, rather than importing, as a method of stocking aviaries therefore cannot be over-emphasised.

Until recently, most aviculturists have neglected attempting to breed from neo-tropical parrots, with the result that they have earned a reputation of being hard to breed. One had only to study the breeding results obtained by a certain British enthusiast with the larger parrots to realise that this is not so. With patience, perseverance and intelligent management perhaps more might emulate these results.

Most breeding pairs, with the exception of some of the smaller species, should be housed one pair per aviary. Due to the high cost of building aviaries, and the fact that modern gardens are small, the aviculturist naturally tends to keep one pair each of a number of species, to add as much variety and interest to his collection as possible. This, unfortunately, is not conducive to good breeding results. It is extremely difficult indeed to build up a strain of birds using one pair only. The ideal would be to buy half-a-dozen birds, or even three or four. One is then more likely to obtain a true pair and if a bird is lost a replacement is at hand. Replacements are often a problem with birds imported in small numbers; valuable time can be wasted in searching for a suitable partner.

The greatest advantage of having two or more breeding pairs, however, is that if young are reared one does not have to pair them back to a parent or nest-mate, as an unrelated outcross is available. It never ceases to amaze me that aviculturists almost invariably sell the young they breed, even those of rare species. Too often one of the members of the breeding pair is lost, no partner can be found for it, and no more youngsters are bred. Had the young birds been retained one could have been paired back to its parent. Breeders will argue that they have not the space to keep the young; while this obviously applies with Australian parrakeets and other prolific birds, American parrots are seldom as free-breeding and some at least of the offspring should be retained, those which are sold going to someone who will make a real attempt to breed from them.

Few New World parrots require large aviaries, because many are climbers rather than flyers. Only in immense aviaries, the size of which is out of the question for the average bird keeper, will Amazons and Macaws really exercise their wings. Many breeders of the larger Australian parrakeets, which *do* require long flights to ensure breeding fitness and fertile eggs, might be encouraged to keep two or three pairs of neo-tropical parrots if they realised that equally spacious enclosures are not necessary for these birds. I am not advocating that they are kept in small or cramped quarters; only that the conditions provided for Australian parrakeets are not necessary.

In studying reports of breedings of South American parrots I have often noticed that the conditions were not what would be generally considered as ideal – or perhaps I should say ideal for Australian parrakeets. In a number of instances conures have bred in very small quarters, often either actually inside the owner's house or in a cage with no access to outdoor accommodation. One aviculturist has been outstandingly successful in breeding *Pyrrhura* conures in a basement flight, and a friend described to me seeing newly-fledged Golden-crowned Conures in 'murky-dim' aviaries contained within 7ft-high brick walls under conditions which would normally be described as far from ideal.

Dark corners, ledges, small enclosed aviaries in a quiet corner where the birds can feel secure and are seldom disturbed – conures like such things. Never will they roost on a perch if a ledge is built into a corner of the shelter or if a nest-box is provided. They feel secure – and no bird will breed if its surroundings do not provide a sense of security. In the chapter on conures I mention the large aviaries in one zoo which houses flocks of conures without breeding results being obtained. I believe that the aviaries are too large and too *open;* they do not provide the required privacy.

Macaws, the largest of the parrots, nest fairly readily in captivity; none of the aviaries I have seen in which these birds have bred have been large ones. A well-known breeder of Australian parrakeets has rows of neat and spacious aviaries in which many young birds are bred every year, but away from these, in a secluded corner beneath some trees, is a small aviary in which Blue and Gold Macaws breed regularly. Would they, I wonder, breed in an open range of parrakeet aviaries?

Another well-known aviculturist, who keeps many rare and interesting parrots in immaculate brick-built aviaries, has never reared one of the many species from South America which are kept. The conditions appear to be perfect – but are they? Orange-flanked Parrakeets have bred in a dingy shed for someone with no previous experience with parrot-like birds (quite an achievement when one considers how few breeding records there are for *Brotogeris*), while an aviculturist with many years' experience breeds nothing in model aviaries!

There is an element of luck in all breeding successes; nevertheless, it may be time to revise ideas on suitable breeding accommodation for certain parrots. In my opinion, only birds that can fly very fast over a small distance and use their wings in preference to climbing need lengthy aviaries – and these are by no means essential. And, for all species, part of the aviary must be designed to give essential privacy. A quiet area surrounded by trees, even if it is dark and enclosed by foliage, would, in my opinion, give more success than an open situation.

*Sexing.* Unfortunately, very few American parrots are sexually dimorphic, ie, in most the plumage is alike in cock and hen. Obviously the major obstacle to be overcome is in selecting a true pair. There are only two ways of attempting this. The first may be out of the question for many, due to lack of accommodation; it is to house half a dozen birds of the same species in a fairly spacious aviary and allow them to choose their own partners. Some of the smaller birds can be left in a colony for breeding purposes, but this would prove disastrous with many large parrots which, when in breeding condition, must be housed one pair per aviary.

The only other way of finding a true pair is by careful observation of behaviour and appearance. A guide to the sex of a parrot, but by no means an infallible one, is the shape of its head and upper mandible. This applies more especially to the larger parrots. In the male the upper mandible usually appears broader when viewed from the front. In some, but not all, species the cock has more depth above the eye and the head appears to extend further rather than falling away sharply behind the eye. In other words, a bird with a small beak and a small head is more likely to be a hen than a cock. Admittedly, one can sometimes study true pairs and see little difference in the heads. First impressions about a parrot's sex are valuable, since the more one studies an individual the more bewildered one can become!

With adult birds in breeding condition one can try the pelvic bone test. This is often of little use in determining the sex of a bird whose history is unknown, as whether it is adult or immature and whether it is in breeding condition may not be evident on sight. It is not everyone who would wish to test the pelvis of a Thick-billed Parrot, for example, or other psittacines with equally formidable beaks! Theoretically, the pelvic bones of adult females must be wide apart to allow egg-laying; in males and immature birds they are so close together as to almost touch.

Very close study of the behaviour of parrots can also provide valuable clues as to their sex. As the members of a pair must be readily identified – and preferably from a distance – it may be necessary to mark one with a small amount of dye.

The first recorded breeding of Pallid Caiques in Britain came about by the purchase of two birds whose sexes were unknown. After studying their behaviour, carefully examining their plumage for signs of sexual distinction and weighing and measuring them their owner was still completely mystified as to their sex! So he bought another ' pair '. And another. By ' juggling ' them around and observing their reactions to each other, he discovered that the aggressive ones which were later proved to be males, held their plumage in a different manner to the believed females: the feathers were permanently ruffled, not sleeked down, and the tail splayed, not closed. Observation of known true pairs in breeding condition will often show that the female's tail is permanently ' tight ', that of the male being splayed.

Voice can sometimes provide a clue to sex. In some of the smaller birds I have kept, such as Red-capped Parrots *(Pionopsitta)* and Lineolated Parrakeets, the cocks warble in much the same way as Budgerigars. The hens are altogether quieter. In some genera, such as *Amazona* and *Pionus*, both sexes would appear to be equally noisy. It has also been found that in some species, Tovi Parrakeets and Caiques, for example, the voice of the female is higher pitched than that of the male.

In addition to the satisfaction of breeding from one's birds, great pleasure can be obtained from quietly watching them – keeping quite still, so that one's presence is ignored. There is so much to be learned and recorded about the habits of neo-tropical parrots that any observant aviculturist who takes the trouble to record immediately on paper details of behaviour such as display, copulation, appearance of the young (if seen), allopreening, bathing, etc., is being of real use to aviculture. Little detailed information has been recorded relating to even the most commonly kept species.

Unfortunately, compatability in these parrots is no indication of a true pair since mutual preening, and even copulation, occurs regardless of sex, especially in the smaller parrots. In fact, it is unusual for two birds of the same or a closely related species not to behave in a friendly manner towards each other. The breeder of Australian parrakeets should bear this in mind, as many of these birds show little interest in each other outside of the breeding season. The behaviour of the American species is so different that it may lead the fancier who is unaccustomed to these birds to believe that two of the same sex are a true pair.

Having installed the believed pair in an aviary, the most important consideration is the nest-box. Reference to the size of the nest-boxes for the various species will be found in the text.

A number of different forms of courtship and aggression displays are seen in these parrots. The feathers displayed are those of the head, tail and wings. In *Amazona* and *Pionus* parrots the tail is fanned to show the patch of colour at the base; Amazons also lift the wings slightly away from the body to reveal the colour at the bend of the wings. In some, particularly *vinacea* and *autumnalis*, the feathers of the neck are raised quite high to frame the face but they are not specially adapted for this purpose as is the case in the Hawk-headed Parrot. In the latter there is a most striking erectile ruff, composed of elongated feathers, which are red, edged with blue. Another special adaptation for display is found in the lengthened ear-coverts of the Yellow-eared Conure *(Ognorhynchus icterotis)*.

In some birds, *Pyrrhura* conures for example, the display consists of little more than ruffling the head feathers and strutting up and down the perch in an exaggerated manner. These actions can be seen in *Pionus* parrots and in the Purple-bellied Parrot *(Triclaria malachitacea)*, who also include 'bowing' in their display. On showing a Massena's Parrot *(P.seniloides)* another bird of its own species, something which it had not seen for a considerable period, it immediately began to rock backwards and forwards and up and down (stretched to its full height, then leaning forward so that its head was below the perch) in a mechanical fashion. It strutted up and down the perch, fanning its tail, then climbed down the wire front of the aviary to have a closer look at the other bird. In a later chapter I have described the display of my cock Purple-bellied Parrot: 'He fans his tail, ruffles his rather short head feathers, dilates the pupils of his large brown eyes and walks with deliberate tread along the perch, bowing low until his beak almost touches the perch.'

The threat display of the Caique is yet further exaggerated. Its walk, even more upright than usual, is slow and dignified and punctuated by little jumps, the feet sometimes leaving the perch. Bowing takes place: the head is dipped below the level of the perch then raised slowly to its normal position. Often the wings are held open for a fraction of a second in a phoenix-like pose. Another act of aggression in male Caiques is whirring the wings, with both feet gripping the perch. This behaviour is occasionally seen in females when, for example, an intruder threatens the nest.

Prestwich (AM, vol 60, 2) described the behaviour of his Lineolated Parrakeets, a species which has no bright or conspicuous patches of colour. Two pairs were 'seen to stand facing each other, stretching vertically to the fullest possible extent with beaks interlocked. Thus they remained for a few moments and it would appear that this is the courtship display.'

Power (30b) found that the White-winged Parrakeet *(Brotogeris v.versicolorus)*, a species whose only colours other than green are the white and yellow in the wing, stretches the wings to reveal these colours frequently and repeatedly in courtship feeding. This occurs in the feeding bird, which stretches the wing on the side nearest the recipient. He was not certain, however 'whether this was a courtship display or was indicative of ambivalent tendencies in the performing bird.'

Male parrotlets display by walking up and down the perch close to the female, uttering their chattering song and lifting the wings to reveal the blue coverts.

One of the purposes of mutual preening and courtship feeding is to strengthen the pair bond, yet these activities do not invariably indicate the formation of a true pair, even in a flock where there is a choice of partners. In several genera, eg *Pyrrhura, Brotogeris* and *Pionites,* allopreening is not confined to the head but carried out to various areas of the body, including the wings and vent.

It is interesting to note that during copulation most male psittacines place both feet on the hen's back but in some—perhaps most—small neo-tropical parrots, including *Aratinga, Pyrrhura, Forpus* and *Pionites,* the male keeps one foot on the perch.

That many parrots can use the foot as a hand for feeding is well known. This characteristic seems particularly well developed in neotropical species. The only exceptions of which I know are the *Forpus* parrotlets and Lineolated Parrakeets (and also other members of the genus *Bolborhynchus*). Parrots may also use their feet in defence and I have seen Caiques and Amazon Parrots ward off an aggressive bird with one foot.

*Nest-boxes.* New breeding pairs should be offered a choice of several nesting sites. The box is best constructed of strong wood, especially in the case of the larger parrots. Even conures such as *Pyrrhuras,* which are not normally destructive, may do considerable damage to the inside of the box while preparing the nest, or even during incubation. I have known the hen to do so much gnawing that the eggs have fallen out through the side of the box! Lining the inside with wire mesh is therefore a wise precaution with destructive species, especially Amazons and other large parrots.

An inverted turf makes a suitable nest-lining. Peat or a little decayed wood are more often used, sometimes also sawdust and wood shavings. It would be advisable to mix any wood base with a little soil as not only are sawdust and wood shavings very dry but the dust from them could possibly cause aspergillosis. Some hens will tolerate very little nest-lining and lay and incubate on bare wood.

It is a sound idea to offer a choice of nest-boxes, one being positioned in the flight, the other in the shelter. As the shelter offers more seclusion this site will often be chosen, especially if the shelter does not allow a lot of light to enter.

Parrots usually choose the smallest nest available, even one which appears to be too small for their needs. The entrance should be just large enough to admit the birds comfortably. If it is too large the box may be ignored altogether; too much light is admitted, destroying the sense of security which the nest should provide. The entrance hole should, if possible, face away from the source of any possible disturbance; also away from direct sunlight.

The nest should be made as attractive as possible, especially for those birds which do not habitually roost in a box. Careful thought on the requirements of individual pairs will often pay dividends. A Danish aviculturist persuaded the Golden-fronted Parrakeet *(Bolborhynchus)* to nest by constructing a box which simulated the unusual conditions under which these birds nest in the wild.

Once eggs have been laid or their presence suspected, the nest must be left undisturbed. One does not have much choice in this matter where the large birds, especially Amazons, are concerned, for the cock will make quite certain that no one goes near the nest. Nasty injuries may result if his warnings are ignored.

Only the hen incubates, although the cock may sit beside her in the nest for long periods, leading some to believe that he is sharing the duty of incubation.

One can often tell by the behaviour of the birds and the amount of food consumed when young have hatched. 'Leave well alone' is the policy to adopt from then on. The hen will leave the nest only for very short periods indeed at first, so unless the box is situated on the outside of the aviary inspection is not possible. Some of the smaller parrots seem not to resent nest inspection and one soon gets to know how far one can go with individual birds. With rarely-bred and valuable species, however, unless something has obviously gone wrong, patience and restraint must be cultivated and the nest left severely alone! Some birds will not tolerate any disturbance at all and will immediately desert if the nest is inspected.

When chicks hatch, feeding becomes of premier importance. Suitable foods for rearing are discussed in the text. It is possible to breed parrot-like birds on little other than seed but the difference in those young birds that are fed with nourishing extras is so great, especially in size and stamina, that no one who cared for the welfare of his birds would fail to provide the necessary extras.

Neo-tropical parrots are slow to develop and spend longer in the nest than do Australian species. They are blind and covered with a small amount of down for a considerable length of time.

More specific remarks on breeding are given under the appropriate genera or species.

## CHAPTER 4

# MACAWS

THE macaws include the largest and most spectacular members of the parrot family. They are intelligent birds and highly individual and, despite their somewhat forbidding appearance, often gentle and affectionate.

The distinguishing feature of the macaw is the area of bare skin surrounding the eyes, extending to the cheeks and lores. While the large macaws cannot possibly be confused with any other parrots, it seems that the 'dwarf' macaws and the large conures of the genus *Aratinga,* such as the Blue-crowned, have frequently been confused. It is difficult to see why, since no conure has a bare face.

Macaws are the least suitable of all parrots for those who are unable to provide outdoor accommodation. Despite their size they do not need particularly spacious enclosures, as the large species spend most of their time climbing, seldom bothering to fly. For this reason long narrow aviaries, which are recommended for active birds such as parrakeets, are less desirable and wider aviaries are preferable. If space and finances allow there is no reason why a large aviary should not be built.

Large macaws are often extremely destructive and this is important to bear in mind when designing an aviary for them. Later in the chapter reference is made to some Green-winged Macaws which were kept and bred for years in an aviary constructed of timber and ½in wire netting – and no damage was done to it! These birds, however, were exceptional, for most would make short work of ½in netting, which they can crumple as easily as paper if they so desire.

In *Parrots, Cockatoos and Macaws,* E. J. Boosey gave details of an aviary he had had built which he considered perfect for these birds. It is worth describing, for a better design would be hard to find. 'It is 28ft long (8ft of this being accounted for by the shelter) by 5ft wide by 7ft 6in high, and is to my mind an ideal macaw aviary. It is constructed on a framework of tubular metal piping covered with a very strong gauge chain-link netting. The shelter is made of stout sheets of asbestos and contains a single central perch, each end of which is set into the middle of a large square of sheet zinc to prevent the birds sitting and biting at the asbestos. The perch is made of teak as are two others at each end of the flight, and branches of softer wood will periodically be supplied.'

Chain link is normally employed for macaw aviaries. It is very expensive and the only material which can be guaranteed to withstand an onslaught from their massive beaks. The use of chain link poses a problem, for sparrows – and, of course, small vermin – can gain access without any trouble, resulting in the seed bill being doubled. The only answer, which is expensive initially but will soon repay its cost, is to double-wire the aviary with ½in netting. This should be attached to a frame sufficiently far from the chain link to prevent the macaws from reaching through and destroying it.

If timber is used in the aviary construction, 2in x 2in should be employed for the framework, oak and cedar being the most hard-wearing – and expensive. If 2in strips of aluminium are used to protect the framework it will be virtually indestructible. The aluminium must be painted to prevent an electro-galvanic effect which will cause both wire and aluminium to rust very quickly. Unprotected woodwork will quickly be destroyed by large macaws, causing frequent and tedious repair work and possible escapes. A little thought given to the initial design will save a lot of trouble and expense later on.

The shelter – also, if desired, the lower part of the flight – can be constructed of asbestos. This can be boarded on the outside, or the asbestos may be painted to give a more pleasing effect. The edge of asbestos sheeting must also be covered with aluminium, for once a grip has been gained by the macaws, it will be easy for them to damage it. Other alternatives are the use of tubular scaffolding poles or angle iron. If painted with bitumen these will not rust and will never need to be renewed.

The smaller macaws are less destructive, and can normally be housed in an aviary constructed of welded mesh rather than chain link.

All macaws are extremely hardy when acclimatised, and will live outside throughout the year without heat. The aviary shelter can be open-fronted or enclosed; if it is enclosed it must be spacious and light or the macaws may prefer not to use it.

The ideal method of keeping these birds is at liberty; I can think of no other foreign bird which does so well under these conditions and which looks so magnificent. A macaw in flight is one of the loveliest sights in nature, surpassed only by a pair or a group of these impressive birds. Their effortless grace is almost unreal, reminding one of brightly coloured kites as they speed through the sky, their long tails streaming behind.

Unfortunately, it is not possible to give macaws their freedom in built-up areas (in fact, it is not advisable to keep them at all) where these inquisitive and mischievous birds would be likely to meet a sad end. In rural districts anyone with a large garden and no near neighbours has the ideal conditions for liberty macaws. These birds are now among the foremost attractions at many bird gardens and some zoos, where the public are thrilled to see them under natural conditions.

One of the most picturesque places to see them is at Waddesdon Manor, near Aylesbury, Bucks. The aviaries of the 19th century Renaissance style manor are of an 18th century French design and have a frontage of 60yds. In the centre is a grotto with a marble fountain. It is here that the macaws are fed. I watched one day as a pair of Scarlets, a pair of Blue and Yellows and a single Green-winged swooped down for walnuts, grapes and sunflower seed. After feeding they walked over to the edge of the fountain; the sight of three species of macaw drinking together from a fountain group of Minerva and attendant Tritons must be unique, and made a most colourful and unusual picture. The macaws then flew off into the wooded parkland, which extends over hundreds of acres.

Few are fortunate enough to be able to keep these birds under such perfect conditions, but in suitable areas they are easily trained to stay at liberty. Newly-acquired birds should have their wings clipped. They can then be placed in a large nesting barrel in a tree, after part of the front of the barrel has been removed and replaced with welded mesh. After a few days they can be let out to climb among the branches, and will return readily to the barrel where the food supply is located. By the time their flight feathers have grown they will be so familiar with their immediate surroundings that they will be most unlikely to stray.

Usually only the large macaws – Scarlet, Blue and Yellow, Green-winged, Military and Hyacinthine – are kept at liberty. I know of no one who has experimented with the smaller species.

*As Pets.* The large macaws are kept on stands, as no cage has been produced commercially for these birds. I was greatly impressed by

1 Liberty macaws, such as this Green-winged Macaw *Ara chloroptera* photographed at Rode Tropical Bird Gardens, are a popular feature of many bird gardens.

2 The Hyacinthine Macaw *Anodorhynchus hyacinthus* is one of the most spectacular and sought-after of all South American Parrots. The one on the left was photographed at Twycross Zoo.

3 The rarely imported Lear's Macaw *Anodorhynchus leari* is a smaller and less colourful version of the Hyacinthine Macaw. This is one of a pair exhibited at Birdland, Bourton-on-the-Water.

4 Two sub-species of the Military Macaw *Ara militaris* showing clearly the difference in the size of the beak. Owner Kelling Park Aviaries.

5 The Blue and Yellow Macaw *Ara ararauna* is the most widely kept of the macaws and has been known in captivity since the 16th century. The one above lives free in Rode Tropical Bird Gardens.

6 The Severe Macaw *Ara severa* can be distinguished from the other 'dwarf' macaws by the chestnut-coloured forehead. Owner: Gunnar Strömberg.

7 The Illiger's Macaw *Ara maracana* makes a delightful pet, being very intelligent and easily tamed. Owner: Solveig Jensen.

the very large cages designed by one aviculturist for macaws and cockatoos, and specially constructed by an engineering company. The framework was made of angle iron and an extra strong welded mesh (gauge 11 or 12) was used. These were intended as temporary quarters for newly-imported birds and were ideal for the purpose, being virtually indestructible. They were built on runners which made them easy to move around, indoors or out.

Those who are house-proud should not think of buying a macaw, for although these birds seem quite contented to spend most of the day on a stand, they should – under supervision – be allowed some freedom of the house daily for exercise. The prospective owner should also realise that he is choosing one of the noisiest birds available and he cannot reasonably expect near neighbours to tolerate the screams which macaws emit – often in the early hours of the morning. Perhaps he will not be able to tolerate them himself!

Macaws must have plenty of affection and attention and it is unfair to keep one unless one has the time to devote to it. A young bird should be obtained if possible, as these are usually very gentle and like to be handled. They will clamber all over people – even strangers – and like to have their heads scratched.

The dwarf macaws usually make enchanting pets and are really more suitable than the large ones. They are playful and affectionate and will often learn to speak a few sentences, whereas their larger relatives rarely learn more than a few words. Unfortunately, the small macaws do not have correspondingly smaller voices.

In an aviary they are quite active and fly rather than climb. Several pairs can be kept together in a fair-sized aviary; like the *Pyrrhura* conures, they agree well in groups and will even breed under these conditions. They have the same habit of sleeping in their nest-boxes, which should be left in position throughout the year.

*Breeding.* The aviculturist who is seriously interested in breeding macaws has quite a good chance of success, provided he has a true pair! Unfortunately, all macaws are extremely difficult to sex. Being quite expensive birds to purchase, few people can afford to buy several pairs in the hope that they will 'sort themselves out'.

An enormous amount of patience and a good portion of luck is required in breeding these birds – luck in acquiring a true pair and patience in waiting for them to mature and settle down. It may be several years before the larger species make any attempt to breed. Some of the smaller macaws, the Hahn's, for example, are very willing to go to nest. The Hahn's could almost be described as prolific and there is no reason why it should not be established in aviaries.

Any aviculturist who has fertile eggs from a pair of macaws would be most unwise to part with the birds, for they are almost certain to breed successfully sooner or later. Perhaps the most difficult part of the procedure is obtaining a true pair.

If young are hatched, the owner should not expect them to be reared on an ordinary seed diet. All kinds of extras may have to be tried until the parents are provided with the food which they consider suitable for rearing the young. Once a pair have bred successfully they will often continue to do so for many years.

*Feeding.* Most large macaws ignore small seeds such as canary seed, white millet and hemp, although these should be offered in the hope that they will sample them. All these birds will eat sunflower seed and peanuts, sometimes also hemp, wheat and groats or oats. They often appreciate nuts and some are even able to crack brazil nuts unaided. Because sunflower seed and nuts only make a nutritionally unbalanced and very monotonous diet it is absolutely essential to offer a wide variety of fruits and vegetables. A good and varied diet offered to one pair of Scarlet Macaws consisted of sunflower seed and as much fruit as they would eat – oranges and bananas being enjoyed most – unshelled peanuts, corn-on-the-cob, carrots, celery and once a week, raw onion. Cooked oatmeal, hard-boiled egg and dry toast were given occasionally.

Macaws should also be offered apple, grapes, pear, spinach beet and sods of grass with earth and roots attached. They can also be given a piece of sweet or dry biscuit, sponge cake, stale bread soaked in sweetened milk, and toast or stale bread which most birds will immediately 'dunk' in their drinking water.

When they are rearing youngsters they may be rather difficult to please. It is essential to provide 'bulky' foods as they cannot be expected to rear young without them. Almost any food, including meat and fish, can be offered. Many are particularly keen on spinach beet, especially the stalk. Other cultivated greenfoods such as cabbage can also be offered throughout the year.

The smaller macaws will usually accept a more varied diet. They should be offered sunflower, peanuts, groats or oats, buckwheat, white millet, canary seed, hemp and spray millet. Sprouted oats and sprouted millet sprays were eaten every day by a pair of Severe Macaws. They liked apple, orange, grapes and raw carrot but ignored banana. While breeding, these birds were given hard-boiled egg and biscuit, boiled rice with milk sweetened with sugar and jam.

Individuals vary enormously in their likes and dislikes. One pair of Hahn's Macaws, for example, would sample only sunflower, apple, wild greenfoods and blackberries. E. N. T. Vane fed his Noble Macaws on sunflower, buckwheat, peanuts, canary seed, hemp and oat screenings. They would eat groundsel, shepherd's purse, sow-thistle and spinach and, while rearing young, large amounts of chick-weed. Sprouted seed was also provided and crusts which had been roasted and crushed and made to a crumbly consistency by adding boiling water.

### Genus: *Anodorhynchus*

These are the most distinctive of the macaws, being wholely blue or bluish, with enormous beaks, even for macaws.

HYACINTHINE MACAW *(Anodorhynchus hyachinthus)*

*Description:* The plumage is a rich, deep shade of hyacinth blue throughout; the feathers normally have a high gloss. The very large beak is black. The eyes and the lower mandible are surrounded by bare skin, bright yellow in colour; a line of bright yellow decorates the tongue. Length: about 36in.

This is undoubtedly one of the most imposing and striking of all parrot-like birds.

*Distribution:* The interior of Brazil, south of the Amazon, in the states of Pará, Piauhy, Goyaz, Minas Geraës, São Paulo and Mato Grosso.

In 1863 H. W. Bates (3) wrote of this species: 'It occurs in the interior of Brazil from 16°S lat. to the southern border of the Amazon valley . . . It flies in pairs and feeds on the hard nuts of several palms but especially of the Mucujas *(Acrocomia lasiopatha)*. These nuts, which are so hard as to be difficult to break with a heavy hammer, are crushed to a pulp by the powerful beak of the macaw.'

According to C. Hilary Fry (12): 'These birds inhabit the taller and denser types of forest associated with rivers, although they are also found in seasonally dry woodland savanna called 'cerrado', again usually where the growth is good and fruits are available.' Gallery forest in cerrado – the 120 foot tall bands of impenetrable forest which grows by swamps and watercourses – is particularly favoured by this and other macaws and parrots.

'Naturalists have produced few observations on the feeding of Hyacinthine Macaws in the wild state and it is not at all common even to see the birds perched. Generally they are seen as small parties in flight when their extraordinary cries attract attention. The voice, an extremely loud and raucous monosyllable, seems to soak up the myriad lesser sounds of the forest.

'The Hyacinthine lays its four or so round eggs in an unlined tree cavity; the sexes share in incubation and the young are hatched blind and naked.'

*Remarks:* This is one of the most sought-after of neo-tropical parrots and commands an extremely high price. It is normally found only in zoos and bird gardens. Birdland, at Bourton-on-the-Water, Gloucestershire, is famous for its Hyacinthines, several pairs of which are at liberty.

Despite its dangerous-looking beak, this is normally a very gentle and affectionate species. Undoubtedly the ideal way to keep it is at liberty; it would be unfair to cage a bird of this size and a large and very strong aviary would be required.

*Breeding records:* The first known breeding of this species occurred in Poznan Zoo in Poland (AZ *Nachrichten,* vol 14. 1967, 141-2). No dates or details are available. The birds were successful on more than one occasion in breeding in an indoor compartment measuring only approximately 5ft x 5ft x 6ft in a wooden chest placed on the floor.

At Chicago Zoo, a female Hyacinthine paired to a Scarlet Macaw laid one egg on April 30 1967 but the egg was very small and was broken. A year later a male Hyacinthine was obtained. On April 15 the hen laid one egg; the third was laid on April 22. Two were infertile and one disappeared. Two more were laid on May 13 and 16, one of which hatched on June 13. Three days later the chick had disappeared, probably having died soon after hatching. Two more clutches of two eggs were laid that year. In 1971, Ralph Small was successful in hand-rearing one chick. At nine days old it weighed 100g.

In 1970 three Hyacinthines were reared in Bratislava, Czechoslovakia and, in the same year, a hybrid between a male Hyacinthine and a female Blue and Yellow was bred in Salt Lake Tracey Aviary.

GLAUCOUS MACAW *(A.glaucus)*

*Description:* Slate-blue with a greyish tinge to the head and neck and a browner tinge to the breast. The flights and the underside of the tail, also the under wing-coverts, are blackish. The naked skin surrounding the eye and at the base of the lower mandible is yellow. The bill is black. Length: about 28in.

*Distribution:* South-eastern Brazil, Paraguay, Uruguay. According to de Schauensee (33b) there is no authentic Argentine record for this macaw.
*Remarks:* An extreme rarity in aviculture.

LEAR'S MACAW *(A.leari)*
*Description:* A small version of the Hyacinthine Macaw, distinguished by the duller blue of the plumage, smaller size and the U-shaped area of bare skin by the lower mandible (which extends further in the Hyacinthine). It is mainly dull cobalt, the head and underparts being slightly less brightly coloured, with a tinge of green. The inner webs of the flights, the under wing-coverts and the underside of the tail are blackish. A small area of bare skin surrounding the eye is yellow, also the area between the lores and the lower mandible, but less bright in colour. The beak is black and the tongue is black with a yellow stripe down each side. The iris is deep brown. Length: about 29in.
*Distribution:* Eastern Brazil; known with certainty only from Joazeiro on the Rio São Francisco, Bahiá on the Pernambuco border. Nothing has been recorded about it in the wild.
*Remarks:* Very rare in skin collections and in aviculture. Only isolated specimens have reached Britain, including two which were owned by the late Duke of Bedford, one owned by R. C. J. Sawyer and the pair belonging to P. H. Maxwell which can be seen at Birdland, Bourton-on-the-Water. A few have been imported into the USA.

Hubert Astley had three of these birds, one of which was very tame. He wrote that it showed ' joy at seeing me and having a game of play, more keenly than any bird I have ever met with.' It could talk a little and imitate various noises.

The Duke of Bedford tried this species at liberty but found it to be a poor stayer. Two strayed after a few months and were both shot. He wrote of the hen that she ' used to gratify her taste for society by flying daily to a town three miles distant where she amused herself by pulling at the pegs on people's clothes lines and playing with the dogs.'

Altogether these macaws are most attractive and it is regrettable that they are so rarely available.

## Genus: *Ara*

The large, flamboyant members of this genus are familiar even to those with no interest in birds, and with the Amazon parrots, are the best known of the neo-tropical parrots.

SPIX'S MACAW *(A. (Cyanopsitta) spixii)*
*Description*: A soft shade of cobalt blue, greyish on the head and neck, even more so on the forehead and ear-coverts. Most of the feathers of the upper surface have pale grey margins. The upper part of the breast is tinged with brownish-grey and the underparts are dull greenish-blue. The inner webs of the flights are blackish, also the underside of the tail. The bill is black. Length: about 22in.

This is a very distinctive macaw which cannot be confused with any other. Salvadori considered that it should be placed in the separate genus, *Cyanopsitta;* certainly, in appearance, it is nearer the *Anodorhynchus* macaws than those of the genus *Ara.* It resembles neither genus in having a comparatively small beak and in erecting often the greyish, elongated feathers of the head and neck. It is better proportioned than most macaws, having a long tail and a less prominent head, due to the smaller beak.
*Distribution:* Eastern Brazil in the states of Piauhy (Parnagua) and Bahia (Joazeiro). Nothing seems to have been recorded about this macaw in the wild. After Spix's discovery of it there was no record of a further sighting until 1903, over 100 years later. Excluding the island Amazons, it must be one of the rarest of all the parrots from Central and South America.
*Remarks:* An extreme rarity in aviculture. There was a pair at Paignton Zoo in 1927 and three years earlier Mrs. Dalton Burgess recorded that her single specimen had laid an egg. At the present time there is one pair in Ireland, which was originally brought from Brazil for the World Show of the IOA in Rotterdam in 1965. In 1971 eggs were laid by the female.

The Spix's which belonged to Karl Plath in the USA could speak quite distinctly in a feminine voice and was able to repeat several sentences. It was described as being lovable and tame, rarely nipped, and squawked only occasionally and in a voice less harsh than the larger macaws. This bird was received in February 1928 and met an untimely end in March 1946 when attacked by two Amazon Parrots with which it was temporarily housed.

BLUE AND YELLOW MACAW *(A. (ararauna) ararauna)*
*Synonyms:* Blue and Gold Macaw, Yellow-breasted Macaw
*Description:* This species is generally considered to be the most

beautiful of the more commonly imported macaws. It is a rich sky-blue above, darker on the flights and tail, golden yellow below. The forehead and crown are tinged with green and the sides of the neck are yellow. The under tail-coverts are blue and the underside of the wings and tail are yellow. The naked white skin of the facial area is adorned with three very narrow lines of tiny black feathers under the eye and surrounded by a broader circle of black around the throat. The beak is black and the iris is pale yellow. The extremely long tail accounts for more than half of the total length of about 32in.

Immature birds have some of the wing-coverts and upper tail-coverts pale brownish-grey; the under tail-coverts are a paler and duller blue.

According to Walter Goodfellow, the birds from Bolivia are larger and more brilliantly coloured than those from the other parts of its range.

A bird of this species devoid of yellow pigment – ie, entirely blue and white – was exhibited at a small zoo at Entretat in France many years ago.

*Distribution:* Eastern Panama to Ecuador, eastern Peru, Bolivia, northern Paraguay and Brazil (extending to São Paulo and Rio de Janeiro); in addition, de Schauensee gives the Guianas, Venezuela south of the Orinoco, north of it only in Monagas, and Colombia, except the Cauca Valley and western Nariño.

These macaws are usually seen in pairs, less often in groups. Little seems to have been recorded about their wild life. One ornithologist watched them feeding on a yellow fruit called 'yatiaty'.

*Remarks:* This species, which is frequently and regularly imported, has been known in captivity since the 16th century. It is the most widely kept of the macaws and, if bought when young, makes a delightful and affectionate pet. These birds can be amazingly gentle with their formidable-looking beaks, but some are unreliable and it is never wise to touch one whose character is not known.

The Blue and Yellow Macaw is capable of 'blushing'; one can see the blood colour the bare skin of the cheeks. D. H. S. Risdon noted that this habit was more often seen in the cock of his pair: 'The cock blushes when excited, his bare face assuming a deep pink. He nods his head up and down as a form of greeting, at the same time 'blazing' his eyes by contracting the pupil. The hen is less demonstrative. She seldom blushes and when she does her face hardly colours at all.' (AM Vol. 71, 85).

*Breeding records:* The first recorded breeding reputedly took place in France in 1818, at Caen. It was claimed that 19 clutches were laid by 1822, consisting of 62 eggs, of which 25 hatched and 15 were reared! The eggs in each clutch were said to number from three to six; two or three, sometimes four, is the usual number for this species. This 'record' should obviously be regarded with suspicion!

The first recorded success in Britain took place in 1934 at Romford, Essex. A pair were at liberty in a garden, nested in a coal-shed and reared one youngster. The second (usually quoted as the first) success was the hatching of two chicks and the rearing of one in 1939 at Edinburgh Zoo. The parents did not nest again until 1946, but no young were reared then.

In the USA, two pairs of young birds were bred in 1933 or 1934 by Mr. and Mrs. E. T. Stotesbury of Palm Beach. The nest was on the ground under a large half-barrel.

In Germany a pair nested in a cupboard in 1901 and reared one youngster which fledged at 94 days old. A pair bred at Essen Zoo. Three eggs were laid at two-day intervals. Both parents were said to incubate – but without result. On September 5 another egg was laid, followed at two-day intervals by a second and third. Again both parents incubated and one of the eggs hatched on October 5. The chick was naked except for a very small amount of down and was described as being 'noteworthy for its huge beak, a really astonishing outsize thing in beaks.'

In addition to parrot food, boiled egg, bananas and bread soaked in milk were provided and the youngster was successfully reared.

Chessington Zoo bred one young bird in 1958; four eggs were laid, one of which hatched 28 days after the first was laid. A pair at Rode Tropical Bird Gardens produced one youngster in 1964. Two eggs were laid and at no time was the cock seen to incubate, although he was often in the box sitting beside the hen. The incubation period in this instance was thought to be between 24 and 26 days. As the youngster grew it became evident that bulky food, which was easy for the parents to swallow and regurgitate, was needed. Bread liberally smeared with butter was a favourite, closely followed by cake and sweet biscuit. Large amounts of cooked meat and fat were eaten avidly.

For the first four weeks the young bird grew rapidly without showing any signs of feathering. The quill feathers broke through first, then the eyes opened and the beak darkened. The wings and back were the first to feather, then the tail, head and body. At ten weeks old the young macaw was well feathered, but the tail and flights were still short. At 12 weeks old it clambered out of the nest-box and perched on the rim. At 13 weeks it left the nest permanently. It resembled the parents but was slightly smaller, with a smaller beak and dark eyes.

Another aviculturist who bred this macaw recorded that it left the nest after 94 days. The Blue and Yellow has hybridised with the Scarlet and with the Green-winged Macaw.

WAGLER'S MACAW *(A. (ararauna) caninde)*
*Description:* It differs from the above by lacking the greenish tinge to the forehead. The area of naked skin on the cheeks is much smaller and surrounded by a broad green band, which covers the whole of the throat. The feathered lines on the lores and the upper parts of the cheeks are more numerous and of a lighter green. Length: about 32in.
*Distribution:* Paraguay and the northern part of the Argentine Chaco.
*Remarks:* This should surely be considered as the southern representative of *A.ararauna*.

The present classification of the *militaris* and *ambigua* species is difficult to understand. The two races of *ambigua* (and even the scientific name suggests this) should be considered as sub-species of *militaris* and their range does, in fact, divide the *militaris* sub-species.

MILITARY MACAW *(A.militaris militaris)*
*Description:* The dark red feathers of the forehead are very short, giving a somewhat bristly appearance and immediate recognition of this species. The large area of bare skin on the cheeks is decorated with several fine lines of black feathers. The head is light green, there is a bluish tinge on the hind-neck and the chin is brown. The rump and upper tail-coverts are light blue, also most of the flight feathers and some of the greater wing-coverts. The rest of the wings, also the mantle, are of an olive shade of green; the under wing-coverts are also green. The tail feathers are maroon, tipped with blue, the underside being yellow. Length: about 27in.
*Distribution:* North-western South America, east of the Andes in Colombia, western Colombia, also the Santa Marta region, Ecuador and northern Peru.

This species often frequents cultivated land and damages growing crops. It also feeds on the blossoms of various trees. Small groups of two or three birds are usually seen together. They are said to be very cautious and easily disturbed, and to nest in hollow trees and lay two eggs.

*Remarks:* This is the least common of the large macaws (not including the blue species) in confinement. It is irregularly imported, although it cannot be described as rare. Both Birdland at Bourton-on-the-Water and Birdworld at Farnham have pairs at liberty.

*Breeding records:* Early records infer that young of this species have been hatched but not reared. In *Vogelkosmos* (1969, 138-139), M. Meissner mentions obtaining a young Military Macaw, one of four bred in Holland, probably in 1968. F. S. Scheer, of the Miami Parrot Jungle, produced hybrids between the Military and the Scarlet Macaws, reported in 1950. The lack of breeding records is probably due to the small number of *pairs* owned by aviculturists.

### ECUADORIAN MACAW *(A. (militaris) guayaquilensis)*

*Synonym:* Chapman's Green Macaw

*Description:* It differs from *A. (militaris) ambigua* (see below) in its much smaller bill and in having the lower surface of the rectrices (except the central pair) and the remiges, also the longer lower wing-coverts greenish-yellow, instead of golden yellow (greener even than in *A.militaris militaris*).

*Distribution:* Western Ecuador, possibly also south-western Colombia.

### GRAND MILITARY MACAW *(A. (militaris) ambigua)*

*Synonym:* Buffon's Macaw

*Description:* From the examination of skins, it would seem that it is difficult to separate from *A.m.militaris* except by its larger size and yellower shade of olive green. Length: average about 33in. Immature birds are less brightly coloured with indistinct margins of yellowish-green on the scapulars and inner secondaries.

*Distribution:* Nicaragua, Costa Rica, Panama and western Colombia. Slud (35) found that this species is restricted to the Caribbean slope in Costa Rica, mainly in the lower tropical belt. It is seen most often in well-wooded regions, inside virgin forest and in adjacent clearings with tall trees, in groups of a dozen or so, or in twos and threes, but rarely alone. The birds usually keep very high in the trees and are well camouflaged by the foliage. They are very noisy. Slud recorded seeing one worried by a tiny Bat Falcon whose territory it had invaded. Its beak can apparently open even the most tough-shelled fruits, such as the monkey pot *(Lecythis costaricensis)*.

MEXICAN MILITARY MACAW *(A. militaris mexicana)*
*Description:* Differs from *A.m.militaris* only in its larger size: average 29in.
*Distribution:* Mexico: Sonora, Chihuahua, Tamaulipas, Sinaloa, Zacatecas, Nayarit, Jalisco, Coluna, Guanajuato, Mexico, Michoacan, Guerrero and Oaxaca.

It is found in mountains and arid lowlands, where it replaces *A.macao*. It occurs on the coastal slopes and up to an altitude of 8,000ft in pine and oak forests.

BOLIVIAN MILITARY MACAW *(A.militaris boliviana)*
*Description:* Said to be slightly larger than *A.m.mexicana,* which it otherwise resembles.
*Distribution:* Bolivia, extending to the Argentine border in the province of Salta.

SCARLET MACAW *(A.macao)*
*Synonyms:* Red and Yellow Macaw, Red, Yellow and Blue Macaw, Red-breasted Macaw.
*Description:* Predominantly rich scarlet, and easily recognised by the rich yellow, often tinged with green, of the centre part of the wing, including the greater wing-coverts. The flights and the lower edge of the wing are blue and the lower back, rump and tail-coverts are light skyblue. The tail is scarlet, tinged with blue at the tip of the central feathers, the outer ones being almost entirely blue. The underside of the wings and tail are orange-red and brownish. The upper mandible is white, tipped with black, the lower mandible being black. The large area of flesh-coloured skin below the eyes and covering the cheeks is bare of markings. The iris is yellow. Length: about 36in.

Some immature birds have more green on the wing than do adults. When they leave the nest they resemble the parents except for the slightly smaller bill, which has the lower mandible greyish.

The sexes are generally described as being alike, but E. J. Boosey noticed that the small feathers on the forehead of the hen of his pair were shorter than those of the cock, which were bristly and brush-like. This may, however, have been a feature of this pair only.
*Distribution:* Mexico from Oaxaca south through Colombia to eastern Ecuador, eastern Peru, Bolivia, and Brazil south of the Amazon in the states of Amazonas and Pará; de Schauensee gives additionally the Guianas and Venezuela.

This macaw is found in large noisy flocks, feeding on fruit such as figs and cultivated foods including the fruit of the tonca bean tree while it is still small and green. It also feeds on palm trees, especially the coucorite palm. It nests in holes in trees and lays two, sometimes three, eggs.

According to Slud (35) it does not go far into forests but frequents the forest borders and patches of woodland, also open or semi-open country with scattered stands of tall trees. It normally keeps high in the trees.

*Remarks:* This is a very beautiful macaw and never fails to attract attention in zoos and bird gardens. It has always been regularly imported and is, with the Blue and Yellow, the macaw which is best known to the general public. It is kept as a pet less often than the Blue and Yellow, probably because its temper is less certain.

*Breeding records*: The first recorded breeding of this species in Britain appears to be that of the liberty macaws on Lord Lilford's estate. They bred on numerous occasions; in 1933, after two unsuccessful attempts, one youngster left the nest on December 19. Unfortunately, it died from internal injuries, probably received on its descent from the nest, which was in a hollow cavity near the top of a very tall and partly decayed elm. One youngster was reared in 1934, a male, which left the nest at the end of September. (On several occasions it was stated that these macaws were *A.chloroptera* but Delacour is certain that they were *A.macao*.)

In the USA, the Scarlet Macaw was bred several times from 1916 by L. H. Chamness. The hen laid nine or eleven clutches consisting of two to four eggs. Three was the highest number reared in one nest. The birds were housed in an aviary 10ft x 12ft. In Australia, Sir Edward Hallstrom bred this macaw on many occasions; at one time he had six or seven pairs, most of which were the progeny of one prolific pair.

This species has hybridised often with the Blue and Yellow Macaw. Hallstrom had 20 of these hybrids at the same time, all of which were bred in his aviaries. In the USA, two bred from a male Scarlet and a female Blue and Yellow were described as having the forehead bright red, merging into a patch of yellow. The head and neck were green and the breast and wing-coverts were green tinged with yellow. The underparts were bright red, the primaries blue above, gold below. The upper side of the tail was 'red-blue', the underside gold. These birds were bred in a cage only 4ft square and 6ft high.

The Scarlet Macaw has also crossed with the Green-winged and the Military Macaw.

GREEN-WINGED MACAW *(A.chloroptera)*
*Synonyms:* Crimson Macaw, Maroon Macaw, Red and Blue Macaw, Red and Green Macaw.
*Description:* The head, underparts, under wing-coverts, tail and part of the mantle are crimson. The flights and secondaries are blue and the feathers next to the crimson mantle are olive green, those at the side of the rump being tinged with olive. The rump and under tail-coverts are pale blue and the central tail feathers are tipped with blue. The tail appears to be too short for such a large bird, giving it rather a top-heavy appearance. The flesh-coloured skin of the cheeks is decorated with five or six lines of very small red feathers. The upper mandible is mainly horn-coloured with black on the upper part of the cutting edge; the lower mandible is black. Light yellow is the colour of the iris. Length: average 36in.

Newly-fledged young have the iris dark and the beak partly grey.
*Distribution:* Eastern Panama and the greater part of tropical South America south to eastern Peru and Bolivia, the Argentine Chaco, Paraguay, Misiones and Parana. It is not recorded from western Ecuador.

These birds feed on various fruits and berries, including the fruits of certain climbing plants found only in dense primitive forest. They also inhabit open campos and do not occur in large flocks but in small groups or even singly.
*Remarks:* This species is fairly frequently imported into Britain but is not as common as the Scarlet Macaw. It is believed to have been imported as early as the end of the 16th century and is much better known in Europe than in the USA. It has never been popular as a pet.

In the experience of J. S. Rigge, at least, it is not as destructive as the other large species. He has kept these birds for years in an aviary constructed of rustic poles and ½in wire netting!
*Breeding records:* The first breeding which definitely relates to this species (in the past, there was much confusion over the common names of the large macaws) took place in 1962 in the aviaries of J. S. Rigge of Millom, Cumberland. He received the Avicultural Society's medal for the first breeding.

The pair were purchased in 1956 and were housed in an aviary which measured 17ft x 8ft x 6ft. An oak butter-churn barrel fixed horizontally on a stand was provided for a nest-box. In 1960 three eggs were laid, which eventually proved to be addled. In 1961, laying started on May 18. Two young birds were found dead in the nest, possibly due to the dust from the rotten wood at the bottom of the barrel. The following year a large peat sod, 6in thick, was placed at the bottom of the nest. An egg was laid on April 18 and was removed on May 28, the fully formed embryo being dead-in-shell. The hen remained in the nest and laid again. On July 7 a chick was heard and on July 12 there were two in the nest. Extras in the way of food were provided but the hen refused everything except sunflower, a little hemp and spinach beet. When the young were nine weeks old the family consumed one pound of seed and five large spinach beet leaves daily.

The chicks could be heard squawking when they were fed until the age of two weeks, after which they were silent. At five weeks the red feathers were beginning to show on their heads and the hen left the nest more often. At the age of nine weeks the young were almost fully feathered. The first one fledged on October 18, after 103 days in the nest. The second left four days later. Except for the shorter tail, slightly smaller size, dark iris and greyer beak, the young birds resembled their parents. They did not begin to feed themselves until November 10. By 1972 the total number of young reared by this pair had reached 18. In 1968 for the first time three young were hatched and reared. I saw some of the young birds in 1965. They were all housed in the same aviary – a magnificent sight. Green-winged Macaws which are housed outside and have the benefit of rain and sun on their plumage are a wonderful deep shade of red. This species has hybridised with the Blue and Yellow, and Scarlet Macaws.

### CUBAN MACAW *(A.tricolor)*

*Extinct*

*Synonym:* Tri-coloured Macaw.

*Description:* Forehead red, merging into yellowish-red on the top of the head and shading into bright yellow on the nape; the feathers of the upper back cinnamon-red, edged with greenish. The entire underparts were scarlet, tinged with orange on the cheeks and throat. The primaries and secondaries were bright blue; the upper surface of the tail cinnamon-red, shading into blue at the tip. Length: about 18in.

*Remarks:* It formerly occurred in Cuba and probably also on the Isle of Pines. The last recorded specimen was shot at La Vega, near Cienaga de Zapata, in 1864. It is thought that 15 skins still exist in 11 museums.

RED-CHEEKED MACAW *(A.rubrogenys)*
*Synonym:* Lafresnaye's Macaw
*Description:* Predominantly olive green, lighter on the rump and a purer shade of green on the head and neck. The forehead is red, merging into orange and there is a red spot on the ear-coverts. Red and orange are the colours of the shoulder; the carpal edge of the wing, the under wing-coverts and the thighs are orange. The flight feathers and the primary coverts are greyish-blue and the greater under wing-coverts are olive yellow. The tail is green, bluish towards the tip, the underside being olive and dusky at the tip. The bill is black; the feathered lines on the otherwise bare skin of the cheeks are blackish-brown. Length: about 24in.

Immature birds have much less red on the crown and ear-coverts, no red at all on the smaller wing-coverts, the shoulders and the carpal edge of the wing. The under wing-coverts are of a pale shade of orange and the thighs are greenish, tinged with orange.
*Distribution:* Bolivia, in Cochabamba and probably Santa Cruz in forested areas.
*Remarks:* This species appears to be unknown to aviculture.

GOLDEN-NAPED MACAW *(Ara auricollis)*
*Synonyms:* Cassin's Macaw, Yellow-collared Macaw, Yellow-naped Macaw.
*Description:* Mainly dark green, with the yellow on the hind-neck, which is about ½in in depth, providing a strong contrast to the black forehead and cheeks. The rear of the crown is tinged with blue and the nape is dark green. The flights are blue and the underside of the wings and tail are olive greyish-green, the upper surface of the tail being maroon at the base, bluish-green at the tip. The skin surrounding the eye is white, the beak is black and the iris reddish. Length: 16in.
*Distribution:* Eastern Bolivia, Mato Grosso, Paraguay, and northern Argentina in the provinces of Jujuy and Misiones.

Walter Goodfellow, who was familiar with this species in Bolivia, wrote that small water holes and swampy ground in a certain clearing attracted these macaws in hundreds, morning and evening from May to September. They left Bolivia before the dry season ended, probably to go further south.
*Remarks:* Very rarely imported. A pair brought from Bolivia in 1920 by Goodfellow were the first to be seen in Britain. He presented

them to the London Zoo; one was still there in 1937. A single specimen has been at Wassenaar Zoo in Holland for several years and in 1970 a pair were added to the collection. Jersey Zoo and Birdland, Bourton-on-the-Water, are also exhibiting this species.
*Breeding records:* Busch Gardens, Tampa, Florida have reared at least nine young to date.

## SEVERE MACAW *(A.severa severa)*

*Description:* The forehead, the margin of the cheeks, and the chin are chestnut in colour, the remainder of the head being green with a bluish tinge. The body is also green and the wings, which have the flights and the primary coverts blue. There is some red on the bend of the wing and the outermost smaller wing-coverts are red. The underside of the wings are dull olive, the upper side of the tail is reddish-brown edged with green towards the base and tipped with blue; the underside of the tail is pinkish-red. The bare skin between the eyes and the lores is whitish, the iris is straw-yellow and the bill is black. Length: 20in.

The small macaws can be rather confusing to identify but this one and *A.s.castaneifrons* are easily recognised by the chestnut-coloured forehead. Otto Hirthe, who bred from his pair, noticed that the chestnut on the forehead was more pronounced on the cock.
*Distribution:* From the Orinoco east over the Guianas and south to the Amazon on the Mexiana Island. According to Burmeister it lives in pairs during the breeding season, otherwise in flocks, and exists mainly on the fruit of the jandiroba and another fruit with milky juice. These macaws apparently do much damage to maize crops.
*Remarks:* Irregularly imported but not rare. Severe Macaws make extremely attractive and affectionate pets, especially if obtained when young. Maud Knobel described (AM Fourth series, vol. 7, 190) hers as being '. . . the merriest bird of all my collection, always busy about something, either swinging in his swing, playing with a piece of chain, or lying on his back at the bottom of his cage playing with a piece of wood and laughing to himself all the time. He talks quite a lot but not real words, and he tries desperately hard to whistle.' It is interesting to note that this bird never bathed and hated being sprayed.
*Breeding records:* The first recorded breeding occured in Copenhagen in 1954. The pair were housed in a compartment 20ft long, 3½ft wide and 7ft high. A nest-box was hung in the shelter and another in the flight. They were made of 1½in boards and measured approximately

12in square by 30in high. Moist earth topped with peat moss to a depth of 6in covered the bottom. In 1954 three eggs were laid in August on alternate days in the box in the outside flight. One egg was infertile but the other two hatched; one chick died after about three days. The incubation period was 25 to 28 days and the young macaw left the nest at about seven weeks old. It was not independent until about six weeks after leaving the nest. In 1955 another youngster was reared and three more in 1956.

In Britain, the first breeding was probably that at Whipsnade Zoo in 1961, by a pair which belonged to P. H. Maxwell. The cock eventually bit off all its toes; at the end of August it was found badly injured and died. Meanwhile, the hen, which laid every year, was nesting. About the middle of September a fully-feathered young one was seen looking out of the nest, a slanting tree trunk, which it left a few days later. No special food was provided – only apple and sunflower.

In India, P. Mullick was successful with this species in 1968. In 1965 the pair was housed in a small flight measuring 12ft x 4ft x 6ft, as the cock was unable to fly. They were provided with a barrel 12in long x 12in wide, in which they roosted. On July 6, 1967, two eggs were seen in the nest, one of which hatched at the end of the month after about 28 days incubation. At the beginning of September the adults attacked their owner when he entered the aviary. On October 5 the young bird was still in the nest, possibly because of the presence of zoo visitors close to the flight. It was removed, causing the adults and the young bird to bite their owner. Each day it was removed from the nest for three hours until it seemed less nervous. On October 28 it flew for the first time and left the nest on its own accord on the following day.

Three Severe Macaws were bred in American zoos in 1970 – one in Cincinnati and two in Van Nuys.

CHESTNUT-FRONTED MACAW *(A.severa castaneifrons)*
*Distribution*: Eastern Panama to Colombia, Ecuador, Bolivia and extreme southern Venezuela. Birds from the upper Amazon and the Mato Grosso probably also belong to this form.

RED-BELLIED MACAW *(A.manilata)*
*Description:* This is not a brightly coloured macaw, being mainly green with the lower abdomen maroon. The feathers of the crown are blue with blackish bases, the hind part of the crown and the re-

mainder of the upper parts being green, many of the feathers having black bases. The bastard wing, primary-coverts and the flights are peacock blue, some of the feathers being blackish on the outer webs. The throat and upper breast feathers are tinged with pink and edged with pale blue-grey, shading into light yellowish-green on the underparts. The under tail-coverts are whitish-blue and the under wing-coverts are blue-green tinged with yellowish, and yellow with a touch of orange. The naked skin around the eye and extending to the cheeks is dull yellowish. The rather small beak is black and the iris is dark brown: Length: about 18in, of which the long tapered tail accounts for about 9½in.

*Distribution:* The extreme southern part of Venezuela and the Guianas southward, including Colombia east of the Andes, eastern Ecuador to Peru, and Mato Grosso and Bahia in Brazil; it is also found in Trinidad.

According to G. A. C. Herklots (20) it nests in holes made by woodpeckers in trees and lays two eggs. Its numbers appear to be increasing in Trinidad, especially in the Nariva swamp. Flocks totalling about 100 birds have been seen in the area of the cabbage palms, whose seeds they feed on. Dorothy E. Snyder (36) records that in Guyana it occurs in swamps where moriche palms are plentiful, also in parkland and plantations, where it feeds on berries in the tree tops.

*Remarks:* Considering the large area of South America over which the Red-bellied Macaw is found, it is surprising that until 1971, when one dealer located a source of supply, it was so rarely imported into Britain. The only specimens of which I knew previously were a pair belonging to an aviculturist and the single bird at Birdland, Bourton-on-the-Water, several years ago.

In the USA a female belonging to David West was kept with a male Coulon's Macaw. They appeared to be greatly attached to each other and were observed mating. The Red-bellied was very fond of bathing and would take a dip two or three times daily.

## ILLIGER'S MACAW *(A.maracana)*

*Description:* There is a narrow line of bright red on the forehead; the rest of the head and the nape are greenish-blue, darker blue on the crown. There is a patch of scarlet on the abdomen and another on the lower back. The primaries and primary-coverts are blue, also the secondaries and some of the upper wing-coverts which are tinged with green. The tail is blue, with the base of the feathers tinged with

reddish-brown; the underside of the tail is golden-olive. The bare skin of the cheeks is yellowish, the beak is black and the iris brownish-red. Length: about $16\frac{1}{2}$in, of which the tail accounts for about half the total length. Females are said to show less red on the forehead.
*Distribution:* Eastern and central Brazil from Pará, Maranhão, Piauhy, Bahiá, Minas Geraïs and Goyaz south to Mato Grosso and Rio Grande do Sul; Paraguay; north-eastern Argentina in Misiones. Butler quoted Burmeister to the effect that it preferred the lower plains near the mouths of streams to mountain forests, and was abundant between Cape Frio and the mouth of the river.
*Remarks:* Irregularly imported, but not rare. This species makes a delightful pet; it is very intelligent, easily tamed and will learn to talk. Maud Knobel recorded (AM Fourth series, vol. V, 191) that her specimen was very fond of bathing. ' He will get into quite a big basin and literally lie down in the water, first on one side and then the other. He often gets so wet that I have to turn on the gas fire to dry him up a bit or else roll him in a towel. He is quite different in character to the Severe, though he loves playing about, and will run about on the floor as quick as lightning, and likes being on the floor, which the Severe does not. He gets into the waste paper basket and will carefully take pieces of paper out and strew them over my floor . . . The two I have are far more gentle and reliable than most Amazons, and there is no doubt about their devotion to one.'

Practically nothing seems to have been recorded about this species as an aviary bird.
*Breeding records:* In 1931 two Illiger's were bred in one of the outside aviaries attached to the Parrot House at London Zoo.

COULON'S MACAW *(A.couloni)*
*Description:* According to Salvadori, it differs from *A. maracana* only in lacking the red on the forehead, lower back and abdomen and in having the blue on the head, especially on the cheeks, purer and paler. The tip of the upper mandible is whitish and the area of bare skin around the eye is smaller. Length: 16in.
*Distribution:* Eastern Peru.
*Remarks:* In Peters' opinion it is ' Perhaps only subspecifically distinct from *maracana*, but requires further study.' David West, who apparently owned a Coulon's, found it difficult in the extreme to see how it could be considered as a sub-species of the Illiger's, believing the latter to be ' as vastly different from the Coulon's as an Elegant is from a Rosella.' I can find no other reference to this species in

aviculture and have, unfortunately, never seen a skin or a living specimen.

HAHN'S MACAW *(A.nobilis nobilis)*

*Description:* Predominantly green, yellowish on the underparts. The crown and forehead are blue and some of the under wing-coverts, also the bend of the wing, are scarlet. The underside of the tail is yellowish and the under wing-coverts are yellowish-green. There is an area of bare white skin surrounding the eyes and extending to the beak. *The upper and lower mandibles are black.* Length: 13in. Immature birds are paler blue on the head; there is no red at the bend of the wing but a small patch of pale orange on the edge of the wing below.

*Distribution:* The Caura Valley, Venezuela, east to Surinam (and possibly to Cayenne), south to the Rio Branco. It was formerly found in Trinidad and Guyana.

*Remarks:* It is seldom imported but not rare, as it breeds well in aviaries.

*Breeding records:* This macaw was first bred in Britain in 1963 at Birdland, Bourton-on-the-Water, where it has since proved prolific. In 1964 two pairs were returned to Trinidad, where the Hahn's Macaw died out in the early years of this century.

Due to the confusion caused by the changing of the scientific names it is difficult to know which breeding records relate to *A.nobilis nobilis* (formerly known as *A.hahni*) and which relate to *A.nobilis cumanensis* (formerly *A.nobilis*), the Noble Macaw.

In 1966 A. W. Bolton wrote (Southern Foreign Bird Club Magazine, Sept. 1966) that Hahn's Macaws '. . . breed freely, laying a clutch of four or five eggs and they are double brooded. They can also be kept on the colony system with very good results. With all the Hahn's Macaws that I have kept on the colony system I have never had one fight.

'I have bred these birds in flights as small as 6ft long, 3ft wide and 6ft high, but to see them in full flight is the most wonderful sight and for this you want a much larger enclosure. The nest-boxes I use measure 18in deep by 9in x 9in inside. To form the nest I put a piece of turf cut to the correct size in the bottom of the box with the grass to the bottom.' Soaked peat was placed on top of this.

Lt.-Col. H. W. Clayden bred from a pair obtained from Birdland in 1965, which would almost certainly have been bred there. Two young were reared in 1966 and four in 1967. In 1969 J. Halford bred from a pair which came from Birdland during the winter of 1968/69. The hen laid three eggs, only one of which hatched, after an incubation period of 28 days. The young bird spent eight weeks in the nesting log. The pair were again successful in 1971.

In 1969 T. H. Alston described (Parrot Society Magazine, March 1969) his experience of breeding from this species. His pair nested in a box 4ft deep and 10in square. Five clear eggs were laid during May 1968; the second clutch also proved infertile but the third contained two fertile eggs, both of which hatched. The chicks were covered with white down and their lower mandibles started to turn black at a very early age. They grew slowly and were fully feathered at the age of six weeks, when they resembled the adults, except for the lower mandible, which was only partly black. They fledged at the age of eight weeks.

NOBLE MACAW *(A.nobilis cumanensis)*

*Description:* Distinguished from *A.n.nobilis* only by the colour of the upper mandible which is whitish and by its slightly larger size, ie, 14in.

When the Noble Macaws bred by E. N. T. Vane left the nest the area of bare skin on the face was duller and smaller than in the adults. There was only a small amount of blue shading on the head and no red at the bend of the wing.

*Distribution:* Eastern Brazil south of the Amazon in the states of Pará, Maranhão, Piauhy and Bahiá.

*Remarks:* Irregularly imported. Vane wrote that his original Noble Macaws were very susceptible to 'pneumonia', but after about three years the trouble did not recur and the young never suffered from it. They proved to be so hardy that one experienced no ill-effects from escaping and spending many days flying around in a snowstorm. One youngster, which was brought into the house for two weeks because it had a chill, soon settled down in a cage and learned to say 'hello'.

*Breeding records:* The first breeding in Britain took place in 1949 in the aviaries of E. N. T. Vane. There were three macaws and they were provided with a nest-box 8in square and 30in long, with 6in of peat in the bottom. They were thought to be two hens and a cock; two slept in the box and the third in the aviary shelter. The first egg was laid on June 10, the second two days later; there were three by the 17th and four the following day. The first young one hatched on July 5, the second and third at two-day intervals and the fourth on July 12, giving an incubation period of 24 days. When the nest was inspected on July 22 the eyes of the chicks were open and green tufts of feathering were showing on the body. The parents spent most of their time away from the nest as the weather was hot. On September 3 the first youngster left the nest, returned later in the day and did not appear again until September 9 when all four young fledged together. Two were eventually moved but the others lived together in harmony, keeping together in pairs.

It is interesting to note that while the hen was incubating the cock would sit with the second hen; they were observed mating and often preened each other. At night the cock roosted inside the box and the single hen slept just outside; she was never allowed to enter the nest.

By 1951 Vane's Noble Macaws had reared eight young and in 1956 nearly 30 had been bred. The original pair reared young almost annually, starting on practically the same date every year.

G. Rayson Brown of California believed that the species he bred in 1950 was the Noble Macaw but his birds were probably Blue-crowned Conures.

LONG-WINGED MACAW *(A.nobilis longipennis)*
*Synonym:* Neumann's Macaw.
*Distribution:* Brazil in the states of Goyaz and Mato Grosso.

VEGETATION AND LAND USE
PARAMOS
PARAMOS
PUNA
PUNA
PAMPAS
SUBTROPICAL FOREST
SWAMP FOREST
CULTIVATION [MEDITERRANEAN, TROPICAL AND SUBTROPICAL]
TROPICAL RAIN AND GALLERY FOREST
BUSH AND TALL GRASS STEPPE
WOODED SAVANNA
XEROPHYTIC FOREST
IRRIGATED FIELDS
CEREAL CULTIVATION [UNIRRIGATED]
TUSSOCK GRASSLAND AND DESERT SHRUB
COOL TEMPERATE EVERGREEN AND DECIDUOUS FOREST
CULTIVATED GRASS STEPPE WITH LIVESTOCK REARING
0 500 1000 1500
SCALE MILES
PUNA = UPLAND PASTURE
PARAMOS = MOUNTAIN STEPPE
PAMPAS = TREELESS GRASS-COVERED PLAINS

CHAPTER 5

# CONURES

FREQUENTLY the question is asked: 'What is the difference between a parrakeet and a conure?' The answer is: technically, none. Conure is the name given to some parrakeets from South and Central America, particularly those of the genera *Aratinga* and *Pyrrhura;* this chapter is concerned mainly with these two groups. Sometimes the members of the genus *Brotogeris* are called conures, more often parrakeets, so in fact the term is interchangeable, although it is never applied to Australian or Asiatic species.

Conures have never been very popular birds with aviculturists because certain rather noisy and destructive *Aratinga* species have earned the whole group a bad name – which is quite undeserved. The *Pyrrhura* conures are among the most delightful of parrot-like birds as aviary subjects and many of the larger *Aratinga* species are extremely interesting and intelligent; almost as rewarding to keep as macaws and much less expensive to buy.

I should perhaps explain here that the two genera are quite distinct in appearance and can be distinguished at a glance. The *Aratinga* species range in size from the macaw-like Blue-crowned Conure which measures 13in, and the 14in Queen of Bavaria's Conure to the smaller *pertinax* sub-species which may attain only 7in in length. Almost all are basically green, often light green, and have the head marked with red or orange, soft browns or blues. The *Pyrrhura* species measure between 8in and 11in, are basically dark green and most – certainly those known to aviculturists – have *scaled markings on the throat, hind neck and upper breast.* The tail is maroon or olive green.

The *Aratingas* are by far the most easily obtainable and in a wider variety. The majority of the *Pyrrhuras* are unfortunately unknown to aviculture, like so many desirable parrots.

*Accommodation:* Excluding the few that exceed about 12in in length, conures can be kept and bred in fairly small aviaries – indeed, small aviaries often give better results than large ones. Although they are active birds, large aviaries for single pairs are unnecessary.

Conures are very sociable and usually appreciate company of their own kind. In large aviaries they can be bred on the colony system. Anyone who has been to Portugal and visited Lisbon Zoo is certain to remember the conure aviaries. Never before or since have I seen so many conures in one place. Birds from Brazil are, of course a natural choice for Portuguese zoos and 50 Golden-crowned Conures in one aviary, 30 Jendayas and Nandays in another and 40 Blue-crowned in the next certainly made a colourful picture.

I doubt if many breeding results were obtained as conures seem less inclined to go to nest under such conditions. The ideal arrangement would seem to be to house a colony together, and when two birds are known to have paired up to remove them to a separate aviary.

All conures are absolutely hardy when acclimatised. They *must* have their nest-boxes left in position throughout the year for roosting. In a colony all the birds will crowd into the same box. One aviculturist who had a pair each of White-eared and Jendayas in the same aviary found that they all slept in the same box, even when the White-eared had young inside!

I would not recommend mixing the two genera unless the aviary is a large one. Conures can be rather spiteful and will often attack other parrot-like species, especially if they are in breeding condition. E. J. Brook successfully bred White-eared when housed with a pair of Jendayas in a large aviary and E. N. T. Vane bred the White-eared in a 30ft aviary with Ringneck Parrakeets. There are always exceptions, but it is wise to be very cautious about mixing these birds.

Aviaries for pairs of conures the size of the Red-bellied or Golden crowned, for example, need not be large. A flight 12ft long, 3ft wide and 6ft high is satisfactory, although flights of 14ft or 16ft are really preferable. The aviary can have an open-fronted shelter if it is sited in a reasonably sheltered position, or if desired, a fully-enclosed one.

For the larger species such as Queen of Bavaria's a minimum flight length of 16ft is desirable. For birds such as these, which have macaw-like beaks, although not quite as large, the precautions outlined in the chapter on macaws to prevent extensive damage to the aviary will in many cases be advisable, although not absolutely essential.

A factor which deserves careful consideration when buying some conures is noise. The *Aratingas*, especially the larger ones and particularly Queen of Bavaria's and Nandays, are the chief culprits in this respect. They have extremely harsh ear-splitting voices which carry a great distance. No one in a built-up area should even consider buying Queen of Bavaria's Conures. Before purchasing any member of this family it is advisable to discover the extent of its vocal powers!

*Feeding*. Conures should be offered a very varied diet. The *Pyrrhuras* will sample anything in my experience, but the *Aratingas* are more reticent about trying new foods. When first obtained the following seeds should be offered in separate dishes: sunflower, canary, white millet, hemp, oats, buckwheat and niger. The last three may be ignored, but the chosen seeds should be available at all times in separate dishes. Peanuts can also be offered. Spray millet is invariably relished and should be provided as often as one's finances allow.

*Pyrrhura* conures are extremely fond of fruit and will taste any kind provided. Grapes and apple are the easiest to feed but these birds will also eat soft fruits such as cherries (a great favourite), gooseberries, damsons, plums, pears, orange, tangerines, pomegranates, also figs, which are not easily obtainable these days.

Other conures are more conservative in their tastes, but can be offered any kind of fruit, although perhaps only grapes, apple and cherries will be accepted. Most of my conures are fond of boiled maize. Fruit and greenfood should not be regarded as tit-bits but as an important part of the diet, provided daily.

All kinds of wild and cultivated greenfoods can be offered, of which the most popular are seeding grasses, dandelion heads, young dandelion leaves, chickweed and spinach beet. Shepherd's purse, plantain, sowthistle, lettuce, cabbage and brussels sprouts tops can also be offered. A clod of grass, with earth and roots intact, is especially valuable when other greenfoods are short. When conures have young in the nest as much greenfood as possible should be provided. If this is unobtainable, soaked millet sprays and soaked seeds should be given.

Doubtless on many occasions these birds have been reared on a diet of hard seed and apple only, sometimes even when greenfood has been offered, but the task of rearing the young must be made very much easier by the provision of quantities of greenfood, apple and other fruits.

A breeder in Denmark who has been outstandingly successful in breeding from a pair of rare *Pyrrhura* conures, supplies a rearing diet of sunflower, loose millet and spray millet, wheat, dandelion, chickweed, apple, orange, whole carrot, dried figs soaked for 24 hours before feeding, and poultry pellets. A general mixture consisting of minced carrots, egg, multi-vitamins, crumbs and glucose is supplied throughout the whole of the period that the young are in the nest.

On one occasion the pair reared a nest of nine young. I doubt whether this could have been achieved on a diet less varied and nutritionally sound. A little extra trouble taken over feeding will be repaid many times. This is especially important with *Pyrrhura* conures, which often produce large clutches.

*Breeding*. If a nest-box and a natural log is provided for conures, they will usually choose the natural log. Should only a nest-box be available, however, they will take to this immediately. So great is the curiosity of this genus that anything new placed in the aviary is inspected at once. *Aratingas* are quite different in this respect; much less inquisitive and confiding. They therefore take longer to accept a nest-box. The average number of eggs in a clutch is about four but nests of three and five are common. The Queen of Bavaria's is an exception, usually laying only two or three eggs. *Pyrrhuras* have larger clutches, usually a minimum of four, more often five and frequently six or seven. Seven or eight eggs seem to be the usual numbers for the White-eared Conure.

The greatest virtue of this genus is its readiness to nest and the regularity with which a pair will breed once they have reared young. The most regularly imported species, the Red-bellied, has been bred on numerous occasions. Undoubtedly, if the other members of the genus were available they would nest just as readily.

The incubation period in conures is approximately 26 days and the young remain in the nest for 49 to 52 days normally, sometimes as long as eight weeks. The adults show the youngsters where to feed almost immediately, although they continue to feed them for about two weeks.

Unfortunately, none of the conures are sexually dimorphic; in other words, the plumage of cock and hen is identical. As with macaws, this is the chief problem where breeding is concerned.

Conures are almost always single-brooded in Britain and other temperate climates, as the incubation and rearing period occupies three months. If they nest successfully very early in the year they will sometimes breed again. In 1971 a pair of Black-tailed Conures reared two nests during the first half of the year. In many cases the birds are probably deterred from a second round by the presence of the first round youngsters; the provision of an extra nest-box might encourage them to produce another clutch. These birds often breed as late as September or October or as early as February. I have had young *Pyrrhuras* fledge in November and birds incubating in December. This is difficult to avoid because nest-boxes must be left in position throughout the year for roosting.

*As pets.* Conures are not nearly as popular as pets in Britain as they are in the USA. This is, perhaps, because few hand-reared young birds are available, except for some *Brotogeris*. This should not deter those who wish to keep a pet conure, provided that a fairly young bird can be obtained, even if it is not at all tame to begin with. A conure which is given plenty of attention is likely to lose all fear of its owner and to become quite ridiculously tame.

In the USA, the Petz's Conure or 'Halfmoon', is one of the most popular of all pet birds; in fact, it has attained a quite amazing degree of popularity. There is no reason why the other smaller members of the genus should not make equally good pets. They often learn to speak a few words, will allow themselves to be handled and will do little tricks such as lying on their back in their owner's hand. They can be let out of their cages only under supervision, being mischievous and often destructive. If left unattended and loose in a room these inquisitive birds are certain to get into some kind of trouble. An open door or window will spell disaster.

The prospective pet owner should realise that many of these birds can be very noisy and have regular periods of shrieking. I should imagine that young *Pyrrhuras*, if obtainable, would make exceptionally delightful pets. They have the advantage of quieter, less harsh voices and are noisy only when alarmed.

A conure which is let out regularly for exercise can be kept in a large wire (fancy) cage. A box type cage, with three sides enclosed, is really more suitable for those active birds. If the interior woodwork is covered with ½in wire netting this will prevent them from gnawing and also allow them to climb all over the inside of the cage.

## Genus: *Aratinga*

A wide variety of species are imported, most of which, especially the smaller ones, are very reasonable in price.

### SHARP-TAILED CONURE *(A.acuticaudata acuticaudata)*

*Description:* The forehead, crown, lores, cheeks and ear-coverts are dull blue; the blue is more extensive than in the other sub-species. Some birds show a bluish tinge on the breast. The under wing-coverts are dusky olive and golden olive. The tail is green, olive below, and the lateral feathers are brownish-red at the base of the inner webs. The upper mandible is whitish with a dark tip and the lower mandible is blackish. (Both mandibles are whitish in the Blue-crowned.) The iris is pink and the bare skin surrounding the eye is white. Length: about 14in.

*Distribution:* Eastern Bolivia in the provinces of Santa Cruz and Chuquisaca; western Mato Grosso, Paraguay, Uruguay and northern Argentina south to the provinces of La Rioja, San Luis and Pampa.

E. W. White, who collected skins of this species in 1880 near Andalgala in Catamarco (northern Argentina) wrote that it was not very abundant in that district. It flew very swiftly in flocks of seven or eight, screeching continuously. He saw the birds feeding on the young shoots of the tala tree.

*Breeding records:* In 1971, K. Bastien of Ventnor in the Isle of Wight bred three young from a pair which had been in his possession for three years. In appearance the young birds exactly resembled their parents, except that both mandibles were horn-coloured. This is interesting because various authors have described the young as 'lacking the blue on the head.'

*Remarks:* Seldom imported and probably frequently confused with the Blue-crowned Conure.

MARGARITA CONURE *(A.a.neoxena)*

*Synonym:* Venezuelan Blue-crowned Conure.

Doubtfully distinct.

*Distribution:* northern and eastern Venezuela, possibly also Guyana.

BLUE-CROWNED CONURE *(A.a.haemorrhous)*

*Description:* It differs from the nominate race in the smaller amount of blue on the head, only the forehead and crown being blue tinged with vinous. Another difference is the colour of the beak; both upper and lower mandibles are whitish. Length: about 13in.

*Distribution:* Eastern Brazil in the states of Bahia and Piauhy.

*Remarks*: not often imported and usually in small numbers, although a large consignment arrived in Britain in 1966. This is a very noisy bird; one owner had to shut his pair in the shelter every night because they persisted in greeting the dawn with harsh cries!

Several writers have commented on the intelligence of this species. The Duke of Bedford (38) told of a timid one with an injury which required regular bathing. It learned in four days that its owner's

intentions were good and would voluntarily bend its head forward to be sponged. It could talk and was even trained not to screech by 'cross words and light taps on the beak.'
*Breeding records:* G. Rayson Brown of Los Angeles bought a pair of these conures in 1949, under the impression that they were Noble Macaws. In December they began to show an interest in the nest-box. On February 5, young were heard in the nest and the first fledged on March 17. Four weeks later the second had not left the nest so it was removed. The cock fed both youngsters for some time after fledging. On May 4 the hen was again incubating and two chicks were seen in the nest on June 7. No further reports were made of that pair.

*A.a.neumanni (Blake and Traylor)*
*Distribution:* Bolivia.

WEDDELL'S CONURE *(A. weddellii)*
*Description:* The head is greyish-brown, the feathers tipped with dull blue. The upper parts are olive-tinged green and the primaries are blue, the first being black edged blue, and the primary-coverts deep blue. The greater under wing-coverts are blackish, slightly edged with bluish or green. The tail feathers are blue, green at the base, blackish on the underside. The throat and upper breast are tinged blue and the lower breast and abdomen, also the under wing-coverts, are green. A description of a living specimen gave the beak as 'uniformly black, the feet nearly so, the naked skin round the eyes nearly white, and the iris pale grey.' Length: about 12in.
*Distribution:* Amazonian drainage in Ecuador, Peru, Bolivia and western Brazil (not north of the Amazon) in the states of Amazonas and western Mato Grosso.
*Remarks:* Very rarely imported. The only references I can find to this species in aviculture relate to the first known importation (a single bird received in 1923 by Chapman, which was bought by Mrs. Dalton-Burgess); a 'biggish Conure, "Weddell's"', so described by Dr. Hopkinson as being at Paignton Zoo in 1931 and, thirdly, that owned by A. A. Prestwich in the 1950s. Prestwich informed me: 'I originally had a pair (?) but one soon died. The survivor I gave to the London Zoo. I believe they were some 11in to 11½in in length. I remember I was surprised that they were almost silent and rarely moved – sitting side by side.'

There is a group of conures whose plumage is almost entirely green, except for varying amounts of red on the head and under wing-coverts. They all greatly resemble each other but are, at present, separated into no less than eight species with, using Peters' classification, a total of 18 species and sub-species. If their distribution is plotted on a map it can be seen that, with the exception of part of Venezuela, it covers the entire tropical part of Central and South America but nowhere does the range of any two species overlap. They form a natural group, easily distinguished from all other conures, yet not always easy to identify within the group. They should in my opinion be treated as a single species.

MEXICAN GREEN CONURE *(A.holochlora holochlora)*
*Description:* All green, paler and more yellowish below. Some specimens have a few red feathers scattered on or below the throat or on the neck, but not elsewhere. The flights are partly black, the under wing-coverts and the underside of the tail are pale yellowish. The beak and the area of skin surrounding the eye are flesh-coloured. The iris is brown. Length: about 11in.
*Distribution:* Mexico, in the states of Nuevo Leon, Tamaulipas, Vera Cruz, Puebla, San Luis Potosí, Guaunajuato, Mexico and Oaxaca. It inhabits the foothills and mountains.

Salvin recorded in 1860 that this species fed on the maize that covered the hillsides, causing serious damage to crops. He saw these birds flying low over the plains in flocks which numbered from 20 to 30 individuals; the pairs appeared to keep together.
*Remarks:* Like most Mexican species, it has not been imported frequently or in large numbers, but cannot be described as rare.
*Breeding records:* Probably the first breeding was that which occurred in the aviaries of W. J. Sheffler in the USA in 1934; three were reared in one nest. In 1958, J. L. Throp, curator at the Buteyn Bird Ranch in the USA, wrote that four pairs had laid infertile eggs there during the previous spring. One pair laid a second clutch and reared two young. When they left the nest they were difficult to distinguish from the adults. Four more were reared by two pairs; these did not leave the nest until mid-September.

Practically nothing has been recorded about the sub-species of *A.holochlora* as aviary birds. They are seldom imported and are, in any case, not birds that would attract much attention or interest.

SOCORRO GREEN CONURE *(A.h.brevipes)*
*Description:* Dark green above, darkest on the head, lighter green below. On comparison with skins of *A.h.holochlora* it was found to be appreciably larger and slightly deeper green on the underparts. It lacked any flecks of red on the throat or neck but this may not be a constant feature. Length: about 13in.
*Distribution:* Socorro Island (part of the Revilla Gigedo Group), off the west coast of Mexico.

BREWSTER'S GREEN CONURE *(A.h.brewsteri)*
*Distribution:* Mexico, in the states of Sonora, Sinaloa and Chihuahua. It is usually found from 4,000ft to 6,000ft above sea level.

RED-THROATED CONURE *(A.h.rubritorquis)*
*Synonym:* Red-collared Conure
*Description:* The distinguishing feature of this conure is the orange-red on the throat and part of the upper breast and, in some specimens examined, also on the feathers bordering the lower mandible. The extent of the orange area is very variable and increases with age; some specimens were merely spotted with orange in this area and one showed none at all. The bases of the orange-red feathers are yellow. It is a slightly darker shade of green below in comparison with *A.h.holochlora.*
*Distribution:* Eastern Guatemala, Salvador, Honduras and northern Nicaragua.

NICARAGUAN GREEN CONURE *(A. (holochlora) strenua).*
*Description:* Differs from *A.h.holochlora* only in its larger size and beak. Length: 13in.
*Distribution:* The Pacific coast of Mexico and Central America from Oaxaca to Nicaragua.

FINSCH'S CONURE *(A. (holochlora) finschi)*
*Description:* The scarlet forehead and under wing-coverts are the distinguishing feature; there are also a few red feathers, scattered irregularly on the upper breast and at the bend of the wing. The undersides of the flight feathers are yellowish. The bill is pale horn-coloured or whitish and the iris is orange. Length: 11in. Immature birds show less red, especially on the forehead, where this colour may be completely lacking.

8 Like most *Pyrrhuras*, the rarely imported Emma's Conure *P. leucotis emma* has proved to be very free-breeding. A Danish aviculturist bred nine in one nest. This bird belongs to Göran Bengtsson.

9 Souancé's Conure *Pyrrhura melanura souancei* had seldom been imported into Europe until 1967 or 1968 when large numbers suddenly became available. Owner: Kai Hansson.

10 The Pacific Black-tailed Conure *P. m. pacifica* can be distinguished at a glance from Souancé's Conure by the absence of the conspicuous area of white skin surrounding the eyes. Owner: author.

11 These two Sun Conures *Aratinga auricapillus solstitialis* caused a stir when they were imported by Avon Aviaries in 1971. They were the first Sun Conures to be seen in Britain for many years but about 30 more were imported during the following 12 months.

12 One of the author's favourite species, the Pearly Conure *Pyrrhura perlata* nests readily in aviaries.

13 The White-winged Parrakeet *Brotogeris v. versicolurus* is popular as a pet. It can be distinguished from the Canary-winged Parrakeet *B. v. chiriri* by its greyer, more olive, shade of green, especially on the head and by the bluish area around the eyes. Owner: Inge Forsberg.

14 The colourful Jendaya Conure *Aratinga auricapillus jandaya* would enjoy greater popularity were it not such a noisy bird! This one was photographed in Lisbon Zoo.

*Distribution:* Southern Nicaragua to western Panama; absent in Costa Rica in the western part from Guanacaste southward. According to Paul Slud (35), it prefers open agricultural or pasture lands in which woodland alternates with clearings; it does not enter forest, except perhaps at the edges. In extensively forested sections of the Caribbean lowlands it occurs irregularly or seasonally. It is usually seen in flocks numbering a few individuals to several score. At the height of the dry season (the latter part of April and the beginning of May), Slud observed a flock of about 100 apparently paired individuals in a small patch of very open low woodland. 'The members of a pair billed and snuggled but also nibbled each other besides biting meddlesome neighbours. One of a pair would hang from the bare or sparsely-leaved twig on which the other was perched, or both would hang by one foot, employing the other to grab a free foot of its companion. There was constant noise and activity . . . The usually wary birds were so absorbed in their carryings-on that I was able to approach them closely.'

Alexander Wetmore reported (43b) that in Almirante, Panama, their numbers have increased greatly since 1950. He watched a flock estimated at about 500 birds flying in each evening from a considerable area to roost in the palms. If the weather was wet or dull they departed from the roost an hour or more after the normal time.
*Remarks:* Seldom imported. There was a single specimen at the London Zoo until recently, which was presented by A. A. Prestwich in 1956.

WAGLER'S CONURE *(A.wagleri wagleri)*
*Synonym:* Red-fronted Conure.
*Description:* The forehead and crown are red and there is a red band across the throat or some scattered red feathers. There is no red on the side of the face or in the wings. The rest of the plumage is green, slightly paler below and olive on the under wing-coverts and the underside of the tail. The bill is a pale horn colour. Length: about 14in. The immature bird bred at the Buteyn Bird Ranch showed no red on the forehead.
*Distribution:* Colombia from the Pacific coast to the Cauca and Magdalana Valley and Santa Marta region; northern coast region of western Venezuela.
*Remarks:* Not often imported. A pair labelled as this species has been exhibited at Antwerp Zoo for several years.

*Breeding records:* Three were hatched at the Buteyn Bird Ranch in or about 1957. One soon died and the second had to be destroyed after an Amazon in the adjoining pen damaged its beak. Wagler's Conure has hybridised with the Jendaya Conure.

PETERS' CONURE *(A.w.transilis)*
*Distribution:* Paria Peninsula in north-eastern Venezuela.

CORDILLERAS CONURE *(A.w.frontata)*
*Description:* The forehead, part of the crown, the edge of the wing and the thighs are scarlet; the underside of the tail and the under wing-coverts are greyish-yellow. The rest of the plumage is mid-green, slightly olive in shade and paler below. The bill is whitish. Length: about 14in, half of which is accounted for by the tail.
*Distribution:* Peters gives its range as 'western Ecuador and western Peru south to Lima' while A. W. Johnson (23) attributes to it a slightly more southerly range: 'Peruvian Andes between 3,000ft and 10,000ft from N. border south to Arequipa; and east to Cuzco and upper Marañon River.' He states that it frequents tree or cactus-covered areas of open steppe country from which it makes sorties into cultivated fields or fruit orchards. It is 'by no means common'. Chapman (10b) stated 'evidently a rare species, our rather intensive collecting throughout its recorded range having yielded but one specimen.'

CARRIKER'S CONURE *(A.w.minor)*
*Description:* It appears to differ from *A.w.frontata* only in its slightly smaller size, ie, 13in.
*Distribution:* The Upper Marañon Valley in north-central Peru.

MITRED CONURE *(A.mitrata mitrata)*
*Description:* The forehead and the forepart of the crown, the lores, area surrounding the eyes, part of the cheeks and sometimes part of the ear-coverts, are dark red. Scattered red feathers are found in some specimens over much of the plumage, except the wings. The rest of the plumage is green, olive on the under wing-coverts and the underside of the tail. There is some bluish colouring on the flights. The bill is whitish and the iris is orange-yellow, with an inner circle of grey. Length: about 15in, of which the tail accounts for just over 7in. Immature birds are said to show less red below the eyes.

*Distribution:* Central Peru, east of the Andes and south through central Bolivia to western Argentina.

CHAPMAN'S MITRED CONURE *(A.m.alticola)*
*Distribution:* Central Peru in the region of Cuzco.

RED-MASKED CONURE *(A. (leucopthalmus) erythrogenys) (formerly A.rubrolarvatus)*
*Synonym:* Red-headed Conure.
*Description:* Most of the head, except the hind part of the cheeks, is red, and there are a few scattered red feathers on the throat and bordering the head. The shoulders, under wing-coverts, the edge of the wing and the thighs are also red. The greater under wing-coverts and the underside of the tail are yellowish-olive. The beak is yellowish-white. Length: 13½in. Immature birds show red only on the under wing-coverts.
*Distribution:* The arid tropical zone of south-western Ecuador and north-western Peru, where it is common.

In the late 1890s Walter Goodfellow wrote that he had seen these birds offered for sale at 5d. each in Guayaquil. He shot specimens at an altitude of 8,000ft near the Volcano of Paracé in Colombia. They were very common and 'immense clouds' were seen on a ride from Buenaventura to Cali. He said of the bamboos in Carmen: 'every branch of these giant grasses was literally weighing down with its burden of *C.rubrolarvatus*. The noise was simply deafening!' Some of the conures were nesting in the crevices of perpendicular cliffs.
*Remarks:* This species is occasionally imported. It makes an interesting aviary bird, the only drawback being its loud, harsh voice. Shore-Bailey's birds were able to repeat a few sentences, although kept in an outside aviary. He wrote of them: 'In spite of their habit of screaming they are most charming little birds, and I think one of the prettiest of the conures. I think with a little trouble they could be made good talkers.' His pair learned to copy the cackling of a hen which had just laid an egg.

If obtained when young the Red-masked Conure makes a very good pet, usually becoming extremely tame and often learning to talk. One kept as a pet would go back into its cage as soon as it was told to do so. One August it escaped and lived free for three months. It was reported to be in better condition when finally captured than when it escaped. Delacour kept a pair at liberty at Clères and found them to be good stayers.

*Breeding records:* Two Red-masked Conures were bred at Chester Zoo in 1969. In 1971, Mrs. H. Holtom of Wellplace Bird Gardens in Oxfordshire reported to me that a pair of what, from her description, appeared to be this species, had three chicks, three weeks old. She was able to send me photographs of the chicks, as the adults, which had been in her possession for three years, did not object to nest inspection. Four eggs were laid, one of which was cracked. In Denmark this species was bred in 1969.

WHITE-EYED CONURE *(A.leucophthalmus leucophthalmus)*
*Synonym:* Green Conure.
*Description:* Mainly green; the bend of the wing, the carpal edge and the under wing-coverts are red, except the greater under wing-coverts which are yellow. The under tail-coverts are golden-olive, also the flights which have dusky tips. The bill is yellowish flesh colour and large and powerful. There is an area of bare white skin surrounding the eye. Length: about 13½in. Immature birds have the bend of the wing and the carpal edge yellowish.
*Distribution:* Venezuela, the Guianas southwards over most of Brazil (west to the Solimoës and east to Bahia) and eastern Bolivia, to the Argentine Chaco, Paraguay, Entre Rios and Uruguay.

One observer of this species in the wild found it shy and quick to take alarm, although the plumage makes it most inconspicuous. These conures are usually seen in pairs or in groups of four or five, flying at a great pace and uttering harsh screams.
*Remarks:* Rarely imported; easily overlooked as it is neither colourful nor conspicuous. Equally rare in the USA. J. L. Throp stated in 1958 that the pair at the Buteyn Bird Ranch were the only ones he had seen in the USA.

R. T. Kyme found that it was a long time before his pair would sample any seed other than sunflower. They eventually acquired a taste for apple, spinach beet, groundsel, sowthistle, chickweed and seeding grasses.
*Breeding records:* This species does not appear to have been bred in Britain. The pair owned by R. T. Kyme produced three eggs in 1961, which were broken. In the USA (and possibly anywhere in the world) it was first bred in 1934 by W. J. Sheffler. The birds nested in January and the young ones fledged in April. They proved to be double-brooded and three more left the nest in October. This species was bred in the following year, also in the USA, by J. P. Walker; five eggs were laid and the three young were five weeks old when reported. More

recently, the White-eyed Conure was bred at the Buteyn Bird Ranch in 1957, when four were reared. In Australia one was bred at Adelaide Zoo in 1936-7.

ECUADORIAN WHITE-EYED CONURE *(A.l.callogenys)*
*Description:* From examination of skins it would appear to differ only in size. Hellmayr, however, stated that size, also the presence of red spots on the cheeks and sides of the neck, were purely individual characteristics and of no geographical significance.
*Distribution:* Eastern Ecuador and north-eastern Peru.

*A.l.nicefori* (Schauensee)
*Description:* It differs from *A.l.callogenys* by having a solid band of red on the forehead, and by paler, more yellowish-green plumage.
*Distribution:* Colombia.

HISPANIOLAN CONURE *(A.chloroptera chloroptera)*
*Synonym:* San Domingo Conure.
*Description:* Very much like *A.euops* from which it differs in being larger and generally of a purer shade of green, especially on the lower parts. The red of the under wing-coverts is brighter and extends to the bend of the wing. Length: 12½in. In immature birds, the under wing-coverts are tinged with pale red and there is no red on the bend of the wing.
*Distribution:* The island of Hispaniola (San Domingo), where it is most numerous in the mountains but sometimes found in the lowlands.
*Remarks:* Seldom imported and unlikely to be correctly identified.
*Breeding records:* In 1936 V. Wright bred four 'Haitian Conures' from one pair in the USA. This was probably the species referred to.

MAUGE'S CONURE *(A.c.maugei)*
*Synonym:* Puerto Rican Conure.
*Description:* There appears to be much confusion about this probably extinct sub-species. Only three museum specimens are known to exist. It has been stated that this sub-species could be distinguished from closely related conures by the fact that all the under wing-coverts were red. According to Dr A. Wetmore of Washington, however, it was hardly, if at all, distinct from *A.c.chloroptera*.
*Distribution:* Formerly Puerto Rica – now extinct on that island.

Peters states: 'now known only from Mona Island' but it has been stated that the last specimen was taken on Mona Island in 1892 by W. W. Brown.

CUBAN CONURE *(A.euops)*
*Synonym:* Red-speckled Conure.
*Description:* Mainly green, slightly lighter below; there are scattered red feathers on the head and neck, also on the thighs, sometimes on the abdomen and flanks. The whole of the smaller under wing-coverts and the carpal edge of the wing is red. The bill is whitish flesh-coloured and the area of bare skin surrounding the eyes bluish-white. Length: about 10½in.

A. A. Prestwich noted of his pair, which may have been *A.chloroptera chloroptera* (size being the main difference) 'The female is slightly smaller and slimmer than the male. The male has a larger and flatter head, also his upper mandible is larger, broader and more hooked than that of his mate. Many more red areas are observable in the male, but I do not think that this point could be relied on as an indication of sex, as the areas become more numerous yearly and would seem to denote age. When the under-wing-coverts are compared it is noticed that the male is coloured a rather more brilliant red, also the scarlet band is more extended than in the female.'

Sydney Porter asked (AM Third Series, vol XI, 122): 'Is *Conurus euops* in a transitional stage of evolution, either assuming certain areas of red plumage or losing them? It seems so strange that birds should have such bright colours scattered in patchwork fashion over the body without having it in certain restricted areas. Perhaps they are assuming a green plumage for better protection.'
*Distribution:* Cuba; formerly also found on the Isle of Pines. It inhabits wooded regions and is occasionally found in open country in the lowlands. In the early years of the century its numbers diminished fast as forests were felled. Birds of virgin forest, they could not adapt themselves to changed conditions and had already become extinct on the Isle of Pines, where they were found only 40 years previously in huge flocks. The future of this species must therefore be very uncertain.
*Remarks:* Rarely imported. Both Prestwich and Porter described these birds as amusing, active, destructive, very noisy, inquisitive and intolerant towards other birds, continually bullying them. Porter's birds would eat only apple and sunflower seed while those belonging to

Prestwich fed on sunflower, a little canary seed, but no millet. They liked apple and would sometimes eat orange.
*Breeding records:* Prestwich's pair nested on numerous occasions, usually eating the eggs, which were infertile. Four or five eggs formed the clutch and both birds were said to take part in incubation (but it is more likely that the cock kept the hen company in the nest during incubation).

GOLDEN-HEADED CONURE *(A.auricapillus auricapillus)*
*Description:* Adults differ from the Jendaya Conure (see below) in having only the forepart of the crown yellow; the back of the head and the hind-neck are green, the sides of the head being yellow-tinged green. There is a red tinge on the ear-coverts and around the eyes. The throat and upper breast are green, the remainder of the underparts being red, showing in places the green bases to the feathers. Length: about 12in. Immature birds have the cheeks of a deep, purer green and the red of the lower parts confined to the sides and abdomen.
*Distribution:* Eastern Brazil in the state of Bahia.
*Remarks:* Very rarely imported into Britain; possibly better known in the USA.
*Breeding records:* This species has been bred on a number of occasions in the USA, if the correct name has been given (and if it has not been confused with the Jendaya Conure).

GOLDEN-FRONTED CONURE *(A.auricapillus aurifrons)*
*Distribution:* south-eastern Brazil in the states of Minas Geraës, Rio de Janiero, São Paulo and Paraná.

JENDAYA CONURE *(A. (auricapillus) jandaya)*
*Synonym:* Yellow-headed Conure.
*Description:* The whole of the head, neck and part of the upper breast are a rich, bright yellow, the yellow merging into the rich red of the rest of the underparts. A few red feathers are mingled with the olive of the thighs and there may be a few olive-green ones mixed with the red of the breast. The mantle, wings and rump are green and the lower back is orange-red. The flight feathers and the tip of the tail are bright blue, the basal portion of the tail being bronze-green and the underside blackish. The bill is black. Length: 12in.

Jorge O'Neill, who bred this species in Lisbon, describing the young wrote 'The breast and neck, which in the parents is orange-yellow, is more lemon yellow and sprinkled with green.' Clifford Smith describes the young as 'similar to the parents – except that the yellow feathers on the head, necks and throats, and chests, are edged with green, and the green feathers on their backs are tinged with yellow, this giving a mottled appearance.'

*Distribution:* Eastern Brazil in the states of Maranhão, Piauhy and Ceará.

*Remarks:* Probably never imported in really large numbers it is, nevertheless, usually available and is one of the better-known members of the genus.

*Breeding records:* Of recent years this species has been bred on many occasions. Jorge O'Neill bred it in 1957 (two young), 1958 (four), and 1959 (four). In 1960 one of the adults bred one young one when mated to one of its youngsters and in 1961 three more were bred from this related pair.

V. Dilwyn Jones bred three in Wales in 1954. Three eggs were laid in a log constructed of bark strips; it was 5ft high and filled with earth to a depth of 2ft 6in. The hen alone incubated but both parents helped with the rearing.

In 1953 Mrs A. Morgan of Nottinghamshire bred two from three eggs. One of these died in the nest at the age of about eight weeks; the other left four days later.

Clifford Smith of Bradford reared two Jendayas in 1963. On July 2 three eggs were seen in the box, two of which hatched on July 30. The first youngster fledged on September 21, the second five days later.

There are several records of the Jendaya Conure hybridising with the Nanday Conure. In 1950 two hybrids of this cross produced a youngster in the San Diego Zoo. (This shows how closely related the two species are and that there is no justification for placing the Nanday Conure in the separate genus, *Nandayus*.) In 1960 three Jendaya x Nanday hybrids were hatched, two of which were reared, by birds belonging to Orazio Farina, Bagnara do Romagna, Italy. A Swedish aviculturist, T. Larsson bred (probably) four of these hybrids in 1962 and three more in 1963.

SUN CONURE *(A. (auricapillus) solstitialis)*

*Synonym:* Yellow Conure.

*Description:* This, in my opinion, is the most beautiful of all neotropical parrots. It resembles the Jendaya in size and shape; its colours are singularly exquisite, being mainly yellow and orange or a fiery shade of orange-red, with most of the yellow areas tinged orange. The only two I have seen differed considerably; presumably one was more mature than the other. In the most brightly-coloured bird the head and under parts were very rich red-orange, especially in the area surrounding the eye; the yellow feathers of the mantle were edged with orange. The second bird showed the bright orange only in the orbital area, on the forehead and on the sides of the body, being yellow where the other was orange. The upper wing-coverts are green, irregularly tipped with yellow; the bastard wing and the primary-coverts are dark blue, green on the outer edges. The tail is olive green, sometimes blue towards the tip, and always blue on the outer webs of the outer feathers. The under tail-coverts are green tinged with yellow and the underside of the tail is dusky olive. The beak is black. Length: 12in.

Russ described the plumage of the young birds bred at Rouen as green above at the age of four months, slightly mixed with yellow. The wing and tail feathers were pale yellow at the base, deep blue at the tip. Orange-yellow and greenish were the colours of the crown and the back of the head; the underparts were greenish-yellow and the abdomen red. The iris was dark brown, that of the two I saw being pale brownish. In the transitional stage the green feathers of the back and the wing-coverts change to yellow, as does the olive green on the lower back and upper tail-coverts. At one stage they are said to resemble Jendaya Conures but may be distinguished by the yellow markings on the wings and the yellow tinge on the back.

*Distribution:* The Guianas and the Rio Branco region of north-west Brazil. According to Haverschmidt (18), in Surinam 'It occurs in flocks on the southern Savanna and is said to be common on the Paroe Savanna. It is entirely unknown in the northern part of the country.'

*Remarks:* Extremely rare. Two of four obtained by a collector in Surinam were sent to England in July 1971, the first seen for very many years. These birds must be scarce in the wild, for they were the only ones secured after 12 years collecting. I was fortunate in seeing them after they had been in the country for a few days and was enraptured by their beauty. No artist's portrayal could do justice to their striking and unique colours. The fiery orange combined with golden-yellow would delight the most demanding aesthete!

Many years ago the Duke of Bedford owned a pair, which he did not find to be hardy. The failure of the heater in the aviary shelter one 'quite mild' night resulted in both birds developing severe chills, which proved fatal in the case of the hen. I cannot help feeling that this would not have happened had they been provided with a nest-box to roost in.

*Breeding records:* From 1872 a pair of Sun Conures bred in Rouen, France, where they occupied an outdoor aviary during the summer and a heated birdroom in the winter. During the fifth to eighth years the hen laid 29 eggs, four to six in a clutch and all infertile. The male died in 1881 and was immediately replaced. After two years the new pair nested successfully. The chicks' nestling down was reported to be short and whitish-grey.

More recently, according to David West of California, I. D. Putnam has reared this species. It hybridised with the Golden-crowned Conure in the aviaries of Baron James de Rothschild on several occasions between 1868 and 1870.

## QUEEN OF BAVARIA'S CONURE *(A.guarouba)*

*Synonym:* Golden Conure.

*Description:* This conure is unmistakable; adults are entirely rich golden-yellow, with the exception of the primary and secondary flight feathers which are green. The massive light horn-coloured bill (which is supposedly noticeably larger in the male) and short tapered tail give this bird a top-heavy appearance. There is a small circle of bare skin surrounding the eye. The iris is brown or black. Length: 14in. Immature birds have scattered green feathers on the upper wing-coverts and on the cheeks. One aviary-bred bird had moulted clear yellow by the time it was 15 or 16 months old.

*Distribution:* North-eastern Brazil south of the Amazon, from the Rio Xingu to Maranhão and possibly Ceará. Nothing seems to be known of its life in the wild.

*Remarks:* This is the most sought after of the conures. It is occasionally available and commands an exorbitant price. One dealer in England sometimes obtains £300 for a pair and an American Zoo is reputed to have paid $3,000 for two birds. Lovely as the plumage of this bird is, its beauty, in my opinion, is spoiled by its ungainly shape. However I find its character even more attractive than its colours. These conures are among the most playful and intelligent of all parrot-like birds and endear themselves to one instantly.

Their one fault is their extremely loud and harsh voice, which must be heard to be believed! David West recorded of his: 'The four birds greet each new dawn with a full assortment of terrible shrieks and cries . . .'

Three Queen of Bavarias were acquired by the Duke of Bedford in 1925; the 'cock' chewed off the tails of its two companions. By 1929 the hens were plucking themselves and then started on their mates (a fourth bird had been obtained). One pair were trained, with little trouble, to fly at liberty. They returned to roost in the aviary shelter every night, never left the garden and did no noticeable damage to trees, spending most of their time on the aviaries, yelling at the inmates or destroying the woodwork of the shelters.

Queen of Bavaria's Conures are such inquisitive birds that they were, no doubt, more interested in the activities of the other birds than in exploring the surrounding area. Although they were cowardly if any bird stood up for itself, they became very vicious with timid birds and finally mutilated an Amazon and killed a nestling Crimson-winged Parrakeet. Needless to say these exploits ended their days at liberty. Despite these shortcomings they apparently looked very attractive in flight and never molested non-psittacine birds. The two pairs could not be kept together.

Conures of this species spend many hours playing together like kittens, rolling over and pretending to fight. There is something about them which suggests that they are rather superior to most other birds, both in intelligence and personality. Certainly they are among the most desirable (for people without neighbours) and expensive of all parrots. They are hardy and can winter outside without heat when acclimatised. Newly-imported birds may require heat, especially young ones which can prove quite delicate.

*Breeding records:* The first recorded successful breeding took place in Colombo, Ceylon, in 1939, in the aviaries of Dr Osman Hill. Two young were hatched on about March 21 and left the nest on May 3 and 4.

The first success in Europe occurred in Liverpool during the following year. A pair belonging to G. Turner hatched two chicks in mid-June. One died at the age of five weeks as a result of eating nesting material and the other fledged during the middle of September when it was only half-feathered. Like its parents, it used its wings only as a last resort, preferring to climb or walk. The adults were thought to be the only true pair in Britain at the time.

Mrs G. T. Clark was almost successful in breeding this species in 1947; the one youngster was killed by a rat when it was on the point of leaving the nest. In 1949 three chicks were hatched, two of which were reared. They were fathered by a bird loaned by the Duke of Bedford, Mrs Clark's original cock having died. The Duke's pair had hatched young in 1935 but they were killed by the cock.

In the USA, David West of California bred from a pinioned male and a female with a flight impediment. On July 1 1957 the hen was found to have three eggs. On July 4 'two small bits of fluff and one egg' were seen in the nest. The weather at the time was very hot, the temperature never falling below 80°F, rising on several days to over 100°F. Both parents fed the young from the time they hatched. The chicks were quite noisy and their calls could be clearly heard from a distance of 50ft. The nest-box used measured 18in square and 3ft high.

At 35 days old they were beginning to show pin feathers on the wings and tail. At the age of six weeks they were almost fully feathered and left the nest at the end of the tenth week. The youngest of the three fledged too early and was removed for hand-feeding. They began to eat by themselves about three days after leaving the nest. Although they could fly very well if persuaded to do so, they were reluctant flyers and preferred to climb. The rearing food provided was fresh corn-on-the-cob (at least three large ears daily), sunflower seed and a few oats. A very large amount of water was taken while the young were being reared.

A pair at Wassenaar Zoo hatched young some time during the '60s. J. Louwman informed me: 'The birds were housed in one of our smaller parrot aviaries (about $1m^3$). Although this is not very large we were successful in breeding. Success was quickly followed by disappointment as the female suddenly died when the young were only one day old. As the young conures had not been fed they also died.' Autopsy revealed the hen's death to have been due to intestinal inflammation.

Currently I know of four pairs in Britain which have nested. In 1970 two pairs owned by one aviculturist both produced clutches of four eggs, all infertile, perhaps because the birds were not fully mature, although it is suspected that they were not true pairs.

In 1971, an eight-year-old pair owned by Mrs N. Howard hatched three young, all of which were reared. The hen had laid one clutch of three eggs for the previous four years. These birds are ferocious in their defence of the nest, allowing no one to enter the aviary. While the young were being reared large amounts of 'bread pudding' and sweet biscuits were eaten.

Another natural group of conures is formed by those medium to small-sized species with orange on the head or breast, usually also with blue on the head. At present they are classified as belonging to six species with a total of 21 sub-species. Several are island forms, but nowhere does the range of any two overlap. In several cases the 'species' are not at all easy to identify. *A.cactorum cactorum* from eastern Brazil, for example, greatly resembles *A.pertinax chrysophrys* from Guyana and *A.aurea aurea,* the Golden-crowned Conure from western Brazil, differs from *A.canicularis canicularis,* the Petz's Conure, from Central America, only in the colour of its beak and in the area of orange below the eye.

AZTEC CONURE *(A.astec astec)*
*Synonym:* Olive-throated Conure
*Description:* In some specimens there is a narrow band of orange, composed of very small feathers, which covers the cere. The throat and upper breast are brownish-olive and the abdomen is yellowish to yellowish-olive. The upper parts are green, except for the flight feathers which are blue tipped with black; the tail is tipped with blue and is greyish-yellow on the underside. The beak is brownish horn-colour and the iris is yellow. Length: 9in to 10in.
*Distribution:* The Caribbean slope of Mexico and Central America from Vera Cruz to the Almirante Bay region of western Panama. A. G. Butler (9) quoted A. Boucard 'This bird abounds in all parts of Yucatan; but the largest flocks were met with in northern Yucatan, where 400 or 800 were seen in a single flock. In November and December they were feeding upon the seeds of a plant which grows very abundantly in that part of this State. The sharp, piercing cry of these birds is almost deafening when in large flocks.'

Paul Slud (35) wrote that this species is found in partially deforested and heavily forested areas, not in forests but at woodland borders and in neighbouring clearings and plantations. He noted that it usually occurs in groups of several individuals and *not* in large flocks. It keeps fairly low down in the trees and does not fly about above the treetops. Its flight is very swift and twisting.
*Remarks:* One aviculturist described his Aztec Conure as 'decidedly interesting, neat, if not gaudy, not very noisy yet easily taught to say a few words – a parrot nearby being the instructor. Its appetite is moderate – except where chewing wood comes in; and altogether it is deservedly a favourite'.

It is not very commonly imported, either in Britain or in the USA.

*Breeding records:* In 1903 Harold Attewell bred this species in Jamaica. He housed seven birds in a cage 3½ft wide at the front sloping to 15in at the back, 18in high and 2ft deep. On the back two biscuit tins hung, each with half a coconut shell in the bottom. One pair laid two eggs and hatched one youngster which lived for only three weeks. In April of the following year four eggs were laid, only one of which hatched. The chick was reared. Another clutch of four eggs was laid, three of which hatched but it is not known whether the young were reared. The chicks were fed almost entirely on soaked canary seed.

EASTERN AZTEC CONURE *(A.a. vicinalis)*
*Distribution:* Central Tamaulipas south to north eastern Vera Cruz.

*A.a.melloni* (Twomey)
*Distribution:* Honduras.

JAMAICAN CONURE *(A. (astec) nana)*
*Synonym:* Dwarf Conure.
*Description:* It is said to differ from the Aztec Conure only in its slightly larger size (despite its name), pale beak and browner throat and breast. Examination of skins proved this to be correct; it is larger and much darker on the lower parts. The throat and the whole of the upper breast are dark brown, merging into dark olive on the lower breast. It is a uniform bright dark green above, from the forehead to the tip of the tail, except the primaries and secondaries which are blue, edged with black. The under wing-coverts are greyish and the underside of the tail is greyish-yellow. Length 10½in. Immature birds have the under parts dull green suffused with brown or olive, with the abdomen dull light yellowish-green.
*Distribution:* Jamaica, usually in the wooded hills and lower mountain slopes. Sydney Porter recorded that it nests in large earth nests made by a certain species of ant, cutting its way into the side of the nests.

PETZ'S CONURE *(A.canicularis canicularis)*
*Synonym:* Orange-fronted Conure.
*Description:* It is often confused with the Golden-crowned Conure but is easily distinguished by the colour of its beak: the upper mandible is horn-coloured, the lower being horn-coloured and black. In the Golden-crowned the beak is entirely black. The Petz's is mainly

green, more yellowish below and on the under wing-coverts and under tail-coverts. The forehead and part of the crown are orange, the latter part of the crown being blue. The wings are green except for the secondaries which are blue, narrowly edged with green. There is an area of bare skin surrounding the eye, whereas in the Golden-crowned the area surrounding the eye is covered with orange feathers. Length: 9½in.

Immature birds have much less orange on the forehead.

*Distribution:* The pacific slope of Central America from the Isthmus of Tehauntepec southward to western Costa Rica. Paul Slud (35) observed 'As a rule it occurs in flocks of several individuals to several score. On the central plateau it is represented by wandering groups, some of them apparently seasonal residents in the plazas of towns, rather than the large concentrations in which it is met in the northwest. It is, of course, strictly arboreal in the ranch lands of the subhumid northwest and the agricultural areas, plantations, and pastures that rise eastward from the entrance to the Gulf of Nicoya to the coffee fincas of the central plateau during the well-marked dry season'.

*Remarks:* This species excels as a pet and in the USA where it is enormously popular, it has no rivals in this category among small parrot-like birds (excluding, of course, the Budgerigar and the Cockatiel). These birds are much more playful and entertaining than are Budgerigars. Young birds are easily tamed, can be taught to do little tricks, will learn to talk and are usually quite fearless. Anyone desiring to buy one for a pet should ensure that a young bird is obtained. Hand-reared Petz's Conures are available in the USA, rarely in Britain.

*Breeding records:* I can trace no record of this species breeding in Britain. It has been described as a 'reasonably free breeder' in the USA, where it will apparently 'breed reasonably well in cages with a nest-box attached', according to William Allen (1). In 1958 J. L. Throp stated that he believed that there had not been more than four or five successes in breeding this species in the USA. The pair at the Buteyn Bird Ranch hatched one youngster which died in the second week. The hen laid again and hatched, and probably reared, four young. In 1970, four were bred in the Birmingham Zoo, USA.

WESTERN MEXICAN PETZ'S CONURE *(A.c.eburnirostrum)*

*Description:* This sub-species is reputed to be slightly larger than

*A.c.canicularis*. On examination of four skins collected from the plains of Colima and Mazathan, Western Mexico, no distinguishing features could be seen, and the size was identical to that of the nominate race. *Distribution:* Western Mexico in the states of Sinaloa, Durango, Nayarit, Colima and Gueriero. E. R. Blake gives its distribution as the arid lowlands from eastern Michoacan south to Oaxaca. C. W. Beebe (4) described the behaviour of this species in the wild. 'They are the most sociable little creatures, calling loudly to each other when on the wing, and keeping up a continuous low chuckling and chattering when perched. One would climb, foot over foot, to a large fruit, take several bites and return to his mate, close to whom he would snuggle and offer his head for an affectionate nibble. The favourite fruit of these birds was very sticky and juicy, and the little creatures were almost always in a disgracefully soiled condition – their bills and heads encrusted with a gummy liquid. These little Parrakeets were not shy, but very watchful, and, when frightened, they always flew to a curious tree which, though bare of leaves was sparsely covered with an odd-looking long, and four-sided fruit of a green colour. Under such circumstances, they alighted all together and, unlike their usual custom of perching in pairs, they scattered all over the tree, stood very upright and remained motionless. From a distance of fifty feet it was impossible to distinguish Parrakeet from tree, so close was the resemblance. A Hawk dashed down once and carried away a bird, but the others remained as still as if they were inanimate fruit. This silent trust in the protective resemblance of the green fruit was most remarkable, when we remembered the frantic shrieks which these birds always set up at the approach of danger, when they happened to be caught away from one of these Parrot-fruit trees. The latter have no common name; botanists know it as *Pileus conica*.'

Beebe found this conure to be 'Numerous in the *barrancas* and in the lowlands' of Colima.
*Breeding records:* Two were bred at San Diego Zoo in 1937.

*A.c.clarae*
*Distribution:* Sinaloa and western Durango south to Colima and Central Michoacán.

GOLDEN-CROWNED CONURE *(A.aurea aurea)*
*Description:* Dark green above and light green, tending to yellowish-olive, in places, on the breast. The forehead, part of the crown and

the feathers surrounding the eyes are orange. The latter part of the crown is blue and the cheeks and throat are olive-green. The flights are bluish, tipped with black. The tail is green, tipped with blue, the under surface being yellowish-green. The beak is black. Length: 10in. (See under Petz's Conure for distinguishing features.)

*Distribution:* Brazil, south of the Amazon and east of the Rio Madiera to eastern Bolivia, Mato Grosso and São Paulo.

E. G. B. Meade-Waldo, who observed this species in the wild in 1907, found it to be very common, and noisy on the wing. It could be approached closely when settled in trees and bushes.

*Remarks:* It is now imported into Britain in smaller numbers than formerly. In the USA it is almost unknown, its place being taken by the Petz's Conure. In Britain this situation is reversed. Despite their destructive ways and harsh voices, Golden-crowned Conures make attractive aviary birds. A pair in my possession showed a marked preference for sunflower seed, eating only small amounts of canary seed, white millet and apple. They ignored greenfood.

*Breeding records:* The first recorded breeding took place in 1880 in Danzig. Two eggs were laid. The incubation period was said to be 26 days and the young fledged after 50 days. In Britain Capt. R. Ward was the first successful breeder. Two eggs were laid (three in the unsuccessful attempt made during the previous year) and one youngster was reared. In the USA this species has been bred by I. D. Putnam and by Mrs Olive Gilmer. E. F. Petsch bred three in South Africa in 1958. Six eggs were laid, three of which hatched. Two chicks died within three weeks of leaving the nest, probably due to the intense heat. It was first bred in Denmark in 1932 and in Sweden in 1959. This species has hybridised with the Cactus Conure, the Jendaya Conure and reputedly with the Quaker Parrakeet.

GREATER GOLDEN-CROWNED CONURE *(A.a.major)*

*Description:* Said to differ from *A.a.aurea* in its slightly larger size.

*Distribution:* According to Peters, it is known only from two localities, about 70 miles apart, on opposite banks of the Paraguay River in Paraguay.

ST. THOMAS CONURE *(A. pertinax pertinax)*

*Synonyms:* Caribbean Conure, Curaçao Conure.

*Description:* This conure is easily identified by the golden yellow-orange of the forehead, the sides of the head and the chin. There is a blue tinge on the crown. The throat and the upper part of the breast are olive-green, the lower breast being greenish-yellow with the centre of the abdomen orange. The upper parts are green, except for the flight feathers which are bluish, edged with black. The under wing-coverts are yellowish-green and blackish. The upper surface of the tail is green, the central feathers being tipped with bluish, and the under surface is golden-olive. Length: 10½in, of which the tail accounts for about 4½in.

*Distribution:* The island of Curaçao. It is, or was, also found on the small island of St. Thomas and on St. Croix, in the Virgin Islands.

In 1895 Dr Hartert wrote in *Ibis:* 'On Curaçao it is very numerous in the western part of the island, but not so common, although by no means rare, in the eastern. The nests are mostly built in large ants' nests placed in trees, into which they dig holes. The Negroes take the young ones from the nest and keep them in cages. Large numbers are sold to the sailors.'

In 1931 Sydney Porter (AM Fourth Series vol IX, 131) described this species as 'extremely rare' on its island homes of St. Thomas and St. Croix. He wrote: 'It has been stated that this bird lives upon the Dutch island of Curaçao, which is quite likely, for St. Thomas and St. Croix were formerly Dutch before they were sold to the USA, and this bird may have been introduced there, for it is very unlikely that it is its natural habitat, for it is over a thousand miles from the other islands, and there are many hundreds of islands in the intervening space.'

According to James Bond (6) it inhabits scrubby woods or thickets in the hills, descending at times on seasonable fruits. It is most numerous on the eastern part of St. Thomas.

*Remarks:* Very rare in confinement. Dealers are inclined to give the name 'St. Thomas' to any sub-species of *A.pertinax*, especially to *A.p.chrysophrys*. In 1931 Sydney Porter observed 'examples sometimes turn up on the market at a reasonable price. I suppose this is because dealers do not realise the great rarity of this bird, and also because there seems to be little demand for Conures . . .'

The St. Thomas Conure is now almost unknown to aviculture. In the early 1950s there was one at Brookfield Zoo in Chicago, the survivor of four. Porter found this species to be noisy and destructive in an aviary, and very quarrelsome towards other birds.

*Breeding records:* It is said to have been bred in California by Putnam, also in Denmark in 1955 by Erik Jensen. In the latter case four young were hatched but only one was reared to independence.

No description of the adults was given, so it may be that it was one of the sub-species which was bred.

BROWN-EARED CONURE *(A.p.ocularis)*

*Synonym:* Veragua Conure

*Description:* It has the lores, throat and upper breast, dull brown (the cheeks being a slightly darker shade) merging into green on the lower breast. The centre of the abdomen is yellow, but not well defined. It differs from *A.p.aeruginosa* in having less blue tinge on the front of the crown and in the orange eye ring, which is broader below the eye than above it, where it is negligible. There is very little orange-yellow on the abdomen and it is altogether much less colourful. The under wing-coverts are pale brownish, faintly edged with yellow and the underside of the tail is greyish-yellow. The upper parts are a uniform dark green. The flights are blue on the inner edge, edged with black. The iris is light yellow. Length: about 9½in. Immature birds have the foreneck and upper breast greener and lack the orange eye-ring.

*Distribution:* Veragua and Panama, on the Pacific side from Chiriqui to the Canal Zone.

It is interesting to note that Immelmann (22) describes a species of moth which lives in the termite mounds where Golden-shouldered Parrakeets *(Psephotus chrysopterygius chrysopterygius)* nest. The caterpillars feed on the excreta of the young birds. He states: 'Caterpillars have similarly been found in the nesting-holes of the Brown-eared Conure *(Aratinga pertinax)* in South America, and have evidently begun a similar symbiosis.'

*Remarks:* Not rare but infrequently imported. I found this species to be very destructive; their beaks had the strength of wire-cutters and ordinary gauge wire-netting was bitten through easily. My pair, unfortunately, were rather nervous birds. They showed a decided preference for sunflower seed but would also eat most kinds of millets, also canary seed. They were very fond of apple and greenfood.

*Breeding records:* Three were reared by Shore-Bailey in 1915.

BROWN-THROATED CONURE *(A.p.aeruginosa)*

*Description:* Examination of two skins which appeared to belong to this sub-species showed that in comparison with *A.p.ocularis* the blue on the head is more definite. The centre of the abdomen was tinged with orange, a wider area being yellowish.

*Distribution:* Colombia in the arid Caribbean portion of the tropical zone, extending eastward into western Venezuela; the upper Rio Branco region of north-western Brazil.

*Remarks:* Once very frequently imported, less so of recent years.

*Breeding records*: The Avicultural Society's medal for the first breeding of this sub-species was awarded to Mrs M. Williams. In 1908 three young were reared which had the eye 'surrounded by a whitish ring and the head is much greener than in the adult birds. The young were reared on soaked bread squeezed dry, soaked canary seed, greenfood and fruit'. Two years previously four eggs were laid: three hatched and one of the chicks died. The remaining two were fostered out to Budgerigars. One died soon after, and the third during cold weather while it was still in the nest. Erik Bagge of Denmark has also bred the Brown-throated Conure, and in Sweden it was first bred in 1965.

This species has hybridised with the Golden-crowned Conure. The breeder, Miss L. Sturton-Johnson, described the hen variously as Yellow-crowned and Golden-crowned. Three young were hatched, the first on June 4. One fell from the box and was killed; the others fledged on July 24 and 26.

## TORTUGA BROWN-THROATED CONURE *(A.p.tortugensis)*

*Description:* It is said to differ from *A.p.aeruginosa* in having more orange on the side of the head and no blue, or very little, on the crown; the lower part of the cheeks are paler.

*Distribution:* Confined to the island of Tortuga off the northern coast of Venezuela.

## MARGARITA BROWN-THROATED CONURE *(A.p.margaritensis)*

*Description:* On examination of skins this sub-species appeared to be intermediate between *aeruginosa* and *chrysophrys*, having much less orange on the centre of the abdomen and in some cases hardly any. The top of the head is similar to that of *chrysophrys* but the cheeks, lores and throat are a pale brown, not a rich shade, and there is more orange on the cheeks. Length: 9½in to 10in.

*Distribution:* The island of Margarita, off the northern coast of Venezuela, and the Paria Peninsula on the Venezuelan mainland.

In 1907 P. R. Lowe recorded (*Ibis*, 1907, 557): 'This is a common bird in Margarita. It frequents the low-lying coast-belt, as well as the hills. Large flocks used to fly over regularly in the evening from the tall mangrove-trees lining the large lagoon at the west end of the island, making their way towards the foot-hills, where apparently they roosted.'

Friedmann and Smith (11) found this the commonest parrakeet of the region, being most abundant at the edge of the dry woods, where it was usually encountered in flocks of 10 to 20 individuals. They laid their three or four eggs in termites' nests 10ft to 20ft above ground.

GUIANA BROWN-THROATED CONURE *(A.p.chrysophrys)*

*Synonyms:* Orange-cheeked Conure, Yellow-cheeked Conure.

*Description:* Dark green above with a fairly well defined area of dull blue on the crown and forehead. The flights are very blue, edged with black on the inner edge. There is a circle of orange feathers below the eye, extending well below in some specimens. The lores may be orange or brown. The cheeks and throat are brown (the shade being quite variable), the upper breast varying from medium brown to olive-brown. The abdomen is yellowish-brown with an orange patch in the centre, the extent varying from a tinge to a large patch of orange. The under wing-coverts are greyish and the underside of the tail greyish-yellow. Length: 9½in. Immature birds show a smaller amount of orange on the abdomen.

*Distribution:* Guyana, Surinam and Cayenne.

*Remarks:* No importations seem to have been recorded before one which occurred in 1952, when it was probably new to aviculture. Six birds from this importation were obtained by A. A. Prestwich, who was offered more specimens until he had 15. He wrote: 'Evidently this sub-species did not prove a particularly welcome newcomer to the aviaries of Great Britain. And probably with good reason. Our experience is that it is one of the less desirable members of the group, being very noisy, destructive, but boisterous rather than really quarrelsome, although on several occasions we have effected rescues only just in time after a sudden collective onslaught. Conure species appear to be great believers in lynch law.'

*Breeding records:* The Avicultural Society's medal for the first breeding of this species was awarded to A. A. Prestwich in 1955. Two pairs were housed in a 30ft flight, eight more birds in another. Converted ammunition boxes, measuring 15in high x 9in x 6½in containing turf and peat were hung at an angle of about 30° from the vertical. Both pairs nested, laying four and five eggs. They failed to incubate them, probably due to the fact that they regarded both boxes as joint property. The eight birds in the second aviary made no attempt to nest. In 1955 one of the two proven hens laid on June 16, four more eggs being laid apparently on *successive* days; incubation began with the second egg and lasted for 25-26 days. The first chick hatched on July 12, the second the next day. The eldest left the nest on August 30: 'A fine strong flier, an exact replica of its parents, but a trifle less brightly coloured.' The second, a poor flyer, sparsely feathered on its back, left the nest on August 31. Successs was not expected as the young were in the nest during a period of heat-wave and drought; the hen seemed to be incubating half-heartedly and the nest-box was described as 'an inferno' while the young were being reared.

The parents were not provided with any extras. Their food consisted of seed, soaked millet sprays, unlimited sweet apple. Greenfoods including chickweed, groundsel, sowthistle and spinach were available but were hardly touched.

ARUBA BROWN-THROATED CONURE *(A.p.arubensis)*
*Description:* It resembles *A.p.aeruginosis* but has more dark orange/yellow on the lower parts and a brighter and better defined patch below and behind the eye. The crown shows less blue, if any blue at all. The lores, cheeks and ear-coverts are dull olive-brownish. The throat and the lower part of the cheeks are dark brown, every feather with a pale shaft.
*Distribution:* The island of Aruba, in the Dutch West Indies.

BONAIRE BROWN-THROATED CONURE *(A.p.xanthogenia)*
*Description:* It differs from *A.p.pertinax* in usually having more yellow, and of a brighter shade, on the head, particularly on the forehead, crown and nape. Individuals vary considerably and some, according to K. H. Voous (42), are indistinguishable from *A.p. pertinax.* He states that there is no constant difference in adult and immature plumage but the beak is light brownish in young birds and blackish-grey in adults. Length: about 9in.
*Distribution:* The island of Bonaire, where it is very common and found in almost all localities. Flocks of 100 or more are seen when fruit is ripening. This conure also eats blossoms for their nectar, and seeds. No animal remains were found in the stomachs of 48 birds examined by one ornithologist. They nest in December and January, during and immediately following the short rains.

Natural crevices, also arboreal termites' nests, are inhabited by these birds. K. H. Voous found that the nesting holes had an entrance of 7cm to 10cm in diameter and consisted of a narrow, curved tunnel, widening into a dome-shaped nesting cavity about 25cm wide. Other nests were found in the decayed trunks of date palms; none had any soft lining, but nests found in a rocky wall were lined with green feathers. Other nests were situated in a steep, sandy wall about 15ft high, bordering a road. They had been excavated in the soft and stony soil about 10ft to 12ft from the ground. Whenever possible nests were placed in small colonies.

Although Aruba and Curaçao are less than 80km apart, no flights between these islands have ever been observed.

Other sub-species which have been described are: *A.p.surinama* (Zimmer and Phelps) from Surinam; *A.p.venezuelae* (Zimmer and Phelps) from Venezuela and *A.p.griseipecta* (Schauensee) from Colombia.

CACTUS CONURE *(A. (pertinax) cactorum)*
*Description:* It is difficult to see what justification there can be for giving this conure specific status; it should be treated as a sub-species of *A.pertinax*. It greatly resembles *A.p.chrysophrys* but has only a tinge of blue on the crown, the feathers of which are pale brown with lighter edges. The lores, cheeks, throat, sides of the neck and upper breast are pale brown. There is a yellow line below the eye and the ear-coverts are green. The amount of orange on the abdomen varies from a prominent area of bright orange in some adults to only a tinge in immature birds. The flanks, thighs and under tail-coverts are yellowish-green and the flights are tinged with blue and tipped with blackish. The upper parts are green, except for the blue tips to the central tail feathers; the under side of the tail is golden-olive. The beak is whitish on the upper mandible, horn-coloured on the lower one. Length: 10in. Immature birds have the crown green, the throat and upper breast olive and the abdomen only tinged with orange.
*Distribution:* Brazil, from Bahia south of the Rio São Francisco and adjacent areas in Minas Geraës. It derives its name from the fact that it feeds on the fruits of cacti.
*Remarks:* A few decades ago it was freely imported into Britain but now it is little known in Europe or in the USA.
*Breeding records:* The first recorded breeding of this species took place in 1914, when Dr L. Lovell-Keays' pair reared three young from four eggs. The chicks were first seen on June 28 and the eldest

fledged on August 7. The following year one more youngster was reared. The nest used was a 6in barrel. F. S. Elliott also bred this conure, probably in the 1920s, and it was bred in Denmark in 1963.

PALE CACTUS CONURE *(A. (pertinax) caixana)*
*Description:* Paler than *A. (p.) cactorum,* particularly below, with the centre of the breast less orange.
*Distribution:* Eastern Brazil from Maranhão and Piauhy east to Pernambuco and south to north-western Bahia.

Peters followed existing classification in placing the Nanday Conure as the single representative of the genus *Nandayus*. It does not differ significantly from the *Aratingas* in appearance or behaviour, originally being separated on account of it having the tail longer than the wing and graduated for more than half its length. The shape of its beak also differs slightly.

NANDAY CONURE *(A.nenday)*
*Synonyms:* Black-masked Conure, Black-headed Conure.
*Description:* The whole of the head, including the cheeks, also the beak, is black; this distinguishes it from all other conures. The upper part of the breast is washed with blue, the remainder of the under parts, also some of the under wing-coverts, are yellowish-green. The thighs are red. The wings are a slightly darker shade of green than the lower parts, the feathers of the upper part of the wings being faintly edged with yellowish-green. The secondaries are blue, the primary flight feathers blue and green. The upper surface of the tail is green edged with blue, the underside being blackish. There is a narrow circle of bare whitish skin surrounding the eye. Length: 13in, of which the long, tapered tail accounts for 6in.

One aviary-bred Nanday was described as resembling its parents when it left the nest, except that its thighs were not red. Other breeders have observed that there is no difference at all in the plumage of adult and immature birds.
*Distribution:* South-eastern Bolivia and southern Mato Grosso to the upper Pilcomayo, Argentine Chaco (Rio de Oro) and Paraguay.

This species is found in very large flocks, sometimes in association with Quaker Parrakeets. One of its favourite foods, according to J. Graham Kerr, is the berries of *Loranthaceœ*. He described it as 'very common in large flocks in the Argentine Chaco'.

*Remarks:* First imported about 1870, since when it has been regularly imported and is usually available. Unfortunately it is *extremely noisy* and has a harsh, loud voice. It is also a rather destructive bird. Despite these faults, it does have some admirers and is one of the best known members of the conure family.
*Breeding records:* This conure nests fairly readily in confinement, and is said to have bred in France as long ago as 1881.

It was first bred in Britain in 1901 by Mrs Johnstone. Five young were hatched but one was killed just before fledging. In 1916 a pair belonging to E. J. Brook reared three youngsters from three eggs. They left the nest at three or four day intervals. Three young were hatched by a pair in the possession of A. C. Brett in 1958. Five eggs had been laid. Unfortunately the young were deserted when the eldest was about three weeks old. They hatched on alternate days and were said to be naked at birth, later growing whitish down. The pair reared one youngster in 1959, but it was badly plucked when it left the nest. They were fed on sunflower seed, oranges, a small amount of apple, also grapefruit. This species has bred in Britain on many other occasions.

In the USA, five were reared at the San Diego Zoo in 1930 and one in 1948. Also in 1930, Mrs C. L. Lewis from near Los Angeles, had young in the nest.

The Nanday Conure has hybridised with the Jendaya Conure on a number of occasions.

## Genus: *Leptosittaca*

The sole representative of this genus is placed by von Boetticher with the *Aratingas*. It is unknown in aviculture.

### BRANICKI'S CONURE *(L.branickii)*

*Description:* (from one skin only, in poor condition, in the British Museum, Natural History): Predominantly dark green, the feathers of the abdomen being reddish in the centre, giving a mottled effect. There is a very narrow line of yellow and brown feathers on the forehead, covering part of the cere; there is a small amount of yellow below the eye and on the ear-coverts, the feathers of which are lengthened. The under wing-coverts are greyish-yellow and the underside of the tail is maroon. Length: 14in, including the 6½in tail.
*Distribution:* The humid, temperate zone of the Central Andes in Colombia and southern Ecuador to central Peru.

## Genus: *Conuropsis*

The single species, and its sub-species, which formed this genus, both became extinct in the early years of the 20th century. They were the only members of the parrot family found in eastern North America.

### CAROLINA PARRAKEET *(C.carolinensis carolinensis)*

*Description:* This species was mainly green, paler below, olive on the wings with the bend of the wing and the front edge yellow. The head and the upper part of the neck were yellow, the forehead, lores, orbital region and the cheeks being orange. There were a few orange feathers on the thighs and the underside of the tail was olive. The beak was a whitish horn-colour and the iris was brownish-grey. Length: about 15in. The female apparently lacked the yellow on the neck which was said to be attained by the cock when two years old.
*Remarks:* In 1879 C. W. Gedney (13) wrote: 'Vast numbers of these birds are annually imported into England (I recently saw 200 loose in one room).' *Twenty-five years later the last wild Carolina was taken.* Few facts could illustrate better the greed and short-sightedness of Man.

In 1832 Audubon wrote that the Carolina was not nearly as common as formerly but even in 1860 they were comparatively numerous throughout the Gulf States and the Mississippi, Arkansas and White River Valleys. In 1959 William H. Allen stated: 'Its annihilation was almost as brutal as needless. Its flesh was edible and considered by some to be a delicacy; its plumage was much in demand, both at home and abroad, as a decoration for women's hats; it was destructive to a variety of cultivated crops, including many fruits and grains; it depended on the large trees lining the river banks, and in swamps, for nesting places; and it was in great demand as a cage bird.

'To top it all, the Carolina Parrakeet was extremely loyal to its companions, and would return again and again to the site where a fallen companion lay, to give the gunner shot after shot, until the whole flock was destroyed.'

It formerly inhabited an area of the south-eastern United States from southern Virginia to Florida and was occasionally found northwards to Pennsylvania and possibly even New York.
*Remarks:* Gedney recommended that a saucer of salt should be placed in the aviary for these birds: 'they have an inordinate love

for it and its effects are highly beneficial. In their wild state they drink large quantities of salt water, always frequenting the neighbourhood of salt springs, and apparently preferring the saline liquid to that furnished by the fresh water rivers and streams which abound in North America.'

*Breeding records:* Nineteenth-century writers invariably described the Carolinas as free-breeding, yet there is not one authentic record of it breeding in Britain. Gedney's information on the subject certainly does not ring true; he stated that both male and female assisted in incubation, which lasted for 14 or 16 days. There are a number of recorded breedings for Europe and the USA. Two French aviculturists, who both bred the Carolina in 1877, were probably the first breeders. In the USA Cincinnati Zoo bred from several pairs over a number of years. The last known Carolina died in this zoo in 1914.

LOUISIANA PARRAKEET *(C.c.ludovicianus)*

*Description:* It differed from *C.c.carolinensis* in its generally paler colouring.

*Distribution:* It formerly inhabited the interior of the USA in the states of Wisconsin, Indiana, Ohio, Nebraska, Colorado, Oklahoma, West Virginia, Kentucky, Tennessee extending to the Gulf of Mexico.

*Remarks:* The date of extinction is unknown. Three of a flock of 11 were shot in Louisiana in 1881 and in Kansas one was shot in 1904. One is reported to have been seen in Jackson country, Missouri, in 1912 but it could have been an escaped cage bird.

Genus: *Rhynchopsitta*

THICK-BILLED PARROT *(R.pachyrhyncha)*

*Synonym:* Thick-Billed Parrakeet

*Description:* This is a very attractive bird, whose general appearance and shape is almost macaw-like. It has a heavy beak, long tail which is not quite in proportion to the body, and pointed wings.

It is predominantly bright apple green in colour, brighter on the cheeks. The forehead, front part of the crown, the lores and a broad streak through the eye are scarlet. The beak is black and the iris is yellow. There is more scarlet on the bend of the wing and on the lower half of the thighs. The under wing-coverts are a bright pure yellow and slate-coloured. Length: about 16in. The plumage has a pleasing iridescent gloss to it.

*Distribution:* This is the only remaining representative of the parrot family in the USA. It is found in the pine belt in the mountains of the Mexican Plateau in Chihuahua, Durango, the state of Mexico, and Vera Cruz, sometimes appearing as far north as the mountains of south central and south-eastern Arizona.

It feeds on the cones of the Mexican stone pine *Pinus cembroides*. In Arizona it has been known to remain during the winter, undeterred by the snow, feeding on acorns when the pine nuts are exhausted. In 1904 C. W. Beebe (4) found that it was common in the barrancas on the slopes of the volcano of Colima in western Mexico, and was tame and abundant among the coniferous trees. 'It is either a very stupid bird or controlled by its curiosity, for the flocks followed us everywhere as we made our way over the slippery ground.'

*Remarks:* This species was probably unknown to aviculture until the 1920s when it was represented in the collection of Washington Zoo. In 1927 Karl Plath had an extremely tame specimen. It disliked women but was very fond of Plath's seven-year-old son. 'He delights in crawling all over the boy, snuggling in his bed and kissing him in the mouth (when permitted). He follows him about like a dog, with a queer shuffling gait, and shaking his tail from side to side.' It was described as having a 'decidedly unpleasant voice'. (AM Fourth Series, vol V, 141.)

In 1959 San Diego Zoo owned three specimens, including the only known pair in the USA. This species was reported to be rare in confinement because of the difficulties and dangers of trapping it, due to its powerful beak, and the fact that when trapped it was difficult to sell. In 1963 David West reported that there were several pairs in California and Arizona. About 1967 it suddenly became available in Europe. Due to its very destructive habits it is seldom found in private collections.

*Breeding records:* The Thick-billed Parrot hatched on September 8, 1965, at San Diego Zoo was probably the first to be bred in confinement. The parents were received in March 1955 and December 1956. Over a period of nine years they were provided with a variety of nesting facilities, including, in July 1965, a wooden nest-box 14in wide and 24in long, suspended by wire from the top of the aviary at a height of 10ft. A 6in opening at the front gave access to the box which was half-filled with soil and pine shavings.

The birds were closely observed and it was found that the female would accept food from the male only after a certain stage in the courtship cycle had been reached. The hen would enter the box and chatter loudly, calling to the male to approve her selection of nesting site. He would fly to the entrance, look in, then enter the box. On

August 12 the hen did not leave the nest to feed, and was fed by the cock. Only the hen incubated the single white egg, which was probably laid on that day. The chick hatched on September 8, giving an incubation period of 28 days. The young bird was examined on September 24, when it had pin feathers in the occipital region and when the tail feathers, enclosed in their sheaths, measured 2in. Patches of white downy feathers on the neck, back and rump were conspicuous and the central, femoral and humeral tracts had begun to feather.

It was decided to place the chick in a small brooder and rear it by hand; the regulator was set at 70-75°F. For three months it was fed with a cereal formula at 8am, 12 noon and 5pm daily.

In December 1970, Robert Nelson of Oregon informed me: 'I have a young Thick-bill just now eating independently and hand-raised him from two weeks of age. He was hatched in the aviary of a friend who didn't want to bother with the hand-rearing procedure.' Two chicks were hatched in Jersey Zoo in 1970. One died at the age of 10 days, the other shortly after.

### MAROON-FRONTED PARROT *(R.terrisi)*

*Description:* It differs from *R.pachyrhyncha* in being of a much darker shade of green with the forehead and supercilliaries brownish-maroon instead of deep red. The patch on the under wing-coverts is dark brownish-grey, not yellow. It is slightly larger, being about 17in in length.

*Distribution:* The highlands of the Sierra Madre Oriental in central west Nuevo-León (Sierra Potosí and the mountains south east of Galeana). It is rare and very limited in its range.

## Genus: *Cyanoliseus*

The largest of the conures, these birds are extremely attractive and showy in an aviary. Due to their large size and powerful voices they are, perhaps, more suitable for zoos and bird gardens than for the average private collection.

### LESSER PATAGONIAN CONURE *(C.patagonus patagonus)*

*Description:* The head, neck and back are dark olive-brown, the lower back, rump, upper tail-coverts and flanks are yellow with a slight olive tinge, especially on the tail-coverts. The throat and breast are greyish brown, with some white on the upper breast. The amount of white is variable and is not the means of identifying the Lesser

Patagonian Conure from the Greater. However, the Lesser probably never has a complete band of white across the breast as do some Greater Patagonian Conures. The centre of the abdomen and the thighs are orange-red, the rest of the abdomen being yellow. The wing-coverts are olive and the flights are blue, tipped with black. The upper surface of the tail is olive-green, the central feathers having a bluish tinge along the middle; the under surface is brown and the under tail-coverts are olive-yellow. The beak is black and the iris white. Length: 17in to 18in.

*Distribution:* It breeds in south-central Argentina from Neuquén Territory and southern Buenos Aires Province to Chubut, migrating in winter north to Mendoza and Buenos Aires, occasionally to Uruguay. It is apparently resident in the mountains of Cordoba.

According to W. H. Hudson, it was abundant many years ago on the southern pampas of La Plata and ranged in winter to Buenos Aires, even as far north as the Parana River. It once appeared in immense flocks in winter, but gradually diminished in numbers until it was rarely seen within 100 miles of Buenos Aires, although 200-300 miles to the south large flocks were still seen in ancient breeding places.

These birds are gregarious even during the breeding season, and nest close together in burrows which they excavate in a perpendicular cliff or high bank. The burrows are 3ft to 4ft deep and four or five eggs are laid inside.

Patagonian Conures feed on fruits and berries, including the berries of *Empetrum rubrum* and the seeds of the giant thistle *(Carduus mariana)* and the wild pumpkin. They are apparently destructive to grain crops. Flocks are very noisy when disturbed, and have been recorded as hovering above horsemen, screaming around their heads.

*Remarks:* This species was fairly often available in Britain in the past and has been frequently imported during the last few years. It is an attractive aviary bird, its main draw-back being its loud, harsh voice. It has seldom been kept as a pet, probably for this reason, yet this very intelligent species would undoubtedly make a good pet if obtained young. There is a record of one which, although very shy when bought, soon learned to talk and became an accomplished mimic. It imitated all kinds of sounds, from the squeak of a stove to the sawing of wood.

*Breeding records:* The Patagonian Conure has bred on a number of occasions in captivity but it is often uncertain which records relate to *C.p.patagonus*.

GREATER PATAGONIAN CONURE *(C.p.byroni)*

*Description:* Distinguished from *C.p.patagonus* only by its slightly larger size, ie, about 20in, and by the heavier and larger bill. In some specimens the white on the upper breast forms an almost unbroken band and is usually more extensive than in the Lesser Patagonian Conure. Often it is extremely difficult to decide to which sub-species a living bird belongs, especially if there is no other Patagonian Conure to compare it with.

*Distribution:* Probably now confined to a few isolated breeding colonies in Chile in the foothills of the Andes or in the coastal range between Atacama and Colchagua. Formerly it was quite abundant from Aconagua to Valdivia.

A. W. Johnson (23) states that this species 'nests colonially in holes in lime or sandstone cliffs, using them as dormitories during the rest of the year. The fact that these colonies can only be reached with ropes is no impediment to the country people who make a habit of visiting them every spring (October or November), pull out the young birds with hooks attached to long bamboo poles, and either sell or raise them as pets. It is this habit, rather than excessive shooting, that has caused the great diminution in numbers . . . The young parrots are easily tamed and soon learn to repeat a few words or phrases. They seem to be temperamental, taking a great liking to some people and a strong aversion to others.

'It is interesting to watch the manoeuvre whereby the parrots approach and enter the holes. Separating into groups of up to a dozen birds, they beat their wings rapidly to pick up speed, wheel in close formation and sail straight ahead at the cliff face, their short, rounded wings held rigid and the long, pointed tail streaming out behind – a squadron of fighter planes in miniature. Just as they reach the cliff the wings are closed and the birds enter the holes on the run. As a rule the holes do not lead straight in but zig-zag here and there, forming an intricate series of underground galleries, many of them intercommunicating, and with their only entrance pointing towards the cliff-face.

'Just what can be achieved by reasonable measures of protection is well illustrated by the case of this parrot. In 1940 nesting colony X was reduced to 6 pairs; we talked to the owner of the farm and he agreed to prohibit the taking of the young until the numbers of the colony could be built up. Twelve years later we were sitting eating some sandwiches at this same farm, accompanied by the British Ambassador to Chile, when a flock of at least 500 of these parrots passed close over our heads. We know of one other colony where the birds are protected. We have never found more than 2 eggs or 2 young birds in any one hole.'

*Remarks:* This species has been fairly freely available since the mid 1960s, before which it was not frequently imported.

*Breeding records:* It was first bred in Britain in 1963 by W. R. Partridge of Evesham. He obtained a pair early in 1960. The male was easily distinguished by the stronger head and beak, more masculine appearance and larger orange-red patch on the abdomen. During the late spring they were transferred to an aviary 21ft long, 5ft wide and 7ft 6in high, which housed various doves, soft-bills and small seedeaters. In 1961 and 1962 they were supplied with a nest-box 11in square and 2ft 6in tall, hung 3ft above ground, which they eventually destroyed.

In 1963 a 29in-high hollowed-out log of very hard wood was provided. The inside diameter was approximately 9in. The nest lining was formed of wood chippings chewed from the inside of the log. On May 20 three eggs were seen inside, although the conures had not been observed to enter. On the next inspection on June 11 all the eggs had hatched, and the chicks appeared to be between three and five days old, giving an incubation period of 24 or 25 days. The eldest two youngsters left the nest on August 4 when they were eight weeks old; the third left two days later. They appeared very intelligent, following the adults in and out of the shelter almost immediately. They exactly resembled their parents except in the colour of the upper mandible, which was ivory-white instead of black. When they were eight months old their beaks had darkened, but were still much lighter than those of the adults.

The cock was not seen to enter the nest until after the chicks had hatched. He assisted the hen in feeding the young for several weeks after they fledged. The only addition made to their usual diet of sunflower, canary seed and apple was several pieces of bread daily and extra spinach beet.

## ANDEAN PATAGONIAN CONURE *(C.p.andinus)*

*Description:* It differs from *C.p.patagonus* by the darker brown throat and breast which has no trace of the creamy-white patch on

the sides of the chest, in the duller, more greenish, rump, and in lacking the bright yellow on the abdomen.
*Distribution:* The mountains of north western Argentina in the provinces of Salta, Catamarca, Tucuman, San Luis and La Rioja.

WHITLEY'S CONURE *(C.whitleyi)*
*Remarks:* In 1926 Herbert Whitley exhibited a conure at the Crystal Palace Museum which no one could identify. It was mainly dark green, with scarlet on the forehead and a large patch of scarlet, preceded by yellow, on the abdomen; the thighs were red. There was some blue on the carpal edge of the wing, in the flights and on the tail. The beak was black and an area of white skin surrounded the eye. (A coloured plate of this bird appeared in *Avicultural Magazine,* Fourth Series, vol IV, opposite 261.)

The conure was examined by three ornithologists who decided that it belonged to a new species and N. B. Kinnear, of the British Museum, named it after its owner. The bird was purchased from Chapman and was thought to have come from Brazil. No similar bird has ever been recorded, so it must almost certainly have been a hybrid. It was originally named *Aratinga whitleyi* but, judging by the illustration of this bird, it more nearly resembled a Patagonian Conure, to which it was paired while in Whitley's possession.

Genus: *Ognorhynchus*

The opportunity to study alive the single member of this genus would be most interesting; one could then more easily assess with which genus it is most akin. Von Boetticher placed it with the *Aratingas.*

YELLOW-EARED CONURE *(O.icterotis)*
*Description:* This large macaw-like conure is dark green above and can be immediately identified by its bright yellow cheeks, lores, throat and forehead. The elongated yellow feathers of the ear-coverts give the bird its name. The under parts are pale greenish-yellow and the under side of the tail is pale maroon. Length: about 16in, of which the tail accounts for about 6½in. (Of the six skins examined one measured only 13in.) The beak is probably black; it is large and powerful with a sharp, narrow tip.
*Distribution:* The sub-tropical zone of the Central and Eastern Andes of Colombia and the Andes of northern Ecuador. (The skins examined were collected in the vicinity of Bogota, New Granada and Zitaguira

on the eastern slope of the eastern Andes, at a height of 5,000ft, and in Intaj, Ecuador.) Chapman (10a) observed this species nesting in colonies in holes 80ft or more up wax palms, which are characteristic of the flora along the Quindio Trail above the rivers Tochecito and Toché in Colombia. In places nearly every palm was occupied by a pair. The nest holes were situated just below the lowest leaves.
*Remarks:* About 1965 a London dealer received two of these extremely rare birds. I believe that they were separated but their subsequent fate is unknown. I can trace nothing relating to this conure in confinement.

## Genus: *Pyrrhura*

With the exception of the Red-bellied and, since about 1967, the Black-tailed Conure, members of this genus are seldom available. This is a great pity, because the *Pyrrhura* conures are among the most attractive and suitable subjects for the aviculturist. Unlike the *Aratingas,* they are not noisy, unless alarmed, and their voices lack the harsh tone of their near relatives. They are not destructive, and I have never known them do any appreciable damage to woodwork; they sometimes whittle away at a batten, but never destroy whole lengths of woodwork, or chew wire-netting, as other conures do.

Immature birds of this genus (unlike many *Aratingas*) resemble the adults, except for their softer, less definite colouring.

For the sake of completeness I have listed all the sub-species which have been named. The status of many, however, is uncertain. Little is known about any but the *frontalis, perlata* and *leucotis* species and some of the *melanura* forms. The other *Pyrrhuras* are more or less unknown to aviculture and are not well represented in skin collections. *P.berlespschi,* for example, is very much like *P.souancei,* approaching in some respects, *P.rupicola.* The latter, with *berlespschi,* should, in my opinion, be considered a sub-species of *melanura,* possibly with *egregia* and *molinae* (and sub-species). The distribution of many of the *Pyrrhuras* is not well-known. When they are better understood the number of species will undoubtedly be reduced.

### RED-EARED CONURE *(P.cruentata)*

*Synonym:* Red-rumped Conure.
*Description:* This is the largest, and one of the most striking of the genus. It is a very beautiful bird, its outstanding feature being the patch of orange-brown behind the ear-coverts, which are maroon. The forehead, crown and nape have the feathers edged with orange,

giving a streaky appearance, especially on the nape. The cheeks are green and the lores maroon. There is a blue collar behind the nape, merging into an extensive blue area on the upper breast. A broad, dark red patch decorates the centre of the abdomen, also the lower back and rump. The bend of the wing is crimson, the primaries are blue edged with green and the tail is golden-olive, the lateral feathers being washed with brownish-red on the inner webs. The underside of the tail is brownish-red. Length: 11in.

*Distribution:* The coastal states of Brazil from Alagoas to São Paulo.

*Remarks:* This conure has been imported very rarely. Two specimens were obtained by the London Zoo as long ago as 1869 and others have been exhibited. During recent years it has become almost unknown to aviculture. Wassenaar Zoo exhibited three in the 1950s. In 1967 a dealer in England imported several, which were offered for sale at £40 per pair. This exceptionally attractive conure would be well worth a place in any collection.

*Breeding records:* Whitley bred *P.cruentata* in 1937. Dr Hopkinson reported that he saw the three young when they were three months old. They were still alive in the following year. In 1953 it was reported that Sir Edward Hallstrom had bred this species in the previous year; this was incorrect – the conure bred was probably *P.frontalis*.

## DEVILLE'S CONURE *(P.devillei)*

*Description:* According to Salvadori it has a narrow frontal band of reddish-brown and the crown is brown with the feathers edged with green. The cheeks are green and the ear-coverts are greyish-brown. The breast is olive-brown, each feather edged with two narrow cross-bands, one light, the other dusky or blackish. There is a brownish-red patch on the abdomen. The bend of the wing, the carpal edge and the smaller under wing-coverts are crimson. The bastard wing, primary-coverts and primaries are blue, edged with black at the tip. The greater under wing-coverts are dusky. The tail is olive above, coppery brownish-red below, each feather tipped with olive. The rest of the plumage is green. Length: 9½in.

*Distribution:* Eastern Bolivia, northern Paraguay and south-western Mato Grosso.

## RED-BELLIED CONURE *(P.frontalis frontalis)*

*Description:* The forehead is maroon and the crown dark green, the feathers of the nape having a lighter edge. The ear-coverts are light buffish-brown and the feathers of the cheeks are dark green. The sides of the neck and the upper breast are scaled in the typical manner, being olive on the breast, edged with yellowish, the feathers of the sides of the neck being tipped with whitish-yellow. The scaled markings vary considerably in colour, one bird in my possession being quite golden-yellow on the upper breast. There is an irregular patch of maroon on the abdomen. The upper parts are dark green, the flights being bluish and the tail feathers are reddish in the centre, green at the base, maroon on the underside. There is some maroon on the lower back, well defined in some birds. The iris, beak and feet are black. Length: 11ins. There is a prominent circle of white skin surrounding the eye.

*Distribution:* South-eastern Brazil from eastern Minas Geraës and Espirito Santo to Rio de Janiero.

*Remarks:* Seldom imported in the early years of the century, but now the only regularly imported member of the genus. The price at which this conure is offered for sale is very reasonable and it is, in my opinion, a species which deserves wider popularity. I would thoroughly recommend it, both for the beginner and the experienced aviculturist. It is an ideal aviary bird in every respect, sometimes called 'Scaly-breasted Conure' by dealers.

*Breeding records:* The Red-bellied Conure has bred in Britain on many occasions, the first recorded instance being in 1925. The hen of a pair belonging to W. Shore-Bailey laid five eggs, four of which had hatched by July 24. The first youngster left the nest on September 13, when it exactly resembled its parents. In 1953 A. A. Prestwich reared three youngsters in a colony aviary housing four pairs. The entire colony would roost in one box, even during nesting operations. Squadron Leader S. A. Luckford's pair reared three young in 1963. It is interesting to note that the hen laid another clutch as soon as the young from the first round were self-supporting. Five eggs were laid by J. Halford's pair in 1970; one egg was broken and another was infertile, but the remaining three hatched between June 13 and 27. Three babies left the nesting log on August 3, 4 and 9. In the last two cases the birds reared young in the same year that they were obtained, which illustrates how willing these birds are to nest in aviaries.

In 1928 Prince Taka-Tsukasa bred this species in Japan. In Denmark in 1953 a pair nested in a cage only 60cm long. Four eggs were laid, two hatched; one chick lived for a short while and the other was killed at the age of three weeks by one of its parents – perhaps because of the small nest-box and cage. In the following year the pair reared two young in a cage only 80cm long. In 1954 Sir Edward Hallstrom bred this species in Australia. Three eggs were laid in a grandfather clock type of nest. Only one chick was reared.

KRIEG'S CONURE *(P.f.kriegi)*

Unable to ascertain distinguishing features from the three skins in the British Museum (Natural History).
*Distribution:* Western Minas Geraës, São Paulo, Paraná and Rio Grande do Sul. The birds from Misiones and Uruguay are probably referable to this race.

AZARA'S CONURE *(P.f.chiripepe)*

*Description:* It differs from *P.f.frontalis* in having no red on the tail, which is golden-olive, or on the lower back.
*Distribution:* Eastern Salta and Paraguay.
*Remarks:* The birds received by Shore-Bailey in 1922 were thought to be the first importation. However, it differs so little from the nominate race that it is unlikely that it would be correctly identified by many, in fact, a large proportion of 'Red-bellied Conures' imported belong to this sub-species.
*Breeding records:* Two of Shore-Bailey's birds nested in 1923. Five eggs were laid and a single egg hatched after an incubation period of 30 days. An Avicultural Society medal was awarded for this breeding.

PEARLY CONURE *(P.perlata perlata)*

*Description:* The forehead and crown are dark grey, the ear-coverts being light greyish-buff. The feathers of the throat and the sides of the neck are grey, edged with a lighter grey and the upper breast feathers are edged with blue, creating the typical scaled markings. The lores are bluish-green. The nape of the neck, the tail-coverts and the feathers surrounding the vent are blue. The wings, back and lower breast are dark green. The bend of the wing and the under wing-coverts are scarlet and the flight feathers are blue. The upper surface of the tail is dull maroon, the underside being blackish. The beak, feet and iris are black. Length: 9½in.
*Distribution:* Brazil: exact range unknown.
*Remarks:* In March 1965 I obtained two Pearly Conures, which were placed in a small aviary with no shelter; at night they roosted in the nest-box. So great is the curiosity of this species and, indeed, of

most *Pyrrhuras*, that a new nest-box will be explored and entered within *seconds* of it being placed in the aviary. If a bucket is left in the aviary during cleaning operations it is immediately explored inside and out, and anything edible is quickly removed! This trait of curiosity led to the escape of this pair on one occasion. I returned from two weeks holiday to find the aviary empty; a rat had burrowed into the floor and the Pearlies, no doubt unable to resist the temptation to explore, had made their exit via this hole. However, I soon heard them calling in the distance and before long they alighted in a large apple tree in the garden. I opened the birdroom door and they returned almost at once. I was less fortunate on two other occasions when Pearly Conures escaped in my absence; I never saw them again.

These birds have a talent for finding a weak spot in the wire-netting, due to their extreme inquisitiveness. It is therefore imperative to check the aviary carefully very regularly, because these conures almost invariably find holes before their owners do.

*Breeding records:* The first recorded breeding took place in Denmark in 1961; two young were reared. Three more were bred in 1963 and 1964. It was first bred in Britain by B. M. Killick of Wellingborough.

Five youngsters were bred in 1963, none in 1964, five in 1966. At the time of writing (1971), Mr Killick continues to breed a number each year, which is typical of the consistent results one can expect from *Pyrrhura* conures.

The two I obtained in March 1965 were probably of the same sex. In November of that year I came across another pair; they were undoubtedly a true pair, one being far bolder about the head and its upper mandible much wider. Since then I have successfully sexed these birds by the shape of the beak and head.

I acquired the true pair in December and placed them in an aviary with an open-fronted shelter, 12ft long, 3ft wide and 6ft high. The following year they chewed out the inside of a hollow branch, which then had to be removed. In July they excavated a hole between the ground and some board which concealed a cavity between their aviary and the next one, and disappeared inside. I had to block the hole to prevent them from nesting there. The birds were observed mating on July 23 and 24. A week later the hen was spending long periods inside the nest-box which was situated on the feeding shelf at the back of the shelter (not an ideal arrangement with some birds but quite satisfactory in this case). The box measured 12in high by 9½in square. On August 5 I looked inside when the hen left the nest and found three white eggs. The cock did not, of course, share in incubation.

On August 27 I heard the sound of a youngster being fed, but did not look inside the box until three weeks later. Inspection revealed three healthy-looking youngsters, almost completely naked, and one very soiled egg, either infertile or punctured. The parents showed no concern when I inspected the youngsters at weekly intervals (strangely enough, a daughter of this wild-caught pair, when paired with her father, resented inspection of the nest. I believe that this caused her to pluck the single youngster). After about three weeks the hen ceases to brood the young during the day but roosts inside at night with the cock.

On inspecting the box on October 8, the eldest youngster, which was almost fully feathered, adopted the same threatening attitude employed by the adults when disturbed in their box, ruffling up the head feathers, stretching the neck and swaying from side to side. The first two youngsters left the nest on October 18, the third on October 24. The two eldest were about three-quarters of the size of the adults, which they resembled, apart from the lighter legs and beak. The bill of the eldest was dark grey on fledging; the second had a light silvery-grey beak, which changed to dark grey within a few days. They fed themselves on apple and hard seed almost immediately.

In 1967 this pair nested even later in the year and reared three more youngsters. The adult hen unfortunately died at the end of that year and in 1968 the old male was paired with a 1966-hatched youngster, his daughter. They did not attempt to breed in 1968 but were successful in doing so in 1969.

In February 1968 I removed two of the 1966 youngsters from the colony. Housed in an aviary by themselves they nested within two weeks and eventually reared one youngster, unfortunately not a good specimen.

PARA PEARLY CONURE *(P.p.pseudoperlata)*
*Distribution:* Eastern Brazil from the city of Pará to Cuman Bay, Maranhão.

MIRITIBA PEARLY CONURE *(P.p.coerulescens)*
*Description:* According to Hellmayr (19d) it is distinguished by its 'larger and bi-coloured (yellowish-green or light green anteriorly, decidedly bluish posteriorly) genal patch, and more bluish foreneck

and chest, with narrower and paler (dingy whitish or dull buffy brownish instead of ocreous brown) apical edges'. He commented 'Judging from the material on hand, this appears to be a valid race, although it affords the only instance of an Amazonian species being represented by two geographic forms in the western and eastern sections of the forest region of northern Maranháo.'
*Distribution:* Known only from the type locality near the coast of northern Maranhão.'

RIO TOCANTINS PEARLY CONURE *(P.p.anerythra)*
*Distribution:* Known only from the type locality on the left bank of the Rio Tocantins.

CRIMSON-BELLIED CONURE *(P. (perlata) rhodogaster)*
*Synonym:* Crimson-breasted Conure.
*Description:* This is an extremely beautiful bird, and by far the most striking of the genus. The whole of the lower parts from the upper breast to the vent are brilliant scarlet, in contrast to the dark green upper parts. The cheeks are yellowish-green; the scalloped feathers are whitish below the throat and blue, black and white at the back of the head. The thighs and part of the wings are blue and there is some blue on the cheeks. The underside of the tail is black, the upper surface being maroon. The under wing-coverts are scarlet. Length: about 9½in.
*Distribution:* Central Brazil south of the Amazon from the Madeira east to the Tapajóz, south to the Jaurú and the Jamauchim.
*Remarks:* London Zoo received the first known importation of this species in 1927, when a pair was collected in Brazil by Chapman's representative. Whitley had one specimen in his collection in the 1930s. (The skin of this bird is in the British Museum.) In 1935 the Duke of Bedford obtained three 'Red-breasted Conures', presumably this species. The believed male paired with both females and two eggs were laid. In 1937 a cock was lent by H. Whitley and housed with one of the hens. The other 'pair' nested and five eggs were laid. Later inspection revealed 14 eggs in the nest. The 'cock' was a hen after all!

In 1951 Wassenaar Zoo exhibited a Crimson-bellied Conure and in 1965 a pair was brought from Brazil for the World Show of the C.O.M. in Rotterdam. These birds subsequently went to Amsterdam Zoo where they can be seen at the present time (1971). It am told that there is another pair in Rotterdam Zoo, perhaps the pair sent from Brazil to the C.O.M. World Show in Lisbon in 1970. I doubt that any others have been imported during recent years. In appearance this species is strongly reminiscent of *P.perlata*. Neumann regarded it as a sub-species – the western representative.

MOLINA'S CONURE *(P.molinae molinae)*

*Description:* The feathers of the crown are brown, edged with blue, and the nape is brown, tinged with blue. The cheeks are green, the ear-coverts greyish-brown and the throat, the sides of the neck and the upper breast light brown, each feather narrowly edged with blackish-brown, preceded by a band of yellowish-buff. There is a narrow maroon patch on the centre of the abdomen and the tail is maroon above, green at the base, the underside being coppery-red. The flight feathers are blue. Length: $10\frac{1}{2}$in. The tail is rather longer than in most members of the genus and measures about $5\frac{1}{4}$in.

*Distribution:* Bolivia, in the departments of Santa Cruz and Chuquisaca.

*Remarks:* Rare in aviculture. The only reference I can find refers to the pair collected by Walter Goodfellow. He described it as 'an altogether delightful species'.

*P.molinae sordida*

*Description:* It differs from the nominate race in being smaller and duller. The crown is a paler, more olive, brown and the green area on the sides of the head is reduced and paler; the maroon patch on the abdomen is also paler and less prominent, and the wings are a paler blue.

*Distribution:* Southern Mato Grosso, Brazil, to extreme eastern Bolivia.

CRIMSON-TAILED CONURE *(P.m.phoenicura)*

*Description:* It differs principally from *P.m.australis* and *P.m.molinae* in having the bases of the central retrices tinged with green for about half their basal length.

*Distribution:* Western-central Mato Grosso.

MATO GROSSO CONURE *(P. (molinae) hypoxantha)*

*Description:* There is only one skin of this conure in the British Museum; on the label is this comment by Salvadori: 'Compared with the type, similar but with brighter colours.' The skin is that of an extremely beautiful bird with a long, pink tail tipped with pale maroon. The head is brown with a few blue feathers at the back of the neck. The flights are blue, the under wing-coverts and the area beneath the wings being bright yellow. There is a scarlet patch on the centre of the abdomen, surrounded by yellow feathers tipped with green. The scalloped effect is most unusual, the feathers being white on the throat and pink tipped with yellow for about an inch below. The cheeks are difficult to describe, being a mixture of several colours, including red and green. Length: $11\frac{1}{2}$in, of which the tail accounts for $5\frac{3}{4}$in.

*Distribution:* The four specimens known were from Urucum and Corumba in western Mato Grosso.

*Remarks:* Peters (29) states that it is known from four specimens only and that it may be merely an aberration of *phoenicura.* More recently de Schauensee (33b) gives the number of specimens known as three.

*P.molinae restricta*

*Description:* It differs from the nominate race in having the green of the cheeks tinged with blue and a prominent blue collar on the hind-neck. The pale edges to the feathers of the throat and breast are wider and much paler, and the maroon patch on the abdomen is smaller and duller; the flights are deep blue.

*Distribution:* Known only from the type locality: Palmarito in Bolivia.

ARGENTINE CONURE *(P.m.australis)*

*Description:* The two skins examined showed scarcely any blue on the nape in comparison with *P.m.molinae*; however, the most well marked feature is said to be the more pronounced maroon patch on the abdomen. The lower parts are a duller shade of green.

*Distribution:* Southern Bolivia in the department of Tarija, and north-western Argentina in the provinces of Salta and Jujuy.

RED-EARED CONURE *(P.hoematotis)*

*Description:* The forehead and the front half of the crown are brown, the feathers with bluish edges; the back of the head is olive-green, the cheeks green and the ear-coverts brown-red. The feathers of the sides of the neck are edged with brown-grey and the throat and upper breast are green with a slight olive tinge. There is a maroon patch on the centre of the abdomen, nearly hidden by the green edges of the

feathers. The carpal edge of the wing is bluish and the primary-coverts and primaries are blue. The under wing-coverts are green and blackish. The tail is maroon, tipped with olive-green, the under-side being coppery-red. Length: 9in to 10in.
*Distribution:* The mountains near Caracas (in Aragua), Venezuela.
*Remarks:* Extremely rarely imported; H. Whitley owned one.

WHITE-EARED CONURE *(P.leucotis leucotis)*
*Description:* This attractive species has the forehead, lores and cheeks of a rich shade of dark brown; the crown and nape are blackish-brown and the hind-neck is blue. The ear-coverts are off-white. The feathers of the breast are edged with white and a narrow line of black to create the typical scaled appearance. There is a maroon patch on the middle of the abdomen and another from the lower back to the upper tail-coverts. The bend of the wing and the under wing-coverts are scarlet; the primaries are blue on the outer webs. The tail is maroon above, green at the base and coppery-red below. The rest of the plumage is dark green. The bill is brown. Length: 8¼in.
*Distribution:* The Brazilian coastal states from Bahia to São Paulo.
*Remarks:* This species has been imported into Britain since 1871, rarely at first and more regularly from 1884 until about 1956. It was considered to be one of the members of the genus most often available but is now unobtainable. A single bird from the last importation lived at the London Zoo until 1970. It had an unusual companion in a male Plumhead Parrakeet *(Psittacula cyanocephala)* to which it was paired.

This is one of the most attractive of the *Pyrrhuras* known to aviculturists and it is to be hoped that it will again become available.
*Breeding records:* There are a number of very early records of partial success, including that by Prince Ferdinand of Saxe-Coburg-Gotha in Vienna in 1880 and by a Mr John in London in 1885. The first success in Europe was probably obtained by M. Barnsby of Tours in 1886; seven eggs were laid, four of which hatched. The chicks were reared.

The first recorded successful breeding in Britain took place in 1906 in the aviaries of E. J. Brook. His pair shared a large outdoor aviary with a pair of 'Golden-headed Conures' (Jendayas). The first egg was laid on August 3. The clutch consisted of eight eggs, seven of which hatched. Brook stated 'The first young birds left the nest about five weeks after hatching'. This must be incorrect, as at five weeks *Pyrrhuras* are only partly feathered and do not fledge for a further two or three weks. The incubation period of ' about 21 days ' is also incorrect. He wrote that the youngsters differed from the adults in that ' the inner web of the flight feathers and larger wing-coverts is yellow, and when very young they showed a good deal of yellow on the back '. This is not a characteristic of immature birds; it indicates malnutrition. Brook reported that at night all the occupants of the aviary, including the ' Golden-heads ', roosted in the same nest-box.

A pair of White-eared Conures belonging to T. F. Nixon had seven eggs in 1955, hatched six and reared four young. This was only the third breeding recorded in Britain. In 1956 K. W. Dolton of Worcester bought a pair and placed them in an aviary 18ft long x 3ft wide x 6ft 6in high. They ignored the nest-box provided but immediately took to an old branch with a hole in it. The number of eggs laid and hatched was not recorded, only that the chicks ' were about seven weeks old when they first left the nest, and it was about a week later that three more came out '. They were fed on sunflower, canary seed, hemp and half an apple twice daily.

During the same year a pair owned by E. N. T. Vane, which were housed in a 40ft flight with a pair of Ringnecks, went to nest and hatched some young. Unfortunately the hen died when the chicks were about three weeks old. On inspection the nest was found to contain three dead young, one fertile egg and two clear ones. The pair were not wintered outdoors as the cock suffered from frost-bite and had lost three toes on one foot.

This species normally lays large clutches, seven and eight eggs being recorded more often than not.

## EMMA'S CONURE *(P.leucotis emma)*

*Synonyms:* Blue-naped Conure, Salvadori's Conure.

*Description:* It is distinguished at a glance from the nominate race by the blue which extends from the forehead, which is reddish-chestnut, to the middle of the crown. There is more blue on the lower part of the cheeks, the sides of the neck and the throat than in *P.l.leucotis*. The light edges to the feathers of the throat and upper breast are often broader than in the latter. It is slightly larger, ie 9¼in.

*Distribution:* The Caribbean coast of Venezuela from Caracas east to Sucre.

*Remarks:* Very rarely imported. It was described as probably being new to aviculture in 1929 when received by Chapman. Presumably this bird was bought by Whitley, as one was exhibited by him at the Crystal Palace show in 1931.

*Breeding records:* In 1968 Carl Wentrup of Lyngby in Denmark bred *nine* in one nest. Six of the young went to Sweden. Wentrup's original pair were obtained in 1962 but the male died in 1964. A replacement was found soon after and the pair nested in 1966 when five young were reared. This may have been the first recorded breeding of this sub-species. No young were reared in 1967, nine were bred in 1968 and six in 1969. The birds were housed in a small flight in a basement cellar which was lit by artificial light. The hen rejected a nest-box in favour of a natural log with the entrance at the top. Incubation lasted about 27 days. In 1968 the youngest of the nine chicks fledged a full month after the first. The young were fed by the adults for 14 days after leaving the nest.

PFRIMER'S CONURE *(P.l.pfrimeri)*
*Distribution:* Known only from the type locality in the western central part of Goyaz, Brazil.

BRAZILIAN GREY-BREASTED CONURE *(P.l.griseipectus)*
*Distribution:* Eastern Brazil in the state of Ceará.

PAINTED CONURE *(P.picta picta)*
*Description:* The top of the head is black, the forehead and the lower part of the cheeks are blue and there is a faint band of blue on the nape. The upper cheeks are maroon, the ear-coverts are grey and the throat and the sides of the neck brown or blackish, greenish on the upper breast. The feathers of the throat and upper breast are broadly edged with light greyish, brown and olive to produce the usual scaled effect. There is a maroon patch from the lower back to the upper tail-coverts and on the abdomen. The bend of the wing is red and the outer webs of the primaries are blue. The tail is maroon above, coppery-red below. Length: 9½in. Immature birds are said to have the bend of the wing green with a few scattered red feathers.
*Distribution:* The Caura Valley in Venezuela, eastward through Guyana and Surinam to Cayenne.
*Remarks:* Very rare in aviculture. In 1972 a pair was imported by a London dealer.

*P.p.orinocensis*
*Description:* It differs from the nominate race in having the crown

paler and the margins of the feathers of the throat and breast narrower and therefore less pronounced.
*Distribution:* Venezuela from the Orinoco Valley to the Guyana frontier.

JARAQUIEL CONURE *(P.p.subandina)*
*Description:* Todd (39b) described it as follows: 'Above, including secondaries externally and wing-coverts, bright parrot green; rump and median upper tail coverts garnet brown; primaries externally Pario blue, with black tips and wide black inner margins, and narrow pale green outer margins; outermost primary entirely black; tail dark red (between garnet brown and maroon), with the feathers extensively green on their outer webs towards the base; pileum and nape dark brown (near bister), succeeded by an ill-defined band of Jouvence blue; lores and a narrow frontlet garnet brown; cheeks dark Russian green; ear-coverts dull ochraceous tawny; throat and breast with broadly squamate markings of soiled buff, the feathers with dusky centres; rest of underparts (including wing-coverts) bright parrot green with a slight bluish shade, the middle of the abdomen extensively garnet brown; " iris straw-colour; bill and feet blackish ".' (Carriker).
*Distribution:* Rio Sinu region of north-western Colombia.
*Remarks:* This conure, which appears to be unknown to aviculture, was considered by Todd (39b) as a separate species, as it is completely isolated from *P.p.luciani* by the Andes.

*P.p. caeruleiceps*
*Description:* It differs from *P.p.subandina* (of which Todd considered it to be a sub-species) in having the entire crown dull blue with the nape more dusky; the lores, cheeks and region surrounding the eye are garnet brown. The edgings to the feathers of the throat and breast are broader and a paler 'soiled white'.
*Distribution:* Known only from the type locality, on the western slope of the Eastern Andes of Colombia. It would appear to be rare.

SANTAREM CONURE *(P.p.amazonum)*
*Description:* Adult birds are described by Hellmayr (19b) as having the forehead pale blue, extending to just beyond the eye, with no crimson. The bend of the wing is green (some of the feathers edged with red in one specimen). The four central tail feathers are narrowly margined with green from the base for a third or half of their length.

The ear-coverts are bright brownish-buff. According to Todd (39b), the breast feathers are usually green instead of dusky as in the nominate race.

*Distribution:* The valley of the lower Amazon from the Rio Madiera to the Tocantins and extending up the valley of the Rio Tocantins to northern Goyaz.

*P.p.microtera*

*Description:* It differs from *P.p.amazonum* in being smaller and in usually having less blue on the forehead. The ground colour of the throat and breast feathers is darker and dusky rather than greenish.

*Distribution:* The south bank of the lower Amazon.

PRINCE LUCIAN'S CONURE *(P.p.luciani)*

*Description:* It differs from *P.p.picta* in having the forehead bluish instead of distinctly blue, in showing less maroon on the lores and cheeks, and in lacking the scarlet at the bend of the wing. The crown is brown, the ear-coverts buff and the feathers of part of the cheeks and those of the throat are brown with buff edges. The upper breast feathers have brown centres and white edges. Length: about 9in.

*Distribution:* Upper Amazonia from eastern Peru to the Rio Jururá in western Brazil.

*Remarks:* Very rarely imported. At the Crystal Palace shows of 1928 and 1932 a pair and a single bird were exhibited. As far as I know it has not been imported into Britain in recent years. In 1926 Delacour and Berlioz described this conure as 'common in captivity and easily reared'. This was incorrect; it appears that the Red-bellied Conure (then named *P.vittata*) had been confused with it.

*Breeding records:* The early records, especially those relating to breedings in France, all refer mistakenly to *P.frontalis*. In 1926 a pair of Prince Lucian's Conures, which belonged to F. R. Child, went to nest. Four eggs were laid and after an incubation period given as 21 days two hatched; the other eggs contained chicks which were dead-in-shell. Child stated 'unfortunately the young died at the age of one week', but also stated 'When found dead, their crops were quite empty, and do not appear to have been fed from the time of hatching.'

The only successful breeding that I can trace took place in the aviaries of L. B. Thompson in British Colombia in 1960. The hen laid six eggs; all hatched and six young were reared. Their owner wrote: 'They are fantastically tame and we have really enjoyed them.'

*P.p.roseifrons*
*Description:* It differs strikingly from *P.p.picta* in having the feathers of the forehead and part of the crown scarlet, with buff coloured-webs.
*Distribution:* Jurura, Brazil, also Peru. (One specimen examined was labelled as having been collected in Tarapoto, on the edge of the Andes in northern Peru.)

*P.p.cuchivera*
*Distribution:* Venezuela.

SANTA MARTA CONURE *(P.viridicata)*
*Description:* There is a very narrow frontal band of red, the throat- and ear-coverts are reddish and the remainder of the upper parts are dark green, except the flights which are bright blue on the outer webs, blackish on the inner webs. On the abdomen is an uneven line of yellow-tipped red feathers, below which are a few scattered maroon ones. The bend of the wing is yellow and the under wing-coverts scarlet or orange towards the edge of the wing, where a couple of yellow feathers are found. The underside of the tail is pale maroon. The iris is brown and the bill flesh-coloured at the base, dusky at the tip. Length: $9\frac{3}{4}$in to 10in.
*Distribution:* Known only from the type locality in the sub-tropical zone of the Santa Marta Mountains.

DEMERARA CONURE *(P. (melanura) egregia)*
*Description:* The feathers of the head are brown, tipped with green, the flights are bright blue and the tail is dark maroon. The throat is reddish and the scaled feathers below are green tipped with yellow, the feathers below the cheeks being tipped with white. The most beautiful feature of this bird is the under wing-coverts. There is a small patch of red at the top of the wing, followed by a large area of orange and a large area of yellow. Length: 10in.
*Distribution:* Guyana: Mount Roraima, Merumé Mountains, Kamarang and Carimong, Annai; south-eastern Venezuela; possibly also Surinam. It frequents wooded areas.

BLACK-TAILED CONURE *(P.melanura melanura)*
*Synonym:* Maroon-tailed Conure.

*Description:* The feathers of the forehead are brown and the crown feathers are brown with green edges, giving the head a mottled appearance when closely examined. The scaled markings on the upper breast are brownish-green, with narrow lighter edges, the remainder of the breast being dark green, sometimes with a few scattered maroon feathers on the abdomen. All the three specimens examined differed from *P.m.souancei* in having a less extensive area of red on the primary coverts, the red feathers having almost hidden *yellow tips, the hidden feathers being completely yellow.* The under wing-coverts are scarlet. The upper surface of the tail is black except at the base, which is green; the underside of the tail is very dark maroon. The bill is light brown and there is a *prominent area of white skin surrounding the eye.* Length: 10½in.
*Distribution:* According to Peters it is found in north-western Amazonia, north to the upper Orinoco (Rio Cunucunuma), east to the Rio Negro and south to north-eastern Peru (Pebas) and the Rio Solimoës.
*Remarks:* This species was rarely imported until about 1967 or 1968 when large numbers were received by dealers in Britain. Some, possibly most, of these birds belong to the sub-species *souancei.* It is now usually available but has not proved as popular as other *Pyrrhuras.* In my experience it lacks the confiding nature which makes the Red-bellied Conure, for example, so attractive.
*Breeding records:* See under Souancés Conure.

SOUANCÉS CONURE *(P.m.souancei)*
*Description:* Distinguished from *P.m.melanura* by the primary wing-coverts which are scarlet, with no trace of yellow; the red is more extensive, reaching further along the edge off the wing. The scaled feathers of the upper breast and the sides of the neck are dark green with broad buffish-white (pinkish-buff in one specimen examined) edges, which are much more conspicuous than in the nominate race. Length: 9½in.
*Distribution:* Amazonian Ecuador.
*Remarks:* see under Black-tailed Conure.
*Breeding records:* The first English breeding of *P.melanura* occurred in 1970 when Mrs B. Rhodes of Yorkshire reared two young from what she described as 'Maroon-tailed Conures'. From the description of the birds with which she provided me, they would appear to be *P.m.souancei.* The pair were obtained in July 1968 and housed in an inside flight 3ft long x 3ft 6in high. A nest-box which measured 18in

deep and 9in square, with a 2in layer of peat, was provided. In January 1970 the conures were seen mating; the first egg was probably laid on February 1. On February 26 young were heard in the nest and six weeks later came the sounds of their wings being exercised. After a further week the first left the nest, to be followed by a second a few days later. The nest-box was found to contain an egg, making the total clutch four, as one egg had been dropped on the floor two weeks earlier. The young resembled their parents except for the fainter and less extensive markings around the neck and the darker feet.

The adult went to nest again in December 1970. Four of the five eggs laid hatched in January and all four chicks were reared. At four weeks old they were covered with dark grey down with some quills coming through. The young birds were housed on their own in a large cage where 'they roll about and fight just like a bunch of puppies'. The parents nested again, laying five eggs in April.

In 1968 it was reported that one young *P.berlepschi* was bred in Denmark and in 1969 four were reared in Sweden; both records almost certainly refer to Souancé's Conure.

## PACIFIC BLACK-TAILED CONURE *(P.m.pacifica)*

*Description:* It has the forehead green (not brown as in *chapmani*) and the feathers of the upper breast dull green at the base, very narrowly edged with pinkish-buff. There is no maroon on the abdomen and no yellow on the wing-coverts; the edge of the wing is scarlet. The flights are bluish-black and the tail is maroon above, black below. The small area of bare skin surrounding the eye is greyish and barely noticeable, which distinguishes it at a glance from *souancei*, in which the orbital area is white. The beak is pale brown: Length: 9½in.

*Distribution:* Tropical south-western Narinõ district of Colombia. It is the only *Pyrrhura* recorded from the Pacific coast region.

*Remarks:* In November 1968 I saw three birds in a consignment of Souancé's Conures which differed from the others – and I bought them for that reason. I did not discover their true identity until a few months later. One bird looked very unhealthy but I bought it because it appeared to be paired to one of the other two. I was surprised that it survived for 15 months. The three were housed with my colony of *Pyrrhura* conures but the two fit birds had to be removed as they were responsible for the deaths of two Pearly Conures. (One was housed in an adjoining enclosure and had its tongue slit

through ½in wire netting.) Due to shortage of aviary accommodation the two *pacificas* had to be housed in a flight inside an outdoor bird-room from autumn 1969 until June 1970.
*Breeding records:* Towards the end of October 1970 my pair went to nest. The hen laid four eggs, two of which hatched. When the nest was inspected in December the hen was still incubating the two clear or addled eggs, and two long-dead, probably newly-hatched, young were seen. In February the male's legs became paralysed and the bird unfortunately died two days later. The hen had been caught up with the cock and laid an egg two days after the cock's death. So ended my chance of breeding *pacifica*.

BERLEPSCH'S CONURE *(P. (melanura) berlepschi)*
*Description:* According to Salvadori (who described the type from Chyavetas, eastern Peru), it is very much like *P.m.souancei* but has the light edges of the feathers of the throat and breast very much broader, approaching *rupicola* in this respect. This would appear, however, not to be a consistent feature, as Chapman (10a) described specimens of *souancei* with wider margins than those of *berlepschi*. The ear-coverts are of a brighter green with an olive tinge, and the blue of the primaries is purer and brighter. The green of the upper parts is said to have a yellower tinge and the maroon patch on the abdomen is more distinct and apparently constant. Length: 9½in.
*Distribution:* Eastern Peru.
*Remarks:* It has been reported that this conure has been brought into Europe during recent years, and this may be correct, but it is extremely difficult to distinguish from *souancei*.

ROCK CONURE *(P. (melanura) rupicola)*
*Description:* The cheeks and ear-coverts are green, with the feathers of the crown and hind-neck brown edged with green. The scaled markings of the throat and upper breast are brown, very broadly tipped with whitish. There are a few maroon feathers on the abdomen and the flights are black. Scattered red feathers are found on the carpal edge of the wing, which may be completely red in adult birds. The bastard wing and primary-coverts are also scarlet. The tail is green above, blackish-brown below. Length: about 10in.
*Distribution:* Tropical zone of south-eastern Peru (Chanchamayo Valley), 'Yungas country' of Bolivia, south-west Brazil in Acre.
*Remarks:* Very rarely imported. Whitley had one in his collection at Paignton Zoo in 1931.

CHAPMAN'S CONURE *(P. (melanura) chapmani)*
*Description:* Recognised by Bond and de Schauensee (7) as being closest to *calliptera*, from which it differs in having the feathers of the upper breast dark brown instead of green, broadly edged with whitish instead of vinaceous brown. The crown is darker brown with only a small amount of green. The inner coverts are maroon at the base and green distally, instead of entirely maroon, and there is no yellow on the wing-coverts. There is less maroon on the centre of the abdomen, the tail is darker below and the sides of the tail are green at the base.

It differs from *souancei* in the colouring of the upper breast, as described, and in having the green feathers between the collar and the mantle distinctly bluish. There is some maroon on the ear-coverts and less green on the crown and at the base of the tail.
*Distribution:* The eastern slopes of the central Andes of Colombia.

FLAME-WINGED CONURE *(P. (melanura) calliptera)*
*Synonym:* Beautiful Conure.
*Description:* The head is ashy-brown, also the scaled feathers of the breast and throat, which are tipped with reddish-brown. The cheeks are green with a touch of maroon on the ear-coverts and there is a maroon patch on the abdomen. The lesser wing-coverts are orange and the greater wing-coverts are golden-yellow. The skin of one male examined showed quite a lot of red on the wing-coverts. Length: about 9½in.
*Distribution:* Both slopes of the eastern Andes of Colombia.

WHITE-THROATED CONURE *(P.albipectus)*
*Description:* The crown is brown, the feathers streaked with green, with paler edges. The ear-coverts are orange and there is a broad whitish collar on the hind-neck. The throat and upper breast are pinkish-white, without any scalloping, shading to yellow on the lower breast. The primary coverts are scarlet and the tail is maroon, the central feathers being edged with green. The rest of the plumage is dark green. Length: 10in.
*Distribution:* Known only from the humid tropical zone of south-east Ecuador.

ROSE-HEADED CONURE *(P.rhodocephala)*
*Description:* Immediately identified by the head, which is entirely

scarlet. The scaled breast and throat markings so typical of the genus are absent. There are a few red feathers on the abdomen, the flights are blue and the tail is maroon. The rest of the plumage is green. Length: 9½in.
*Distribution:* Apparently confined to the mountains of western Venezuela: the Andes of Merida and Sierra Nevada.

HOFFMANN'S CONURE *(P.hoffmanni hoffmanni)*
*Synonym:* Sulphur-winged Conure.
*Description:* The head appears to be green flecked with yellow, as the centre of each feather is marked with yellow; the ear-coverts are red and the area below the beak is yellowish. The flights are blue and there is a small patch of yellow on the secondaries. The rest of the plumage is dark green, the scaled neck and breast markings being absent. Length: 10in.
*Distribution:* The mountains of Costa Rica. Slud (35) states that it is distributed through the highlands over the southern half of Costa Rica, from the hilly Caribbean approaches to the central plateau and the mountains along the southern edge of the plateau southward. It frequents forested ridges and hillsides in brokenly wooded country, usually in small flocks which are hard to locate. 'The birds chatter without screeching and the unparrot-like cries of a flock can sound like a weak whirring or bring to mind a noisy group of songbirds.'

CHIRIQUI CONURE *(P.h.gaudens)*
*Description:* It differs from *P.h.hoffmanni* by the more abundant greenish-yellow markings on the crown and hind-neck, mixed with a varying amount of dull red to orange red, extending in some individuals to the edges of the feathers of the back, foreneck and chest. The beak is said to be pale brownish-white. Length: 10in.
*Distribution:* The mountains of western Panama, east to Veragua on the Pacific slope and to the Chiriqui Lagoon on the Caribbean.

Genus: *Enicognathus*

The large parrakeets of this genus have the most southerly distribution of any neo-tropical parrot. *Ferruginea* was formerly placed in the monotypical genus *Microsittace*.

MAGELLAN CONURE *(E. ferruginea ferruginea)*
*Description:* Dark green above, with the feathers of the head fairly heavily edged with black and with less prominent black edges to those

of the back. The under parts are green, slightly olive, with very faint black margins to the feathers. The forehead is reddish and the centre of the abdomen, also the tail, is maroon. The beak is black. Length: about 14in (skins examined varied from 13in to 15in). In some ways this bird is rather reminiscent of a large Red-bellied Conure.
*Distribution:* The island of Tierra del Fuego and a limited area in Chilian territory, north of the Magellan Straits. It is an abundant resident species throughout the forested areas of Tierra del Fuego, nesting late in the year and laying from four to seven eggs.
*Remarks:* A great rarity in captivity. The London Zoo exhibited this species as long ago as 1866 and has owned one or two since then, but not during recent years. In Australia Sir Edward Hallstrom had several specimens in 1953. In 1971 I saw six of these conures in East Berlin Zoo.

CHILIAN CONURE *(E.ferruginea minor)*
*Description:* It differs from the nominate race only in being smaller. The four skins examined measured between 11½in and 12½in.
*Distribution:* Chile from Colchagua to the Guaitecas Islands, and the eastern slopes of the Andes in Rio Negro Territory, Argentina. Ambrose Lane, writing in the *Ibis* in 1897, described seeing large flocks in the forested areas of Maquega and Valdivia. He stated that these birds were eaten by the natives. During recent years its numbers have apparently increased greatly in forests of oak and 'canelo' *(Drynis winteri)* in the cordilleras of Lontué. The conures feed on the seeds of the trees and nest in them during December, when four to six eggs are laid.
*Remarks:* Also very rare in aviculture. The only pair seen in Britain for many years, as far as I know, were those at Pan's Gardens, Ashover, Derbyshire. The curator, F. H. Keeling informed me: 'Unfortunately the Chilean Conure (it was indeed *M.ferruginea)* died on December 9 1970 during a power cut caused by the electricity strikes. No other psittacines in the bird house were affected, which is significant as this individual was always extremely intolerant of low temperatures. Apparently this was not an individual characteristic, as the specimen which arrived with it on August 2 1967 died during an unexpectedly early cold spell in October of the same year. It seems worthy of note that birds from such a comparatively cool and high part of South America should be so affected by even relatively low temperatures.

'By far and away the most interesting characteristic of these

Conures was their habit of spending the bulk of their time clinging to the weldmesh of their aviary, although, of course, branches were provided in the usual way. In this position they invariably used their tails as 'tripods' in almost woodpecker-like fashion, with the unfortunate result that this part of their body was always stumpy and bedraggled. Just over a year ago I was intrigued to notice the same behaviour and tail condition in the solitary specimen in the Amsterdam Zoological Garden.'

The birds at Amsterdam and Ashover were presented by the Chillan Viejo Zoo in Chile. One of those in Amsterdam Zoo also died during a cold spell shortly after its arrival.

SLENDER-BILLED PARRAKEET *(E. leptorhynchus)*
*Synonyms:* Long-billed Parrakeet, Slight-billed Parrakeet.
*Description:* This species is not unlike the Magellan Conure, from which it is easily distinguished by the long, black beak. The bill is very narrow, only slightly curved, and the upper mandible is as long below the lower mandible as above it.

The plumage is dark green with a faint dusky edging to most of the feathers, more heavily pronounced on the crown. The lores, an indistinct area surrounding the eye and the forehead, are maroon; there is a small indistinct patch of the same colour on the abdomen and the tail is maroon with a greenish tip. There is an area of white skin surrounding the eye. The primary coverts are bluish-green. The iris is orange. Length: about 16in, including the 7in tail.

According to Blaauw, who bred this species, young birds are darker, all the feathers having dark edges. The upper mandible is shorter than in the adult and the tip and the top part of the lower mandible are white.

*Distribution:* Chile, from Aconagua to Llanquihue. It breeds locally throughout its range. South of latitude 40°S it is probably a summer visitor only.

In 1897 Ambrose Lane recorded in the *Ibis* that these birds were very numerous in Southern Chile, especially in the interior. They fed on forest trees, being rarely found in cultivated fields. In some years they raided gardens and orchards. In 1911, F. E. Blaauw came across many while riding across country to Puerto Varas. He reported 'The trees were full of Long-billed Parrakeets which screamed loudly and were very active, flying about in small flocks or perching on the tops of giant trees. These birds were probably feeding on the seeds of the Urumus trees, which are very numerous, and on the countless other seeds and berries as well (the Urumus fruit looks like a small olive).'

During recent years these parrakeets have declined greatly in numbers, partly as a result of the reduction in forested areas, also due to shooting and, apparently, to Newcastle disease. In *Birds of Chile* it is stated that they feed on the cones of araucaria pines, also on wild and cultivated plants, including thistles and wheat, doing considerable damage to cultivated crops. They nest in November or December, laying five or six eggs in a hole in a tree devoid of lining and at a safe height.

*Remarks:* This is an extremely rare bird in confinement. Sir Edward Hallstrom owned a single specimen in 1955 and Mrs Howard of Wolverhampton has had one since about 1965, a most interesting bird which is reasonably tame and talks. It was bought from a sailor as a 'woodpecker' for the sum of 12s 6d! Tailless and completely unrecognisable, it was several months before Mrs Howard discovered its true identity. This bird is extremely fond of mealworms and corn-on-the-cob.

While in Chile in 1911, F. E. Blaauw saw a tame Long-billed Parrakeet in an inn near Puerto Varas. He bought it for a few pesos and purchased another for the sum of one peso in Osorno. He took them back to Holland, where they became very tame. They imitated all kinds of noises and Blaauw thought that they could have been taught to talk. The female copied her owner's whistle and the noises of Oven Birds, their travelling companions on board ship.

*Breeding records:* For two years the pair lived in a large garden aviary during the summer and spent the winters in a birdroom, demolishing the woodwork of their flight. In 1913 they went to nest in a roomy log towards the end of May. After about three weeks the cries of young birds, described as resembling the sounds made by young Green Woodpeckers, were heard. On August 3 a strong young one fledged, followed by another a day later. Two addled eggs remained in the nest. In 1916 four more were reared.

Extras provided while the young were being reared were bread soaked in milk, pieces of *Berberis dulcis,* and grass roots. It is interesting to note that although Blaauw never observed these birds feeding on the ground in the wild they delighted in digging up the turf in the aviary.

15 The Red-masked Conure *Aratinga erythrogenys* is one of a large group of conures in which the plumage is mainly green, with varying amounts of red on the head and under wing-coverts. Owner: Borje Hedström.

16 The most frequently imported of the *Pyrrhura* Conures is the Red-bellied *P. frontalis*. It is an ideal bird for the beginner. Owner: author.

17 The Greater Patagonian Conure *Cyanoliseus patagonus byroni* breeds in holes in cliffs or banks in its native Chile, where its numbers have been greatly reduced. These two are part of a colony at Rode Tropical Bird Gardens.

SOUTH AMERICA
SCALE OF MILES
0 100 200 400 600 800
NORTH ATLANTIC OCEAN
SOUTH ATLANTIC OCEAN
PACIFIC OCEAN
EQUATOR
TROPIC OF CAPRICORN
ARUBA
BONAIRE
CURACAO
TORTUGA
MARGARITA
PARIA PEN
BARBADOS
TOBAGO
TRINIDAD
SANTAMARTA
BARRANQUILLA
COSTA RICA
PANAMA
CARACAS
CUMANA
Guanare
Orinoco
VENEZUELA
GEORGETOWN
PARAMARIBO
CAYENNE
GUYANA
SURINAM
FRENCH GUIANA [CAYENNE]
Oyapock
Maroweine
Corantyne
Essequibo
Caroni
Cauca
Magdalena
BOGOTA
COLOMBIA
DUIDA
Guaviare
Vaupes
ICANA
UAPES
Branco
Paru
AMAPA
MEXIANA Is.
ILHA DE MARAJO
BELEM [PARA]
CUMAN BAY
BAHIA DE CARAQUEZ
QUITO
ECUADOR
Napo
Putumayo
Japula
Negro
OBIDOS
MANAUS
SANTAREM
Amazon
IQUITOS
Maranon
Ucayali
AMAZONAS
PARA
Tapajos
Iriri
Tocantins
MARANHAO
CEARA
CAPE SAO ROQUE
Jurua
Parus
Madeira
Parnaiba
Araguaia
TRUJILLO
ACRE
PERNAMBUCO
ALAGOAS
PERU
RONDONIA
BRAZIL
Xingu
MATO GROSSO
GOYAS
Sao Francisco
BAHIA
LIMA
CUZCO
Mamore
SALVADOR [BAHIA]
Parana
L. Titicaca
AREQUIPA
BOLIVIA
LAPAZ
BRAZILIA
COCHABAMBA
Grande
SANTA CRUZ
MINAS GERAES
SUCRE
CORUMBA
Pilcomayo
Grande
PARAGUAY
Paraguay
SAO PAULO
ESPIRITO SANTO
TARIJA
GRAN CHACO
RIO DE JANEIRO
SAO PAULO
AUTOFAGASTA
JUJUY
SALTA
ASUNUON
PARANA
Iguacu
TUCUMAN
SANTIAGO DEL ESERO
SANTA CATARINA
CATAMARCA
Salado
CORRIENTES
RIO GRANDE DO SUL
CORDOBA
SANTA FE
ENTRE RIOS
PARANA
SALTO
Negro
ACONCAGUA
MENDOZA
URUGUAY
SANTIAGO
BUENOS AIRES
ROCHA
PLATA
MONTEVIDEO
LA PAMPA
ARGENTINA
CHILE
Negro
VALDIVIA
L. Llanquihue
I. CHILOE
Chugut
GUAITECAS Is.
Chico
PATAGONIA
Chico
FALKLAND ISLANDS
TIERRA DEL FUEGO
CAPE HORN

CHAPTER 6

# PARRAKEETS AND PARROTLETS

ALL the small parrakeets and the parrotlets are included in this chapter. It covers the *Forpus* parrotlets, which are among the best known of the neo-tropical parrots in aviculture, and the *Touit* parrotlets, which are almost unknown; also the seldom-kept (with two exceptions) *Bolborhynchus* parrakeets and the popular *Brotogeris*. As their habits and requirements differ widely, general remarks are given with each genus or species.

Genus: *Myiopsitta*

QUAKER PARRAKEET *(M.monachus monachus)*

*Synonym*: Grey-breasted Parrakeet, Monk Parrakeet

*Description:* The upper parts are a medium shade of green, brightest on the wings and tail, except the forehead and most of the crown, which is pale greenish-grey. The lores, cheeks and throat are grey, merging into pale grey, white-tipped breast feathers, which merge into the greyish-green of the abdomen. The flight feathers are blue edged with black; the under wing-coverts are pale grey and pale bluish. The thighs and under tail-coverts are bright light green and the under surface of the tail is pale green, with pale blue on the outer edge. Length: about 11½in.

There is a blue mutation of the Quaker, and also a very beautiful and even rarer yellow mutation. The latter is pure yellow above, the colour of a lutino Budgerigar, with the forehead and under parts greyish-white. The flights are greyish and the underside of the tail is bluish-green. The beak is pinkish-brown.

*Distribution:* Eastern and central Argentina in the provinces of Cordoba, Santa Fé, Entre Rios and Buenos Aires; it also inhabits Uruguay.

The Quaker is common in the wild and found in large colonies. In *Argentine Ornithology*, W. H. Hudson stated 'They are extremely sociable and breed in communities. When a person enters the wood [a tala wood near Cape San Antonia] their subdued chatter suddenly ceases, and during the ominous silence a hundred pairs of black, beady eyes survey the intruder from the nests and branches; and then follow a whirring of wings and an outburst of screams that spreads the alarm through the woods. The nests are frequented all the year, and it is rare to find a large one unattended by some of the birds any time during the day. In summer and autumn they feed principally on the thistle; first the flower is cut up and pulled to pieces for the sake of the green kernel, and later they eat the fallen seed on the ground. Their flight is rapid, with quick flutters of the wings, which seem never to be raised to the level of the body. . . .

'The nests are suspended from the extremities of the branches, to which they are firmly woven. New nests consist of only two chambers, the porch and the nest proper, and are inhabited by a single pair of birds. Successive nests are added, until some of them come to weigh a quarter of a ton, and contain material enough to fill a large cart. Thorny twigs, firmly interwoven form the only material and there is no lining in the breeding chamber, even in the breeding season. Some old forest trees have seven or eight of these structures suspended from their branches, while the ground underneath is covered with twigs and remains of fallen nests. The entrance to the chamber is generally underneath, or, if at the side, is protected by an overhanging eave, to prevent the intrusion of opossums.' Nevertheless, these animals are sometimes found in the upper chambers, and Teal also breed in the nests. The breeding season apparently begins in November and up to seven or eight eggs are laid.

Cultivated fruits such as apples, pears, peaches and medlars form part of the diet.

*Remarks:* The Quaker has always been a common bird in aviaries, although due to its destructive and noisy habits, it is more often found in zoos than in private collections. Undoubtedly the ideal way to keep this species is at liberty. On quite a number of occasions this has been discovered by accident, because it takes a strong aviary to contain Quakers!

One which was 'at large' in the New Forest many years ago wove a nest in the thatched roof of a farm-house, close to the warmth and shelter of a chimney-stack. The tunnel to the nest, which was about a yard long, was used as a sleeping place throughout the winter. Twigs from a hawthorn hedge were used to add to the size of the nest until it was 7ft or 8ft long!

This bird lived for about two years, when it disappeared.

At the present time several British aviculturists keep these birds at liberty. One such flock breed in some large trees and feed on corn and pellets provided for the waterfowl in the collection, ignoring seed.

Quakers make excellent pets, apart from their destructive habits. They sometimes learn to speak a few words. One, an accomplished talker could repeat

> Merrily danced the Quaker's wife,
> With all her bairns about her.

Many of its sayings were self-taught and it could perform several tricks. At the command 'Act daft!' it would ruffle its feathers, hold one leg up, open its beak wide and nod its head. It was affectionate towards its owner but 'a terror to the visitors'. This bird was not caged during the day and enjoyed hanging over the door and pulling off the servants' caps as they entered, then laughing at them.

Quakers have been housed with other parrot-like species but this is not advisable. One aviculturist who was unwise enough to put a pair in an aviary containing Budgerigars and Cockatiels was soon left with only Quakers occupying the aviary. These birds will not hesitate to kill others. Their beaks can cut through ordinary gauge wire-netting as effectively as wire-cutters, so an extra strong gauge wire or welded mesh must be used.

It is interesting to note that in 1959, on the death of M. J. Bruyneel of Steenokkerzeel, Belgium, his birds were auctioned. They included eight normal Quakers which fetched £28 and nine rare blue Quakers which were sold for only £53. In 1964 a collection of 12 blues was offered in Belgium at £175 per pair, the buyer having to take the whole collection. These birds were descendants of Bruyneel's. The cost of blue Quakers is now many times that figure.

*Breeding records:* This species must have been bred more often than any other South American psittacine. It has reared young on countless occasions during the past 100 years, frequently at liberty. It was bred in Vienna as early as 1867 and in the late 19th century, Herr von Prosch of Saxony had a flock of about 40 breeding at liberty.

No detailed breeding reports of this species appear to exist – probably because it has been bred so often. One breeding report is of interest because the male finished rearing the young with no assistance. The pair were housed in an aviary with large softbills and the hen laid five eggs, all of which hatched. When the young were between two and three weeks old the hen was killed in a fight with a Glossy Starling. The cock reared the young birds, which left the nest at the age of six weeks. They were fed on sunflower seed, canary, millet, hemp, groats, apples, carrots, sprouts, dandelion and insectile mixture.

Quakers must, of course, be supplied with large quantities of twigs if they are to build their own nests. It may be necessary to make a wire base or to reinforce the nest with wire later when the structure has been added to. They will also use a box for nesting.

On one occasion a pair of these parrakeets which were on board ship bound for Australia hatched and reared two youngsters in their travelling box. The eggs were laid in the sand and seed on the floor. This demonstrates how readily they will nest in captivity. They are prolific and have been known to rear seven young in one nest; they are often double- and even treble-brooded.

The blue mutation has not proved so free-breeding. I know of the existence of only a few on the Continent, four in Britain and one, from the same source, in the USA. A. V. Marques of Bedfordshire has for some years been trying to build up a strain of blues from some of Bruyneel's birds. At first the blues were mated together, with no results at all. As soon as they were paired with normally coloured birds breeding results were obtained and there is now a good nucleus of split blue youngsters. The father of these birds is a magnificent blue and, unlike some mutant birds, is particularly strong and large.

## BOLIVIAN GREY-BREASTED PARRAKEET *(M.m.luchsi)*

*Synonym:* Luchs's Parrakeet

*Description:* It differs from *M.m.monachus* in having the crown, throat and feathers of the upper breast a very pale soft whitish-grey and *not* scalloped with dark and light grey. The lower breast is pale olive-green and not greyish-green.

*Distribution:* It has been collected in northern Bolivia, in the region of Perereta and Luribay, Cochabamba. De Schauensee (33b) gives its distribution as ' Bolivia in eastern Cochabamba '.

## PARAGUAYAN GREY-BREASTED PARRAKEET *(M.m.cotorra)*

*Distribution:* South-eastern Bolivia in the department of Tarija, and south-western Mato Grosso, south to the Argentine Chaco and Paraguay.

MENDOZA GREY-BREASTED PARRAKEET *(M.m.callita)*
*Description:* It differs from *M.m.monachus* in being smaller, with a smaller beak. The colour of the breast is more whitish and the abdomen is paler.
*Distribution:* Western Argentina in the provinces of La Rioja, Mendoza and San Luis. Birds from Tucuman, Santiago del Estero and northern Pampa probably belong to this sub-species.

Genus: *Bolborhynchus*

With the exception of the parrotlets, the *Bolborhynchus* parrakeets are the smallest of the Central and South American psittacines. Most have wedge tails and small beaks which appear thick and swollen. The genus now includes the Sierra Parrakeet (formerly given a separate genus: *Amoropsitta*) and *aurifrons* (formerly *Psilopsiagon*).

They are quiet, inoffensive and softly-coloured. Only the Lineolated Parrakeet and, recently, the Sierra (Andean) are regularly available but not in large numbers.

SIERRA PARRAKEET *(B.aymara)*
*Synonyms:* Andean Parrakeet, Aymara Parrakeet
*Description:* The forehead, crown and upper ear-coverts are dark brownish-grey and the cheeks, the sides of the neck and the throat are whitish-grey. The upper parts, from the back of the head to the tip of the tail, are dark green and the breast, abdomen, under tail-coverts and smaller under wing-coverts are a light yellowish-green. There is a bluish tinge on the primary-coverts, on the flights which are dusky, and on the central tail feathers. The bill is whitish. This parrakeet is reminiscent of a wild Budgerigar in shape and has a long tapered tail. Length: about 7½in.

Males probably have darker caps and brighter-coloured breasts than females. The plumage of immature birds resembles that of adults, and it is interesting to note that when this species was bred at the Keston Foreign Bird Farm in 1964, W. D. Cummings noted: 'They are easier to sex as they come out of the nest, because the cocks have distinctive silver breasts and darker caps.'
*Distribution:* The highlands of Bolivia, south through the mountains of Argentina in the provinces of Salta, Catamarca, Tucumán, La

Rioja, Mendoza and Córdoba. Peters states that they may also be found in northern Chile, but Johnson disagrees.

In March 1921 Alexander Wetmore (43a) watched Sierra Parrakeets on the slopes above the city of Mendoza '. . . by following back on the line of flight of a small flock we found a water-hole, perhaps the only one in an otherwise wholly arid tract. On March 19, near El Salto, at an altitude of nearly 2,000 metres above Potrerillos, Mendoza, these parakeets were common. Here they ranged over the hills in small bands that fed on berry-bearing bushes, or descended to search for fallen fruit in the grass below. The birds were highly social and were always found in parties. Their flight was swift and direct. Their chattering notes were high-pitched and, at times, suggested the excited calls of barn swallows'.

This species is apparently still abundant along the eastern slopes of the Andes.

*Remarks:* Sierra Parrakeets were first brought to England as recently as 1959. Gerald Durrell obtained eight in a bird market in Mendoza. So many were on sale there that Durrell did not realise that they had never been exported to Europe, so obtained only a small number. These birds are popular pets in that part of the Argentine.

One of those brought to England by Durrell went to the Parrot House at the London Zoo where it lived for about 10 years. It was a most delightful little bird, so tame that it would sit on a finger offered through the bars of its cage, nibble gently at the finger and chatter to itself.

In the early part of 1962 a few pairs of these birds arrived on the Continent and a London dealer obtained some. Having been completely captivated by the London Zoo's bird, I bought two. I believe, however, that they were two hens; they never tried to breed.

These birds must be provided with a nest-box in which they can roost all the year round. A feature of this species – and not only of my pair – is that it retires to roost very early. They do well in outdoor aviaries, which need not be very large. I found them to be quite destructive for such small birds, although others have found them to be inoffensive when kept with other seed-eaters.

My birds consumed sunflower to the exclusion of all other seed until they had been in my possession for three years, when they suddenly began to eat panicum millet. Even spray millet was destroyed, then ignored. They would eat apple and seeding grasses.

Other aviculturists have found that this species is reluctant to sample seed other than sunflower, but small seeds should be provided.

These birds have the great advantage of being very quiet, and would therefore be ideal for a flat-dweller. A young bird would undoubtedly make an extremely attractive pet and would probably be quite easy to tame.

Since the first importation this species has been imported fairly regularly, but cannot be described as common in confinement.

*Breeding records:* I think there is little doubt that this parrakeet will prove to be one of the most prolific of South American parrots. In the first year these birds were imported, 1962, A. V. Marques reared one youngster and a pair owned by K. Russell hatched three young which were not reared, due to rain penetrating the nest-box. In 1963 the pair hatched and reared six youngsters from eight eggs. They were quite hardy and roosted in the nest-box. In the same year two were reared at Clères, France, in the collection of J. Delacour. They bred for several years until a pair of large dormice got into the aviary and killed them all in the nest-boxes.

During the following year five were bred at the Keston Foreign Bird Farm. A spare hen was paired to a green Budgerigar; the eggs were infertile. Also in 1964 C. D. Beckett bred four young Sierras. The nest-box used was 9in square and 9in high, lined with 2in or 3in of peat. It was hung 5ft from the ground under cover. The newly-hatched chicks were lightly covered with whitish down; at the age of two weeks the down was thick and blue-grey in colour. Their development seemed very slow and Budgerigar rings would not stay on their legs until they were three weeks old. The first chick hatched on July 12 and left the nest on August 22 when it resembled the adults, except for the shorter tail.

In Denmark four were bred in 1961 – a possible 'world first' – and a pair owned by S. F. Jorgensen laid seven eggs in 1964. Six hatched and all the young were reared. Another prolific pair is owned by A. R. E. Hill. They had been kept in a cage as pets and were placed in an aviary 8ft long x 3ft wide x 6ft high in 1970. A small shelter attached was seldom used. A nest-box 10in square and 12in deep was hung in the covered part of the flight during the end of June. About 5 inches of rotten wood covered the bottom of the box. Within minutes of the box being placed in position the birds had entered and were excavating a hole. Ten eggs were laid in the first clutch and every one was fertile. The adults fought continually throughout the incubation period; nevertheless the hen started sitting after the third egg was laid. When the clutch numbered six or seven both cock and hen stayed in the box. After 19 or 20 days the first egg hatched – the first of nine, the tenth being dead-in-shell. The two youngest were trampled on, but the remaining seven were successfully reared. The young birds exactly resembled their parents when they left the nest.

GOLDEN-FRONTED PARRAKEET *(B.aurifrons aurifrons)*
*Description:* The forehead, lores, part of the cheeks and the throat are yellow in the male. There is some yellow on the breast and sides. The primary coverts are greenish-blue and the primaries are blue on the outer webs. The upper parts are dark green, and the underparts light green. The bill is yellowish and the iris is greyish-yellow. Length: just over 7in, including the 3in tail. The female lacks the yellow on the head, except on the chin. There is a yellowish tinge on the sides of the breast and the lower breast.
*Distribution:* The temperate zone of the Cordillera of central Peru. It is evidently found at a high elevation; the skins in the collection of the British Museum (Natural History) are labelled as having been collected at Chusgon and Cajabamba (9,000ft) and others at 8,000ft, 6,600ft and one at 2,760ft. According to Maria Koepcke (24) this species is common in the steppes and shrubby places of the coast and Andean slopes. It is also found in the cultivated fields, tree plantations, gardens and the parks of Lima. During the winter it is abundant on the coastal hills and in wooded and shrubby places.
*Remarks:* This little parrakeet is extremely rare in aviculture. A pair were received at London Zoo in 1958. Mrs. N. Howard of Wolverhampton obtained six in 1969, only two of which were alive two years later, two unfortunately being lost due to accidents. In 1969 about 50 pairs were taken into Sweden but they proved extremely difficult to keep alive.
*Breeding records:* The first recorded breeding of this species took place in 1967. Streimer reported (AZ January 15, 1968) that he had already been successful in breeding Tuis, Tovis and parrotlets, always obtaining large numbers of each species. In October 1967 he bought some White-winged Parrakeets. While sorting them he discovered two birds which were quite unknown to him. He placed them in a separate cage without taking much more notice of them. Both birds instantly disappeared into a Budgerigar nest-box. They were provided with hemp, sunflower, grass seed, apple, carrot, banana,

orange and plenty of greenfood. They were so shy that they would eat only at night or when no one was about, so that their owner was convinced that they were nocturnal birds. At night he was in the habit of watching the fish in his aquarium, the room being lit by the lights of the aquarium. The birds then appeared in the cage and were seen eating, playing and chirping.

After they had been in his possession for three weeks an egg appeared in the cage. In the following 12 days two more were laid and the birds were no longer seen in the cage at night. On the 23rd day after the first egg was laid chirping was heard in the nest. Rearing diet of cod liver oil food and grated carrot was provided. Five days later a dead, naked youngster was found on the cage floor but more young were heard in the nest. When the two youngsters fledged Streimer saw, to his amazement, that they were wearing closed rings. His wife had ringed them, fearing that no one would believe that they had been bred in captivity!

Nine days later the hen laid again, resulting in seven more chicks being reared.

This species has also been bred in Denmark by Erik Keszler Hansen of Copenhagen. The breeding report appeared in *Steufuglene* (vol. 45, 175-8). In May 1969 a second pair were obtained and housed with finches, which they never attempted to harm, in an outdoor aviary. A number of nest-boxes were inspected and the birds were observed mating. They always perched close together, preening each other and chattering.

In the autumn they were transferred to an indoor flight cage with five pairs of rare waxbills, where they continued to inspect the nest-boxes provided. The owner then read in *Papagöjebogen* by J. L. Albrecht-Möller that *P.a.orbygnesius* digs deep tunnels into soft earth, ending up in a nesting cavity. So he made a square wooden tube 3ft long with an inside dimension of about 2in by 2in. This was fixed parallel to the front side of a nest-box and sloped gradually to the entrance hole. The box itself, situated at a height of about 6ft, measured 6in square and 12in deep. Inside there was an upper section 6in deep with a hole in one corner leading to the lower section.

This was presented to the birds at the beginning of January 1970 and they took great interest in it but could not find the way in, so a hole was cut on the upper side of the entrance tube, 10in from the entrance hole of the box. Three days later the box was entered for the first time and between January 29 and February 26 the female was rarely seen. On February 27 a chick was heard and was seen on April 3.

It was a male, paler in colour than its father, but with a clearly yellow front. The same nest contained another male and two more females. The pair have since bred more young and another Danish aviculturist has been successful with this species.

ROBERT'S PARRAKEET *(B.a.robertsi)*
*Distribution:* Known only from the type locality in north central Peru.
*Remarks:* In or before 1958 David West of California obtained four birds which he tentatively identified as belonging to this subspecies. He wrote: 'They are unusually charming birds, being the size of Budgerigars and having a green body with the forehead, edge of the cheeks and throat yellow and a slight trace of blue on the primaries. The females are solid green, with no trace of yellow, but with a slight trace of blue in the primaries. They have an interesting little alarm note and appear to be quite hardy and will probably prove rather pugnacious . . . They appear to be quite fond of fruit and also crawl about upside down a good deal. The two pairs I have tend to stay very close together and all sleep side by side.'

RED-BILLED PARRAKEET *(B.a.rubrirostris)*
*Description:* Mainly green with a slight yellowish tinge on the throat and the centre of the breast and abdomen. The sides of the breast and the flanks are yellowish-green. The primary-coverts and primaries are dull blue, the under tail-coverts being tinged with this colour. The thick bill is rosy-red. Length: $7\frac{1}{2}$in.
*Distribution:* The mountains of western Argentina from Catamarca south to Mendoza and the Andes of Santiago in Chile.

A. W. Johnston (23) states: 'For many years this parakeet was thought to occur only on the Argentine side of the Andes, but small flocks seen and two specimens obtained by us near Lo Valdes and Lagrina Negra proved conclusively that it sometimes crosses into Chilean territory.'

These birds apparently arrive regularly in the Argentine Andes in September and have been found nesting in the cliffs above the Yeso valley at an altitude of 8,000ft. They have yet to be recorded in any other part of Chile.

*B.a.margaritae* (formerly *B.a.orbygnesius*)
*Description:* It differs from *B.a.rubrirostris* in having the bill horn-coloured instead of pink and by the more conspicuous yellow line on the forehead. It is slightly larger, i.e. about 8½in.
*Distribution:* The high Andes of Chile from Arica to Antofagasta, and in south-western Peru (Pimo), western Bolivia and north-west Argentina in the provinces of Jujuy to Tucumán. It is rare in Chile, found only at altitudes of 10,000ft and above. Flocks of 15 to 20 birds have been seen. These parrakeets live in colonies in holes in high banks or escarpments.

## LINEOLATED PARRAKEET *(B.lineola lineola)*

*Synonym:* Catharine Parrakeet
*Description:* The forehead, cheeks, ear-coverts, throat and under parts are light apple green. In some specimens the feathers of the crown and ear-coverts are narrowly edged with black. All birds have the feathers of the nape and the sides of the neck, extending entirely beneath the wings to the flanks and rump and the edges of the tail-coverts, edged with black. The black edgings become broader towards the tail and on the rump, to give a pronounced barred effect. There is a black patch on the shoulder and the smaller wing-coverts are broadly edged with black, the secondaries and primaries being more narrowly edged with black. There is some faint black barring in the area of the vent and the flanks have a brownish tinge. The shade of green is darker on the wings. The beak is pinkish flesh-coloured and the iris is dark grey, giving the eye a bold appearance. Length: 6½in to 7in.

Females are said to show less black in the plumage – the rump less strongly spotted with black and all the black edges to the feathers narrower, especially on the lesser wing-coverts. The tail is said to be entirely green and not broadly tipped with black, as in the male. This would indicate that Lineolateds are easy to sex, but this is not so. I am not at all certain of the sex of the three in my possession at the moment, especially as a fourth, which I had always believed to be a hen, was reported on post-mortem to be a cock. I carefully examined skins of this species for signs of sexual distinction but unfortunately most were not labelled as to their sex. Of three labelled as females, however, one was precisely what a hen is supposed to look like, while the other two had some black on the tail and wide black edges to the wing-coverts!

*Distribution:* The sub-tropical zone of the mountains of Central America from southern Mexico to western Panama. This species is frequently found at high elevations. In 1871, Salvin recorded seeing a flock in the Volcan de Fuego, at a height of about 8,000ft above sea level. In 1953, E. R. Blake described it as 'a rare bird in Mexico', occurring only in dense forests at high elevations.

According to Slud (35), in Costa Rica it is found mostly in the central highlands, also along the Talamanca Cordillera. 'This bird is seen only occasionally, usually in flocks that vary in size from six to 12 to 50 or 75 individuals, generally in high rapid flight. The species evidently prefers well-wooded partially deforested areas, including the parklike pastures with tall trees on the big volcanoes. Usually it keeps high in the trees. Its rapid flight is accompanied by cries of the sort associated with a flock of small songbirds.'

*Remarks:* This little parrakeet is irregularly imported in small numbers but cannot be described as rare. Due to its small size and protective coloration it must be difficult to detect in the wild. It is an ideal aviary bird, being exceptionally quiet and gentle, requiring only a small flight and possessing a beak which is incapable of doing any serious damage to woodwork. It is gentle and inoffensive and altogether a most charming bird.

David Seth-Smith stated that it was delicate and 'should never be subjected to a lower temperature than 60 deg. F'. Other writers have repeated this statement. My pairs have wintered for several years in an aviary whose shelter was inside a birdroom without heat or in an outdoor birdroom where the water froze on occasions. When the temperature drops to about freezing they sometimes look uncomfortable but have proved absolutely hardy.

The first sight of snow by one pair sent them into ecstasies of delight; they hung upside down from the perch, flapping their wings and opening them wide. These birds appear to dislike sunshine intensely and are often found on a sunny day perched along the ledges in the shelter, well out of the sunshine.

Prestwich recorded that his Lineolated preferred to sleep with their heads pointing downwards, but he did not state whether from the perch or clinging to the wire-netting. They have a fascinating manner of creeping stealthily along perch or ledge carrying themselves almost horizontally.

These birds will eat sunflower seed, white millet, spray millet, canary seed, hemp and greenfood. They show a great liking for apple but can seldom be persuaded to try any other fruit. Their normal diet may result in a vitamin deficiency, so 'nectar' with added vitamins should be provided and will be taken readily.

In 1952 E. N. T. Vane wrote about losses in grass parrakeets when frightened by marauders or unfamiliar with their surroundings. He experienced this trouble and some of the birds that died were six or seven years old and regular breeders. He wrote 'Victims are usually perfectly fit one minute and dead or apparently paralysed an hour or even a few moments later; they never live more than twenty-four hours. Incidentally, Lineolated Parrakeets also appear to be subject to this failing'.

In 1969 I had two pairs in an outside aviary. One pair took to a nest-box and lined it to a depth of about ¾in with small feathers and tiny strips of wood from the inside of the box. They spent hours inside the box but no eggs were laid. I looked into the box one day in May and found both birds laying rigid inside; their bodies were stiff and their legs were protruding at right angles to their bodies. They appeared to be in considerable pain. Immediately I took them into the house into a temperature of about 75°F.

By the evening one had died; postmortem gave enteritis as the cause of death. The other bird appeared to be in much pain for some time but it could feed itself a little and offered no resistance when I handled it to give it nectar in a dropper. Gradually the legs resumed their normal position and lost their rigidness.

After about two weeks this Lineolated was practising therapy – raising itself by holding on to a twig with its beak, or leaning its breast against the twig and putting its weight on the feet. For some time the toes were clenched and for months the feet were useless. Gradually the toes unclenched and after over a year the bird could perch, but not grip with its toes. During this period, however, it could fly normally but would usually roost lying on the floor. Now, two years afterwards, it is still unable to grip with its toes.

An aviculturist of my acquaintance had similar trouble with a large number of grass parrakeets newly-imported from the Continent. He had autopsies carried out by three different people – all gave varying causes of death, one being the complete breakdown of the nervous system. As my two pairs of Lineolated Parrakeets were living under identical conditions in the same aviary when the trouble occurred and were eating the same food, I favour Vane's theory that the cause in this case was psychological and of nervous origin, and not due to poisoning. (The splayed position of the legs suggests a form of cerebral stimulation, possibly food poisoning, the symptoms of which are fits and a tense body.)

*Breeding records:* In 1913 a pair belonging to a Miss M. E. Baker reared one youngster which left the nest but was accidentally drowned before it was independent of its parents.

The Avicultural Society's medal for the first breeding of this species was awarded to A. A. Prestwich for his success in 1953. Approximately 30 pairs were imported during 1951-52, of which he secured three pairs. One pair died but the survivors were housed outside from the late spring to autumn 1952. On being returned to the outdoor aviary in 1953 both pairs immediately re-occupied the nest-boxes which they had previously used for roosting. On several evenings both pairs were seen to stand facing one another, stretching vertically to the fullest possible extent with beaks interlocked. Thus they remained for a few moments and it would appear that this is the courtship display.

The hen of one pair laid five eggs, three of which were fertile, two clear, and all were deserted. The lining of the nest-box consisted of about an inch of peat moss and a few feathers. The hen of the other pair laid four eggs; all were fertile and one hatched. The chick was reared to maturity. On leaving the nest it was rather paler in colour than the adults and had a slight bluish tinge on the head. In 1957 three more were reared. In 1958, a hen belonging to Prestwich vanished for weeks into a hole under a concrete step in the aviary. It was not known whether any eggs were laid but no young were reared.

The next successful breeder in Britain was Mrs D. K. Draper of Basingstoke. In 1954 two young were reared from three eggs. Both adults spent most of their time in the nest-box. When it was inspected on June 2, two chicks and one egg were seen. Both youngsters fledged on June 30. The cock looked after them while the hen incubated a second clutch.

In the USA seven were reared at San Diego Zoo in 1938. Rayson Brown also bred this species. The cinnamon hen owned by David West had two young ones in 1960, but unfortunately died in that year.

In Denmark in 1955 J. Dalborg Johansen reared three, after two previous failures in which the young were deserted when about 10 days old. A Swedish aviculturist bred one Lineolated Parrakeet in 1968.

BARRED PARRAKEET *(B.l.tigrinus)*

*Description:* Bond and de Schauensee (7) described this as a 'somewhat variable species' but did not give any distinguishing features. They found that the males had more black on the central rectrices and were more yellowish-green below than the females.

*Distribution:* Range imperfectly known; apparently the Andes of Colombia and Merida.

PERUVIAN BARRED PARRAKEET *(B.l.maculatus)* (Ridgway)

Regarded by Bond and de Schauensee as not distinct from *B.l. tigrinus.*

*Distribution:* Eastern Peru; actual range unknown.

RUFOUS-FRONTED PARRAKEET *(B.ferrugineifrons)*

*Description:* There is a narrow band of rusty rufous on the forehead the colour of the lores and upper throat. The rest of the plumage is dull green, brightest on the upper tail-coverts, tinged with olive on the breast. Length: 8in to 9in.

*Distribution:* Found only in Colombia on the scrubby mountain slopes from the Paramo zone of the central Andes in Tolima, according to de Schauensee.

ANDEAN PARRAKEET *(B.andicolus)*

*Description:* It differs from *B.lineola* in lacking all black barring. It is a bright dark green above, brightest on the tail and tail-coverts and more yellowish-green below, especially on the throat, also with a yellow tinge on the forehead and the sides of the head. According to Salvadori the female has scarcely any yellow tinge on these areas. The flights are bluish on the outer webs and the under wing-coverts are grey edged with pale blue. The bill is horn-coloured, whitish at the tip. Length: 6½in to 7in.

*Distribution:* The Andes of Peru in the subtropical and temperate zones.

This is another species found at a high altitude. Skin specimens examined were labelled as having been collected at 8,500ft, 9,000ft and 9,100ft.

Genus: *Forpus*

The Parrotlets have often been described as the American counterparts of the African Lovebirds which they resemble in shape, being small with short tails. Their colouring is quite different: light green,

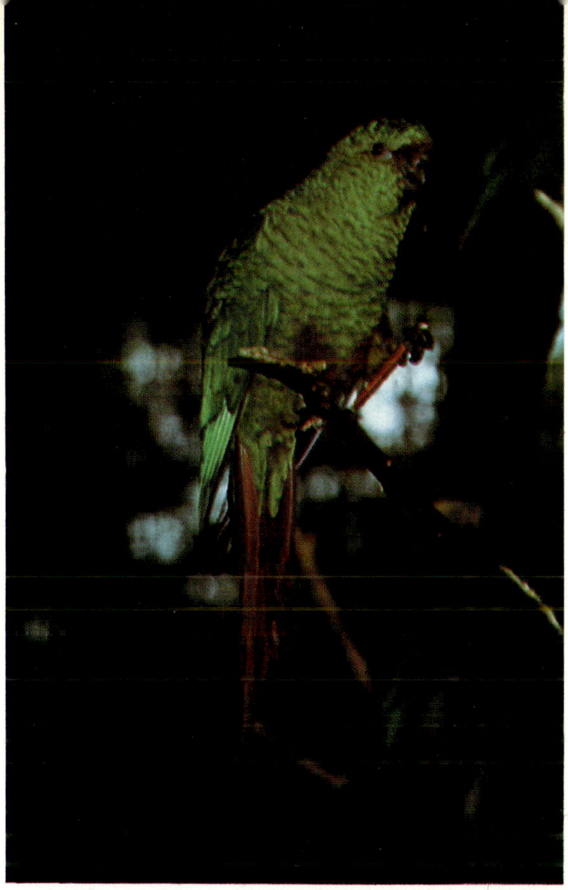

18 The Magellan Conure *Enicognathus f. ferruginea* is extremely rare in captivity. This is one of six seen by the author in East Berlin Zoo in 1971.

19 A delightfully quiet and inoffensive little bird is the Lineolated Parrakeet *Bolborhynchus lineola* from Central America. Owner: author.

20 The Sierra, Andean or Aymara Parrakeet *Bolborhynchus aymara* was first imported into England as recently as 1959. Owner: Erik Ekman.

21 The Golden-winged Parrakeet *Brotogeris jugularis chrysopterus* is one of the more rarely imported members of the genus. Owner: Avon Aviaries.

usually with blue on the rump or wings in the male. Members of the genus do not differ greatly and most of the hens are extremely difficult to distinguish from each other. Because identification is not easy, it is a little uncertain how often some of the Parrotlets have been imported and bred. Hybrid breedings will almost certainly have occurred inadvertently, which adds to the problem. Known hybrid pairings should be avoided.

These birds have much to recommend them, especially to the beginner and those with limited resources. They are not noisy or destructive and are usually very willing to go to nest. Some fanciers keep parrotlets in cages but this is definitely to be discouraged as they very often attack, kill or inflict terrible injuries on each other if closely confined. They should, therefore, be housed in a large compartment or in an aviary. It is safest not to mix more than one pair, but they can be kept in mixed collections with larger birds. Housing is, in my opinion, one of the most important considerations in keeping these miniature parrots. They are perfectly hardy and can be wintered outside without heat, provided that the aviary has a dry and draught-proof shelter.

Most parrotlets are very conservative feeders and may eat only seed. They should be offered the following seeds in separate dishes: canary, white millet, sunflower, hemp, linseed, oats or groats, also spray millet. Greenfood and apple are often ignored completely but one should experiment with the usual items in the hope that they will be tempted to taste them. One aviculturist who bred parrotlets as long ago as 1904 had no problems regarding diet, for the adults reared their young on bread and milk, fresh ants' eggs, blackberries and a little orange, as well as the usual seeds. The birds showed a preference for bread and milk and hemp. Parrotlets have also been known to sample spinach, lettuce, plantain heads, seeding forget-me-nots and moistened sponge cake. Soaked millet sprays and other soaked seeds are a valuable addition to the diet when there are young in the nest.

These birds usually breed readily, and normally get as far as laying even if no chicks are reared. They may be bred in a large compartment or in a small aviary of which they are the sole occupants. They are often very aggressive in a mixed collection and I have known them to turn a pair of Cockatiels out of a nest-box which would have been ten times too large for the parrotlets. A Budgerigar nest-box is quite suitable for them.

The hens lay on alternate days and the clutch numbers from

three to seven, normally five or six. Incubation is carried out by the hen and differs slightly in length according to the species. Helmut Hampe found it to be 20 days in the Blue-winged, 21 in the Green-rumped and 22 to 23 in the Mexican. The latter were always single-brooded, in his experience, unlike other species which may rear two or three nests.

During incubation the cock enters the box often to feed the hen, who is rarely seen. When the chicks hatch they are covered with a small amount of down, whitish or yellowish, according to the species. The young can be sexed when they fledge at about five weeks old, as with the exception of the Mexican Parrotlet, which sometimes does not attain adult plumage until its first moult when about three months old, the young differ from the adults only in their softer colouring.

Some parrotlets are prone to killing their young in the nest and should therefore be disturbed as little as possible. This seems to be a not uncommon vice with Celestials, although I know of one fancier who photographed the chicks at every stage of their development with no ill-effects.

I have never seen a hand-reared parrotlet but they are said to become very tame and affectionate and to learn to talk.

*Renaming:* The original generic name for the parrotlets was *Psittacula*, the name now given to the genus of Asiatic parrakeets which includes the Ringneck, Plumhead, etc. When the name was bestowed on the latter birds it was necessary to rename a number of parrotlets. This means that only fairly recent literature contains the new names, which can cause confusion and adds to the difficulty of determining which species are referred to in some breeding records. Some modern authors prefer to use the classification by Gyldenstophe (15a), in which *xanthopterygius* is used in place of *passerinus* and certain sub-species are re-arranged.

## TURQUOISE-RUMPED PARROTLET *(F.cyanopygius lutescens)*

(Formerly *P.cyanopygius*)

*Synonym:* Mexican Parrotlet

*Description:* The distinguishing features of the male are the turquoise rump and lower back and greater wing-coverts and under wing-coverts. The cock is bright green above, yellowish on the forehead. The sides of the head and the underparts are a lighter, yellowish green. The bill is whitish and the iris is yellow. Length: 5½in. Females have the blue areas replaced with bright green.

*Distribution:* Western Mexico in the states of Sinaloa, Durango, Zucatecas, Nayarit, Jalisco and Colima. It is found in the arid lowlands, usually below 4,000ft.

*Remarks:* The parrotlets from Mexico are not often available in Europe and are probably better known in the USA. Thomas Brosset informed me that a number of Mexican Parrotlets were imported into Sweden during 1969 and 1970. He commented (pers. comm.): 'As far as I know, none of the Swedish pairs have made any attempt to breed, which I think is very strange. All those I have asked are of the same opinion regarding this parrotlet: it is shyer than the other species, less lively and interesting, rather silent, and agrees pretty well with the Lineolated Parrakeet in behaviour; slow in movements.'

*Breeding records:* Mrs G. K. Goddard was awarded the Avicultural Society's medal for the first breeding of *Forpus cyanopygius* in 1927. A pair which had been in her possession for about a year were housed in a large outdoor flight with Nyasa and Black-cheeked Lovebirds. During the middle of August the hen laid three eggs in a nest which was constructed – probably by the Lovebirds – from a few pieces of dry grasses, old millet sprays and feathers plucked from the hen's breast. The first egg hatched on September 5. On October 13 the first chick fledged. Mrs Goddard wrote 'Two are all green and show no blue, and I conclude these must be hen birds, as the third chick has a blue rump and the wings show blue underneath. The blue is a bright turquoise and very lovely (but visible only when the bird is in flight).'

In 1925 a German, E. Schütze, achieved what was probably the first breeding of this species. Young birds left the nest on September 1, 5, 9 and 12. They were caught up on November 2 and all appeared to be females. Three weeks later, however, one showed a few blue feathers on the rump. In 1926 three chicks were hatched but were deserted when the male became ill. The male recovered but a second nest was not attempted.

In Bulawayo, Rhodesia, K. Harrap housed a pair in an aviary containing weavers and whydahs, measuring 21ft x 6ft x 6ft. During the second week in January 1965 the hen parrotlet laid in a nest-box with a 3in layer of sawdust and soil. When the five young fledged they could be sexed immediately as the young males had blue rumps and wing feathers and the young females yellow foreheads. The adults took spinach, lettuce and seeding grasses while rearing.

In the USA Scheffler bred the Turquoise-rumped Parrotlet between 1944 and 1948 and possibly on other occasions. Chicago Zoo reared seven between 1938 and 1950. In Australia three fledged at Adelaide Zoo between 1941 and 1942.

This species has undoubtedly been bred on many other occasions and has hybridised with Spectacled and Celestial Parrotlets. One instance of the latter cross took place in the aviaries of P. Haddock of Ellesmere Port. A male Celestial and a female Turquoise-rumped were placed in a small aviary 8ft x 2ft 6in x 6ft high which already housed two pairs of Budgerigars. They ignored the Budgies and the hen laid four eggs. All hatched and the chicks fledged after approximately six weeks. Three days later the hen died but the young survived.

## SONORA PARROTLET *(F.c.pallidus)*

*Description:* This sub-species is described as being slightly paler than *F.c.cyanopygius* but less yellowish and more ashy in colour. Blake believes it to be doubtfully distinct.

*Distribution:* South-eastern Sonora and northern Sinaloa in north western Mexico.

Joseph Forshaw observed this parrotlet on the outskirts of the town of Alamos in Sonora during January 1965, usually in small flocks numbering about 40 birds. The area is in the foothills of a main mountain range and consists of hills covered by forest and scrublands interspersed with cultivated farmlands. Forshaw wrote (AM vol. 71, 101) that they 'seemed to understand the principles of formation flying when on the wing and they moved in perfect unison. This resulted in the flock twisting and turning as one bird.

'Flying at only 6 to 10 feet above the ground, they showed flashes of bright green while darting through the trees and over the lower shrubs. On leaving the uppermost branches of a tree the flock would literally dive towards the ground, continue to fly at the characteristically low level, then rise suddenly to alight once again in the upper branches of another tree.

'The very swift and direct flight is undertaken with short rapid wing-beats without any noticeable periods of gliding. While in the air the screeching call-note is emitted continuously.'

In the Paradise Aviary at Wassenaar Zoo, a structure so large that it creates virtually natural conditions, there is a flock of parrotlets whose formation flying is fascinating to watch. Here one can see that a flock really does move as one bird.

Forshaw watched the parrotlets feeding only once, when two flocks flew into a large *Ficus* tree. From a position directly below it was virtually impossible to locate individual birds because their plumage blended so well with the foliage. Their manner of feeding was very methodical; the parrotlets worked their way through the outermost branches, examining or even tasting all the fruit and eating that which had reached a satisfactory stage of development. Their preference seemed to be for fruit which was green and beginning to ripen.

TRES MARIAS PARROTLET *(F.c.cyanopygius)* (formerly *F.c. insularis)*

*Synonym:* Grayson's Parrotlet

*Description:* Is slightly larger than the Turquoise-Rumped Parrotlet especially in the bill; it is generally darker and there is a greater contrast between the upper parts and the light under parts. Length: about 5¼in.

*Distribution:* The Tres Marias Islands off the west coast of Mexico.

GUIANA PARROTLET *(F.passerinus passerinus)* (formerly *P. guianensis*)

*Description:* The male is predominantly green, slightly greyer on the back of the head and bright emerald green on the forehead, rump and sides. The under wing-coverts are brilliant dark blue and the bend of the wing and the edge of the wing are also blue. The female has part of the head, especially the sides, distinctly yellow-green, almost yellow in places, but she lacks the blue under wing-coverts and has the rump green. The beak is whitish. Length: 5½in.

(See under Blue-winged Parrotlet for the distinguishing features of the hens of both sub-species).

*Distribution:* Guyana, Surinam and Cayenne, also Jamaica, where it was introduced in 1918 and Barbados, introduced during the early years of the 20th century.

It has steadily increased its range since its introduction into Jamaica and is now widespread in fairly open country in lowlands on the southern side of the island. On Barbados it is rare and evidently decreasing in numbers. Its introduction into Martinique was apparently unsuccessful, although in 1922 Delacour reported that Guiana Parrotlets arrived from the north in February and March and remained on the island for three or four weeks. In Guyana its distribution is extensive, both on the coast and inland.

*Remarks:* It is fairly frequently imported into Britain but not as

often as the Blue-winged or, in recent years, as the Celestial.
*Breeding records:* The first recorded breeding in Britain took place in 1926 when Dr Wildeboer of Hull bred six from eight eggs. The Duke of Bedford bred it at complete liberty and, more recently, H. Murray of Brentwood has bred it to the second generation. He found that these birds were not very hardy, and therefore housed them in heated quarters during the winter. They usually nested early, in February or March, but the first clutch was normally infertile.

The Guiana has hybridised with the Blue-rumped, Blue-winged and Spengel's.

## SPENGEL'S PARROTLET *(F.p.spengeli)*

*Synonym:* Barranquilla Parrotlet
*Description:* The distinguishing features of the male are the royal blue under the wings and the turquoise rump. There is a greyish green tinge on the nape and neck. The crown, forehead and ear-coverts are emerald green and a few feathers surrounding the eyes and nostrils are a lighter emerald green. The chin is bright green, almost emerald. The under parts are a lighter shade, yellowish on the centre of the abdomen and greyer towards the flanks. The rump is turquoise and the upper tail-coverts are turquoise at the rump and grass green towards the tail. The greater wing-coverts are turquoise and green towards the outer edge of the wing, royal blue towards the centre of the wing. The secondary-coverts are turquoise, also a few feathers on the scapulars. A narrow strip at the bend of the wing is mottled with turquoise, green and royal blue. The under wing-coverts are turquoise and ultramarine. The tail is yellow-green. The beak is horn-coloured and large, the build of the head and neck being very heavy.

The female is green, of an exceptionally bright shade on the back and rump. The forehead, part of the cheeks and part of the crown are yellow. Length: 5in.
*Distribution:* The Caribbean coast west and south-west of the Santa Marta mountains of Colombia, also the extreme lower Magderlena Valley. It inhabits the tropical zone in the dry and semi-arid regions.
*Remarks:* Infrequently imported.

The heavy beak and head possessed by this species is put to good use. R. W. Drury's pair tunnelled 3in in depth and width into the decaying wood on the outside of their nest-box. They were provided with a birch log with the centre chiselled out to form a cavity 2in to 3in in diameter and 9in long. The parrotlets gnawed through 4in or 5in of solid wood and widened out the hole at the end of the log and then gnawed through its wall.

*Breeding records:* There are not many records relating to this species in confinement, possibly due to incorrect identification. In 1953 it was listed among the birds bred at Brookfield Zoo, Chicago.

In 1958 R. W. Drury of Essex bred five Spengel's after constructing a special aviary for his pair and taking much trouble with nesting facilities. The aviary was 8ft long, 2ft 6in wide and 5ft 6in high; about one-third of it was enclosed. A Budgerigar nest-box covered with decaying wood and bark was ignored, except to gnaw the wood. The speed with which the birds dashed about the aviary was so alarming that their wings had to be clipped. In October they were housed in a large flight cage in a birdroom for the winter. In the following April they were installed in a new aviary 8ft long, 2ft 6in wide and 8ft high. It was lined with small mesh string netting to prevent them from injuring themselves. About one-half of one side of the aviary only was exposed and this part faced some shrubbery so the parrotlets rarely saw anyone.

During the middle of May it was noticed that they were excavating a piece of elm to a depth of 3in – but inspection proved to be a mistake and stopped their activities. At the end of June a birch log 8in in diameter and 24in long, hollowed out to a diameter of 6in, was hung in the aviary at about 15° out of horizontal. A piece of hard wood was fixed at the end of the log to prevent the birds pecking right through it. They began to take an interest in this log during the first week of July, spending periods of up to half an hour inside, but roosting outside. On July 15 both birds slept inside for the first time and the first egg was probably laid on July 20 or 21. The hen was not seen again until August 2. On September 6 both adults roosted outside the log for the first time and on the 13th a young cock and a young hen were seen in the aviary, both of which were slightly smaller than their parents. The young hen was noticeably less massive about the head, neck and beak. The colours of the immature birds were slightly lighter and, in the case of the hens, the yellow areas on the forehead and cheeks were more restricted. On September 17 another hen left the nest, followed by another hen and a cock on September 25.

While rearing, the amount of hemp was increased but greenfood and apple were refused. A tablespoonful of soaked and sprouting sunflower, hemp and oats was given daily throughout the year, in addition to the usual seed diet of 60 per cent canary, 15 per cent white millet and oats, sunflower and hemp.

That was probably the first occasion on which Spengel's Parrotlet was bred in Britain. During the previous year Mr Drury had been successful in breeding hybrids between a male Spengel's and a female Guiana. The hen nested in a Budgerigar type of nest-box constructed of 1in thick timber. The first of four eggs was laid on May 25 and the two youngsters fledged on July 18. Both birds were cocks and differed little from the male parent except in the colour of the rump. This was a shade between turquoise and emerald green, nearer to turquoise. The colour of the abdomen was lighter and brighter in the young birds.

Spengel's Parrotlet is believed to have been bred in Denmark in 1966; the owner identified his birds, probably incorrectly, as *F. cyanopygius.*

## RIO HACHA PARROTLET *(F.p.cyanophanes)*

*Description:* According to E. N. T. Vane it differs from *F.p.viridissimus* only in the deeper shade of hyacinth blue on the primaries and secondary-coverts.

*Distribution:* The arid tropical zone of the north-eastern part of the Santa Marta region of Colombia, extending to the plains south of the mountains.

## VENEZUELAN GREEN-RUMPED PARROTLET *(F.p.viridissimus)*

*Synonym:* Caracas Parrotlet

*Description:* Males differ from *F.p.passerinus* in the smaller amount of blue under the wings, which does not extend to the edge of the wing. The remainder of the under wing-coverts are glaucous green or pale turquoise. Length: about 5in. The hens would appear to be almost indistinguishable (although Voous stated that hens are not such a bright yellowish-green, with less yellow on the forehead) except for the colour of the legs, which are flesh-coloured and not blue-grey.

*Distribution:* Venezuela from Caracas east to Cumana and south to the Orinoco valley. De Schauensee gives its distribution in Colombia as the valley of the Rio Zulia in Norte de Santander, so it may have a more westerly distribution in Venezuela.

*Breeding records:* Probably the first recorded breeding took place in the USA. In May 1924 three pairs were received by Dr Karl Plath. One pair ignored the nest-boxes provided and laid on the sand behind a log in the shelter in July. Four chicks were hatched from five eggs. The parents were not very conscientious about feeding the young and all but one died.

In Britain H. Whitley was probably the first to achieve success with this parrotlet in 1931. In 1941 it was bred by C. C. Cosgrave in Australia.

HARTLAUB'S PARROTLET *(F.p.cyanochlorus)*
*Synonym:* Schlegel's Parrotlet
*Description:* According to Vane this sub-species differs from *F.p. passerinus* in the yellower shade of green of the underparts, lower back and rump, which would make it rather difficult to identify. Its beak is smaller and weaker.
*Distribution:* The Upper Rio Branco region of north-west Brazil.

CEARA BLUE-WINGED PARROTLET *(F.p.flavissimus) (F. xanthopterygius flavissimus* – Gyldenstolpe)
*Synonym:* Blue-rumped Parrotlet
*Description:* It differs from *F.p.vividus* in being decidedly lighter and more yellowish; the forehead, cheeks and upper throat are suffused with lemon-yellow or wholly yellow. The blue of the rump and wings is lighter – cobalt rather than dark blue. The underparts are a more yellowish-green.
*Distribution:* North-eastern Brazil in the states of Maranhão, Piauhy and Ceara.
*Remarks:* Either rarely imported or seldom indentified.
*Breeding records:* J. Dalborg-Johansen of Denmark recorded (AM vol. 62, 8): 'Blue-rumped Parrotlet, six young reared following the death of the hen when they were only five days old.' This almost certainly referred to *F.p.flavissimus* (and not *cyanopygius*) as Dalborg-Johansen had previously given the scientific name in an account of the hybrid breeding between *F.p.passerinus* and *F.p.flavissimus*. Two pairs, consisting of Ceara cocks and Green-rumped hens, hatched and reared nine young in their first nests. The young cocks after a moult resembled their fathers. The incubation period was 21 to 23 days and the young birds fledged after about 30 days.

DELICATE PARROTLET *(F.p.deliciosus)*
*Description:* It differs from *F.p.passerinus* and *F.p.cyanochlorus* in

having a distinct turquoise tinge on part of the emerald green lower back. The greater upper wing-coverts, instead of being glaucous green, are a delicate turquoise blue with a darker, more ultramarine blue shaft-streak, only the concealed inner webs being yellowish-green like the back. The secondaries are mostly pure ultramarine with a narrow yellowish-green margin on the outer web.
*Distribution:* The banks of the lower Amazon (Obidos, Santarem) and on the lower Tapajóz (Tauary).

LARGE-BILLED PARROTLET *(F.p.crassirostris) (F.xanthopterygius crassirostris* – Gyldenstolpe)
*Description:* A skin in the British Museum shows the male to differ from *F.p.passerinus* in having the rump, under wing-coverts and the edge of the wing rich blue, of a shade rather lighter than cobalt. It has an extremely large and powerful-looking bill for its size and is labelled as having the iris yellow. Length: 5in.

The female is said to differ from the female of *F.p.passerinus* in its larger bill and by having the forehead and the sides of the head purer green, like the back (and not yellowish).
*Distribution:* Amazonian drainage in northern Peru, east to the Solimoës River in Western Brazil.

*F.p.ollalae (F.xanthopterygius ollalae* – Gyldenstolpe)
*Description:* The male is said to differ from *F.p.crassirostris* in having the rump of a darker shade of blue. The under wing-coverts are paler blue and the shade of green on the upper parts is usually darker. The bill is whitish, dusky at the tip.
*Distribution:* The middle Rio Amazon region of west Brazil.

SALVADORI'S PARROTLET *(F.p.flavescens) (F.x.flavescens* – Gyldenstolpe)
*Description:* The male differs from *F.p.vividus* in being lighter green, more yellowish on the forehead, cheeks and underparts. The rump and the underside of the wings are lighter blue. Length: 5¼in. The female is all green, darker above.
*Distribution:* Bolivia.

BLUE-WINGED PARROTLET *(F.p.vividus)* (Formerly *P.passerinus) (F.x.xanthopterygius* – Gyldenstolpe)
*Synonym:* Passerine Parrotlet
*Description:* The male has the lower back, rump, most of the flights

primary-coverts, bastard wing and greater wing-coverts and under wing-coverts rich ultramarine blue. The inner webs of the flights are bluish-green below. The rest of the plumage is green, a brighter more emerald shade around the eyes and on the ear-coverts. Length: 5in. The female has no blue in the plumage; the rump is emerald green and the lower parts are yellowish-green, also the forehead and cheeks which may be yellower than the underparts. The feet are blue-grey, which distinguishes the female from certain other parrotlets.

*Distribution:* Eastern Brazil south of Cape St Roque to Paraguay and north-eastern Argentina.

*Remarks:* Until about 1930 this species was imported into Europe in large numbers. During recent years – and certainly since the Celestial became regularly available about 1963 – few Blue-wings have appeared on the market.

*Breeding records:* The first recorded breeding was that by Russ in Germany in 1867, after which it was fairly frequently bred in Europe, and possibly for the first time in Britain in 1894. The Duke of Bedford bred this species at liberty. The birds were caught up during the winter and housed in aviaries. He wrote that they are 'very savage and quarrelsome and adult pairs must be kept separate'. The Blue-winged has hybridised with the Guiana, Celestial and Spectacled Parrotlet.

SPECTACLED PARROTLET *(F.c.conspicillatus)*

*Description:* The male can be distinguished from *F.passerinus* by the pale blue ring surrounding the eye. The cock is green, brighter on the forehead, crown and cheeks. The lower back, rump, edge of the wing, secondaries, wing-coverts and under wing-coverts are rich cobalt. The bill is whitish. Length: 5in.

The female is entirely green, brighter on the upper parts than the male, especially bright – almost emerald green – around the eyes and on the lower back and rump. The lower parts are apple green. Immature males have no blue surrounding the eyes and the blue on the rump and wings is mixed with green.

*Distribution:* Eastern Darien; Colombia in the tropical zone of the upper Magdalena Valley and at the eastern base of the Eastern Andes. De Schauensee gives its range in Colombia as the tropical zone east of the Andes in Boyacá and Meta and the upper Magdalena Valley north to about 10° N.

*Breeding records:* In 1931 Mr and Mrs A. R. Hood of California bred from two pairs of what they believed to be Celestial Parrotlets; they were however, almost certainly Spectacled Parrotlets. One pair laid four eggs and reared four young. The eggs in the second nest were broken by the other pair. In 1932 the second pair hatched five young, three of which died from neglect due to disagreements between the two pairs. The remaining two young were fostered out with Budgerigars who failed to rear them.

W. Langberg of Copenhagen found this species to be prolific; he bred 14 during 1966 and 1967. A Swedish breeder reared young from wild-caught birds in 1970 and 1971. The Spectacled has hybridised with the Blue-winged and Turquoise-rumped Parrotlets. Seven young from the latter cross were bred by Mrs S. Tomlinson of Long Beach in 1930. When the cock died in 1932 it had reared 24 young.

## CAUCA SPECTACLED PARROTLET *(F.c.caucae)*

*Description:* It differs from *F.c.conspicillatus* in the heavier bill and apparently in the blue areas of the rump, upper and under wing-coverts being decidedly less purple, although on the skins of both forms examined there was variation in the shade of blue.
*Distribution:* Western Colombia in the middle and upper Cauca Valley, west of the Western Andes in the Dagua Valley and the upper Patia Valley.

### *F.c.metae* (Borrero and Camacho)

*Description:* The male differs from that of *F.c.caucae* by its yellower and brighter green, particularly on the forehead, lores and cheeks; the blue eye ring is less extensive, encircling only the rear part of the eye. Length: 5½in.
*Distribution:* The eastern Andes of Colombia in the departments of Cundinamarca and Boyaca. It has a wide altitudinal range from the gallery forests of the plains of the Meta River drainage to the subtropical forest belt of the eastern slope of the Andes.

## SCLATER'S PARROTLET *(F.sclateri sclateri)*

*Description:* The much darker shade of green distinguishes the cock and hen from all other parrotlets. The male is paler below, brighter on the forehead and the sides of the head. The central outer part of the wing, the under wing-coverts, the lower back and rump are brilliant cobalt. The upper mandible is black, the lower one pale. Length: about 5¼in.

The female is dark green, emerald green on the rump, lower back and under wing-coverts. The forehead, sides of the head and the upper breast in the birds examined were yellowish-green, although some hens are said to have a well-defined yellowish frontal band and clear yellow on the throat and the sides of the head. In two skins, one male and one female, there were a few bright yellow feathers on the crown.
*Distribution:* Eastern Ecuador (Rio Napo, Sarayacu) and Eastern Peru (Iquitos, Rio Javari, Rio Ucayali and Cosnipata), also the tropical zone of Colombia at the eastern base of the eastern Andes; also recorded from northern Bolivia.
*Remarks:* This species is rare in aviculture but has been imported into Britain.

SCHOMBURGK'S PARROTLET *(F.s.eidos)* (formerly *P.modesta*)
*Description:* According to E. N. T. Vane (41) its shade of green is even darker than that of *F.s.sclateri* and the rump is a darker blue.
*Distribution:* Eastern Venezuela, the Guianas and western Brazil (upper Rio Negro and Pederneiras on the Madeira). In Colombia it is found in the Rio Guainia region.

CELESTIAL PARROTLET *(F.cœlestis cœlestis)*
*Synonym:* Lesson's Parrotlet
*Description:* The male has the crown and cheeks bright apple green, with a touch of light blue behind the eyes. The rest of the plumage is a soft silvery-green, darker above, except for the brilliant cobalt blue of the under wing-coverts and rump. The beak is horn-coloured. The female lacks the blue markings, except for the merest hint of blue behind the eyes and the slightly bluish rump. The shade of green is duller, paler on the breast and brighter on the crown and cheeks. Length: about 5in.

Young birds can be sexed on leaving the nest but the plumage is of a softer shade. The beak is pink and gradually changes to horn colour.

Examples of a blue mutation have been reported in the wild and may well appear in aviary-bred birds now that this species is so frequently reared.
*Distribution:* The arid tropical zone of western South America from Bahia de Caráques, Ecuador, south to Trujillo, Peru.
*Remarks:* Although plentiful in the wild this parrotlet was rare in aviculture until 1962. Since about 1965 it has been regularly imported

and it is now the best-known member of its family and the only one imported in any numbers.

It often proves fatal to confine these birds too closely. I know of several instances where a caged Celestial has killed and terribly mutilated the other member of the pair. Aviary accommodation should therefore always be given preference.

*Breeding records:* In 1938 R. F. Losky of Peru reported that he found these birds very easy to breed in cage or aviary all the year round. He also noted cannibalistic tendencies in these birds. He had in his possession an $11\frac{1}{2}$-year-old male which had fertilised eggs when 10 years old.

Apart from Losky's success with these parrotlets in their own country, Delacour was probably the first to breed them. In 1958 he reported that two young had been reared.

Since they became readily available in Britain they have been bred on countless occasions. A pair in my possession hatched three young when housed in an outdoor birdroom. Three weeks later the hen ceased to visit the nest-box. The eldest youngster had been killed – its head was damaged – and the other two appeared to have been dead for some days. The cock of that pair proved to be an egg-eater when mated with two different hens.

It is advisable to remove the young from their parents as soon as they can feed themselves, or the parents may attack them, the cock usually objecting to his sons and sometimes the hen to her daughters. This may even happen while they are still in the nest. In 1963 a London fancier, Mrs W. Boorer, owned a pair which hatched six young in a cage in her kitchen. Seven weeks after the first hatched two young were thrown from the nest; one was unfeathered and the legs of the other were bleeding. Both were returned to the nest but the eldest was thrown out again. Shortly after the remains of another young cock were found on the cage floor and one of the young hens was attacked in the box, resulting in a crippled leg. All the youngsters were removed to a separate cage on the morning that the last one fledged. On leaving the nest they were self-supporting and the parents were never seen to feed them. There was a large amount of millet in the box, suggesting that this had been carried into the nest for some time before the young birds left. This is interesting as O. E. Cresswell, who bred Blue-winged Parrotlets in 1895, discovered that the parents took whole hemp into the nest. When he threw in more the nestlings were quick to eat it.

This species has hybridised with the Turquoise-rumped and Blue-winged Parrotlets.

YELLOW-FACED PARROTLET *(F.cœlestis xanthops)*
*Description:* Judging by the skins examined this must surely be the most beautiful, if the least typical, member of the genus. The male has the crown, face and throat lemon-yellow, merging into yellowish-green on the underparts. There is no blue streak behind the eye and the nape is bluish-green. The upper parts are greyish-green and the rump, under wing-coverts and upper tail-coverts are deep cobalt. The female is a lighter shade of blue on the rump and has grey under wing-coverts with a touch of light blue. Length: about 5½in.
*Distribution:* Marañon Valley in northern Peru.
*Remarks:* This parrotlet is unfortunately unknown to aviculture.

Genus: *Brotogeris*

This genus comprises seven small parrakeets, measuring on average 7in to 8in; they are mainly green with a prominent touch of colour on the head or wings, and have pointed tails. Three of the seven are well-known to aviculturists, the remainder being but rarely imported. Hand-tame specimens of the commonly imported ones are easily obtained and are usually kept as pets. Perhaps this has led to their potential as aviary birds being ignored, consequently there are amazingly few breeding records for the whole of the genus.

This may be only part of the reason because in the wild most *Brotogeris* are known to lay their eggs in termitaria. Occupied nests are used because the ants constantly repair the termitarium which would otherwise crack and fall to the ground. Dried termites' nests are brittle and more difficult for the *Brotogeris* to excavate. These nests have the added advantage of being inaccessible to nearly all predators. The Red-faced Lovebird *(Agapornis pullaria)* from Africa, a notoriously difficult species to breed, shares this habit of using ants' nests. Success with this species was obtained by several aviculturists in Africa who used specially constructed nest-boxes resembling the interior of termites' nests. It may be that *Brotogeris* would appreciate a similar arrangement.

The incubation period of these birds is about 26 days. Two to five eggs form the clutch; probably the average number is four. The young remain in the nest for eight weeks. In some very old European breeding records the incubation period is given as 21 days and the length of time the young spent in the nest as five weeks, which makes me wonder whether any breedings actually took place!

Maggots would undoubtedly be a good food to provide for these birds while rearing young. One aviculturist found that his pair of White-wings were extremely fond of them, each disposing of a dozen or more at a time. These were nibbled while held in the foot. One of my Orange-flanked Parrakeets relished the crysalid. It is a good idea to offer both forms of maggots. One American fancier who had a pair of Tovis gave them wheat or cracked wheat bread toasted dry and soaked in water while they were feeding young. They were also provided with canary seed, sunflower and millet, sweet apple, orange and lawn clippings.

All *Brotogeris* are extremely fond of fruit, which is probably the most important item of their diet in the wild. A pair should be given at least a whole apple daily, also grapes, pear, a little orange or banana and any fruit in season. The seed offered should include sunflower, canary seed, white millet, hemp, a few oats and spray millet. Greenfood such as chickweed, young dandelion leaves and seeding grasses can be offered, but will often be ignored. Their favourite foods appear to be sunflower seed and apple.

The available members of the genus deserve the attention of the aviculturist who enjoys attempting to breed from species for which there are very few breeding records. These parrakeets are inexpensive and require little aviary space. Pairs should not be mixed with other parrot-like birds, except other *Brotogeris*, unless the aviary is very large, as they can be rather spiteful, especially towards weaker birds. It is usually safe to mix a single bird with other psittacines, as a loner usually lacks the confidence to attack.

Unfortunately all these little parrakeets are extremely difficult birds to sex. There is no difference in the plumage of cock and hen and one can examine in vain the head and beak for signs of sexual distinction. Those who are seriously interested in breeding from a certain species are advised to buy several pairs and to house them in a fairly large aviary. When they have sorted themselves out into true pairs they can then be housed one pair per small aviary.

Young hand-tame birds make attractive pets and are usually completely fearless, although sometimes spiteful. Even when housed in aviaries they may retain this fearlessness, often becoming very familiar and perching on their owner. Some individuals, especially Canary-wings and White-wings, have one serious fault – they are extremely noisy. A Canary-wing which once lived in my birdroom made such a loud warning, chattering noise whenever a stranger entered that it was almost impossible to hold a conversation. As pets this is their one drawback; they are quite ideal in every other way and often learn to speak a few words.

Some specimens are very fond of bathing and will keep themselves in immaculate condition. They also like to be sprayed. In an aviary they seldom descend to the ground, so food must be placed on a shelf or at perch level.

In the wild this genus must be one of the most successful of all neo-tropical parrots, some being the only psittacines which are common in their area. According to the official government figures 146,000 'parakeets native to the jungle region' were exported from Iquitos, Peru, in 1970. A single shipment may consist of as many as 25,000 Canary-wings and Tuis.

ALL-GREEN PARRAKEET *(B.tirica)*

*Synonym:* Tirica Parrakeet

*Description:* All green, yellowish below, except for the blue flight feathers and the two longish central tail feathers which are bluish. There is a faint olive-brown tinge on the smaller upper wing-coverts. The tail is long, accounting for about 5in of the total length of 10in. A blue mutation has been recorded.

*Distribution:* Eastern and southern Brazil from Goyaz and Bahia to Rio Grande do Sul. Many years ago Burmeister wrote that it was one of the commonest birds in the forested coastal region of Brazil.

*Remarks:* It is known to have been imported by a German dealer in 1873. It later became quite common in confinement but in recent years it has been very rarely imported into Britain. I saw a number in Lisbon Zoo in 1970, which shows that it is sometimes available to those with contacts in Brazil.

*Breeding records:* Dr Lovell-Keays first bred this species in Britain; four young were reared in 1914. Wesley T. Page bred three in 1918 after several broods had died. More recently L. J. Praill was successful; his pair produced four in 1957.

It was first bred in Europe in 1882 in Germany. Most interesting is the appearance of the blue mutation at Schonbrunn Zoo before the First World War. A normal green pair went to nest behind an ornamental cork screen, unobserved by the keepers. Two of the youngsters were blue and two blues and two greens were produced in a second nest. A sad ending befell two of the blues: one was drowned and the other was the victim of a rat. The two remaining birds were sold to a woman in Budapest who raised seven blues from them which, with their parents, unfortunately came to grief during the war. At the present time there is said to be a blue specimen in Brazil.

In Denmark the All Green was first bred in 1961; six young were reared.

WHITE-WINGED PARRAKEET *(B.versicolurus versicolurus)*
*Synonym:* Yellow-winged Parrakeet
*Description:* The White-winged is almost invariably confused with the Canary-winged Parrakeet and is incorrectly identified more often than not. White-wings differ from Canary-wings in being a greyer, more olive, shade of green, especially on the head and they have a bluish area around the eyes. There is white and yellow on the wing, which is not such a bright shade of yellow as that of the Canary-wing. The White-wing is slightly larger: 9½in.

When the wing is stretched the white patch can be seen, otherwise only the yellow on the wing is visible, which is probably the reason why it is so frequently wrongly identified, for its name is misleading.

*Distribution:* Surinam, Cayenne and Amazon valley from eastern Ecuador and north-eastern Peru to Mexiana Island and Pará (Belem). A small population of escaped cage birds has apparently established itself in the area of Lima, Peru.

Goodfellow (*Ibis*, 1902) stated that this species was very common on the Lower Napo, but unknown on the upper parts of the river. It congregated along the banks in thousands during the evenings. 'If disturbed the flocks flew around with such deafening cries that it was impossible to hear each other speak. The Indians delighted in disturbing them. They roosted in trees growing in marshy ground and where the river banks were less dense than elsewhere. They were nesting on the Maranõn in August.'

Another ornithologist saw flocks several hundred strong on the island of Mexiana.

*Remarks:* The White-winged Parrakeet is now one of the most frequently imported of the genus. In the early years of the 20th century it was rare. One owned by R. Phillipps in 1897 was thought to be the only one in Europe.

E. A. Dracup of Bedford described (*Parrot Society Magazine*, October 1967, 1) the aggression display of the cock of his pair. 'He would come close up to the front wire of the cage, put his head down and lift his folded wings from the body an inch or so, slapping them back against the body with quite a sharp " cracking " noise. This would be done several times in succession while he would at the same time shriek at the onlooker.

'They were not especially noisy although when in full " song " their shrieks could be heard several hundred yards away. The song often took the form of a contrapuntal duet with the two birds shrieking in such rapid succession that it sounded like a continuous note from a single bird. They alternated perfectly, however, and neither would miss the beat for a minute or more at a time until both would stop at the same moment as if switched off.' The latter habit, known as anti-phonal dueting, is interesting and has been recorded in other South American parrots, although it is better known in such birds as barbets.

The pair referred to above were together for at least 10 years. After the hen died the cock survived for only a month. His owner was convinced that death was due to pining for his mate as he was in perfect condition but appeared to have lost all interest in life.

*Breeding records:* Surprisingly, I can find no record of this sub-species having been bred in Britain. In the USA R. Schmidt bred one youngster from two eggs in 1930.

The White-winged Parrakeet has hybridised with the Tovi Parrakeet.

## CANARY-WINGED PARRAKEET *(B.versicolurus chiriri)*

*Description:* Rich light green, darker above, yellow tinged below. There is a yellow patch on the wing, formed by the outer greater wing-coverts. The bill is light brown. Length: 8½in to 9in. The iris is dark brown. It is a much purer shade of green than the White-winged Parrakeet (q.v.).

*Distribution:* Eastern Bolivia, central and eastern Brazil from Mato Grosso, Goyaz, northern Maranhão, Piauhy and Ceará south to the Argentine Chaco, Paraguay, Misiones and São Paulo.

It is found in flocks, especially along the banks of rivers. Five or six eggs are laid in the nests of white ants.

*Remarks:* This species is always available and is most inexpensive. It was first exhibited at the London Zoo as long ago as 1868 but even in the early years of the 20th century it was rarely imported. Canary-wings can be thoroughly recommended as aviary birds. They look most attractive in flight when their bright yellow wing patches are visible.

*Breeding records:* This species has only rarely been bred in confinement and the first breeding in Britain took place as recently as 1954. This is mainly because most specimens imported are young tame birds and are sold as pets.

When E. N. T. Vane bred Canary-wings in 1954 the hen laid five eggs, described as being slightly larger than a Budgerigar's and more elongated. After 26 days all five eggs hatched. The young were quite naked and were, like all South American parrakeets, slow in developing. At 10 days old they were still naked but the feather tracts could be seen forming at 15 days, when the eyes were still unopened. The beaks were white at this age. When they were 24 days old the feathers were opening and showing yellow and green. They left the nest in September at the age of eight weeks, when they resembled the adults except for the slightly smaller size. Large amounts of greenfood including dandelion leaves and the seeding heads, groundsel, chickweed, sowthistle and other seeding weeds were consumed while the young were being reared. Apple, pear and banana were also eaten. In 1955 and 1956 nests of five young were reared by this pair.

In Australia, between 1967 and 1968, C. C. Burfield bred from a pair that had been in his possession for 10 years. Their aviary measured 8ft x 3ft and the nest box 7in square and 15in high. Three eggs were laid and three hatched. On leaving the nest the young birds resembled the adults except for the dark beaks. Three weeks later they were independent.

One young Canary-wing was reared by a London fancier, Mrs G. Narraway, in 1970. The pair consisted of an eight-year-old cock which was previously kept as a pet, and a hen bought the year before. They nested in a box in an inside flight and were not disturbed during incubation because they became very nervous. Mrs Narraway reported (pers. comm. May 1971): 'The chick was fed by both parents, and was given the same food as my Cockatiels are reared on, i.e. seed, soaked groats, bread and butter, and the usual fruit.

'The baby left the nest at seven weeks, fully feathered and just a duller version of the parents. The first day the parents left it to fend for itself, but when I went into the aviary to see it properly both parents flew to it, and were with it constantly from then on. They continued to feed it for about four weeks after it had left the nest and then it picked up food itself, although it took a long time before it could hold food in its feet.'

It was then tame enough to take a grape from its owner's hand.

The adults did not go to nest again but roosted in the box and allowed the young bird to roost with them.

### BEHN'S PARRAKEET *(B.v.behni)*

*Description:* Distinguished from *B.v.chiriri* by its larger size and by the bluish-green underside of the tail feathers.
*Distribution:* It is known definitely only from southern Bolivia in the departments of Chuquisaca and Tarija; the northern and eastern limits are not known but the birds from Salta, north-western Argentina, probably belong to this sub-species.

### ORANGE-FLANKED PARRAKEET *(B.pyrrhopterus)*

*Synonym:* Orange-winged Parrakeet
*Description:* Mainly green, a lighter grass green on the under parts. The crown is bluish-green, the forehead greyish and the sides of the head and the chin whitish-grey. The bend of the wing and the small coverts of the underside of the wing are brilliant orange. Length: 8in. Its build is rather heavier than that of the other members of the genus.
*Distribution:* The arid tropical zone of western South America from Bahia de Caráques, Ecuador, to north-western Peru.

Many years ago this species was encountered by Walter Goodfellow in the vicinity of Guayaquil, where it caused considerable damage to banana plantations. He saw large flocks of these birds; individuals could be bought for the equivalent of 2½d each.
*Remarks:* Usually readily available, especially hand-reared tame young birds, which has resulted in it becoming quite popular as a pet. Adults are imported much less often and little has therefore been recorded about it as an aviary bird. My pair were extremely aggressive towards other parrot-like birds, yet a single bird of the same pair made so little effort to defend itself that it was attacked by a pair of Celestial Parrotlets and died from the injuries received.
*Breeding records:* The first breeding in Britain took place in 1925 when a pair belonging to W. Lewis were housed in an aviary 12ft x 6ft x 6ft with a pair each of Canary-winged Parrakeets, Tuis, Tuiparas and Abyssinian and Peach-faced Lovebirds. The Orange-flanks started visiting the nest-box in May and by the middle of June the hen was remaining in the nest. On August 14 one young bird was seen looking out of the nest and by August 23 five had fledged. Two were soon killed by a Peach-faced Lovebird, which was hardly surprising when one considers the crowded conditions of the aviary. The three others were removed to a flight cage where they

fed on canary seed, millet and Quaker oats. They were paler than the adults and lacked the blue on the head. It is interesting to note that the Abyssinian Lovebirds were also successful in rearing two youngsters.

More recently, in 1969, M. J. Cope reared three Orange-flankeds. He bought a hand-tame pair in October 1967. In January 1969 the pair were split, leaving the cock in a cage and transferring the hen to a 3ft flight cage. By April the cock was calling frantically to the hen. The pair were reunited in a 6ft 6in x 4ft flight in a shed. A nest-box 20in deep with a 9in square base was hung on the front wall. No interest had been shown in the box by the middle of May so it was moved to the back wall. The light from the window was no longer shining into the box, which was entered by the birds during the following week. Towards the third week in August four young left the nest. They were similar to the adults but lacked the blue and grey on the head and the blue in the flight feathers. They were fed by their parents for three weeks and were later plucked by them, perhaps due to the small space in which they were housed. One young bird died during the winter but the other two survived in unheated quarters.

Before breeding started the birds ate only sunflower, canary seed and hemp, with large amounts of fruit, their favourite being apple. While they were breeding soaked and sprouted seed was provided.

In the USA, A. R. Hood bred this species in 1935; five eggs were laid, four of which hatched. Two chicks were removed at the age of five weeks for hand-rearing and the other two were removed one week later as the parents were neglecting them. In Denmark it is believed to have bred as long ago as 1902; more recently, two were reared in 1961.

This species has hybridised with the Tovi Parrakeet.

TOVI PARRAKEET *(B.jugularis jugularis)*

*Synonyms:* Bee Bee Parrot; Orange-chinned Parrakeet

*Description:* Mainly green, yellowish below with a bluish tinge on the abdomen; there is a less pronounced bluish tinge on the head, lower back and rump, flights and central tail feathers. There is an orange spot on the chin which, it has been suggested, is lacking in the female, but this is not so. The small upper wing-coverts are bronzy-green and the centre of the back is tinged with olive. The under wing-coverts are yellowish, and the primary-coverts are deep blue. The long, narrow bill is a pale horn colour. Length: about 7in.

An abnormally coloured specimen, mostly light blue, was seen in a flock of normally coloured birds over 100 years ago. The under wing-coverts were blue and white and the throat spot was white.

*Distribution:* The arid tropical zone of south-western Mexico from Guerrero south over the Pacific slope of Central America to northern Colombia, west of the Eastern Andes, east of them in Norte de Santander.

Paul Slud (35) states that in Costa Rica this species is nearly confined to the Pacific slope, thriving in the driest and wettest lowland areas. It frequents semi-open and partially deforested areas, preferring large openings and clearings with tall trees. Small flocks of up to about 20 birds are usually seen, occasionally single pairs. They are noisy birds and fly rapidly with many twists and changes of direction. Wetmore measured their flight speed at 45mph when they were flying parallel to his car on one occasion. He found that they fed on nectar from blossoms, the seeds from the pods of the barrigón *(Bombax)* and the fleshy parts of balsa flowers.

Roosting sites may attract several hundred birds. They nest in arboreal termites' nests, where these are available. It has been suggested, however, that other birds such as *Aratinga holochlora* and non-psittacine species usually occupy these desirable sites and leave the *Brotogeris* to enlarge natural cavities in dead trees or to utilise vacant woodpecker holes. From one to three pairs may be seen digging in the same tree and, in one instance, as many as 12 pairs. They are very prolific and nests of eight young have been found. In many areas of Central America this is the most abundant and widely distributed psittacine.

*Remarks:* This species is quite often imported, often being advertised by dealers as the 'Bee Bee Parrot', misleading unsuspecting buyers to believe that a larger, short-tailed parrot is being offered. Recently it has not been available as often as the Canary-wing in Britain, although it was once the best-known member of the genus. As a pet it is one of the most attractive of the *Brotogeris*.

*Breeding records:* I can find no reference to this species breeding in Britain, but it is difficult to believe that it has never done so. It is said to have been bred in Vienna as long ago as 1873 and 1874, when nests of two and three were reared.

In the USA Mr and Mrs V. Wright had a remarkable degree of success between 1934 and 1940. In 1938 they possessed a colony of over 50 which had been bred in their aviaries. In 1934 one was reared by hand from a nest of nine eggs, six of which contained chicks dead-in-shell. From 1935 they nested freely and in 1936 second generation birds were bred. One of these reared a nest of five when only one year old. In 1938 a four-year-old hen produced eight in one nest. During the same year another pair reared, with assistance, a nest of six.

In the USA the Tovi is a widely kept species yet success in breeding has probably been achieved to any degree only by the Wrights. I do not know whether they bred Tovis on the colony system but this may have been the secret of their success. Such sociable birds need the stimulus provided by the presence of others of their species.

In 1960 another American aviculturist, Ruby Hood, bred from a pair of Tovis when they were introduced into an aviary which already contained one pair. At the end of April four eggs were laid in a box with a floor covering of moss, pressed cane, shavings, rotted leaves and a little earth. After an incubation period which was thought to be about 21 days the first egg hatched. Four young were reared.

During 1963 and 1964 a flock of 28 Tovis was studied at the University of Kansas. The birds were provided with artificial termites' nests made of thick spongy cork, but no eggs were laid.

### EASTERN TOVI PARRAKEET *(B.j.exsul)*

*Distribution:* Peters gives its habitat as the Sierra de Carabobo in northern Venezuela but de Schauensee states that it is found in Colombia in the Ilanos of Casanare in Arauca.

### APURÉ TOVI PARRAKEET *(B.j.apurensis)*

*Description:* It differs from the nominate race only in lacking the orange chin spot.
*Distribution:* The Apuré region of west-central Venezuela.
*Remarks:* It was first brought to Europe by J. Delacour.

Peters considered *B.cyanoptera* as possibly conspecific with *jugularis*, and *gustavi* and *chrysopterus* as separate species. In the light of more recent information (Traylor 40) it would appear that they should all be considered as sub-species of *jugularis*.

### BLUE-WINGED PARRAKEET *(B.j.cyanoptera)*

*Synonyms:* Cobalt-winged Parrakeet, Deville's Parrakeet
*Description:* Dark, olive tinged green above, bluish on the crown,

22 Young, hand-tame Orange-flanked Parrakeets *Brotogeris pyrrhopterus* are imported in large numbers as pets. Owner: Leif J. Skardal.

23 The Slender-billed Parrakeet *Enicognathus leptorhynchus* is very rare in aviculture. This one was sold by a sailor as a 'woodpecker' for the sum of 12s. 6d. Owner: Mrs N. Howard.

24 Caiques are among the most intelligent and playful of all parrots. This Pallid Caique belongs to E. Nørgaard-Olesen.

25 The Yellow-thighed Caique *Pionites leucogaster xanthomeria* differs from the White-bellied Caique only in the colour of the thighs and flanks, which are green instead of yellow. Owner: author.

26 At 39 days old this Pallid Caique *Pionites melanocephala pallida* weighed 113 grams. Bred by G. A. Smith, it was the first known breeding of the Pallid Caique in Britain.

27 The male Spectacled Parrotlet *Forpus conspicillatus* may be distinguished from other parrotlets by the blue ring surrounding the eye. Owner: Erik Ekman.

28 Since the mid-1960s the Celestial Parrotlet *Forpus c. coelestis* has been the most frequently imported member of the genus. It is free-breeding in aviaries. Owner: Verner Sörensen.

lighter green below. The forehead is yellowish and there is an orange spot under the chin. The primary-coverts, primaries and the centre of the tail are bright blue. The upper mandible is brown, white at the base, and the lower mandible is light brownish horn-colour. Length: about 7½in.
*Distribution:* North-western Brazil, upper Orinoco in Venezuela, Colombia east of the Andes, Ecuador and eastern Peru.
*Remarks:* Rarely imported into Britain. A consignment consisting of about 40 birds, received by a dealer in 1969, was probably the only sizable importation for a good many years. Most of these birds, however, went to South Africa.

GUSTAV'S PARRAKEET *(B.j.gustavi)*
*Description:* Bluish on the crown, dark green above, lighter below. There is an orange spot under the wing; the bend of the wing, the carpal edge and the bastard wing are yellow. The primary-coverts and flights are blue, edged with green, and the central tail feathers are blue along the middle, green at the edges. Length: 7½in.
*Distribution:* The Upper Huallaga River in eastern Peru.

*B.j.beniensis*
*Distribution:* Bolivia.

GOLDEN-WINGED PARRAKEET *(B.j.chrysopterus)*
*Description:* Mainly green with the chin spot brownish. The primary wing-coverts are golden-orange and the under wing-coverts are bluish. The beak is white. Length: about 7in.

Prestwich, who owned several examples of this species, stated (AM vol. 62, 44): 'There is a marked similarity but *chrysopterus* differs from *tuipara* in having a narrow frontal margin and chin-spot of dark brown instead of orange; it is also somewhat smaller.' (An excellent coloured plate of Prestwich's birds appeared in the issue of the *Avicultural Magazine* referred to above.)
*Distribution:* Eastern Venezuela and the Guianas, south to the north bank of the lower Amazon. According to Schomburgk it is found in large flocks along the coast of Guyana and eats the flowers of *Erythrina* trees growing in the coffee plantations. It is said to lay from two to four eggs and to nest in trees.
*Remarks:* I know of only four records of this species being imported into Britain. It was exhibited at the London Zoo in 1878 and 1888. The next mention in the avicultural literature appears to be of the

four obtained in 1952 by A. A. Prestwich. In 1971 I saw a consignment of about 20 of these birds. Now that a source of supply has been located by one dealer it may become available more frequently.

RIO NEGRO PARRAKEET *(B.j.tenuifrons)*
*Distribution:* Amazonas, Brazil.

TUIPARA PARRAKEET *(B.j.tuipara)*
*Synonym:* Golden-fronted Parrakeet.
*Description:* This is one of the most attractive members of the genus. It has a small amount of orange on the forehead, an orange spot on the chin and orange primary-coverts. The upper parts are dark green and the underparts a rich light green. There is a bluish tinge on the crown and some blue on the primaries and greater wing-coverts. The bill is greyish-white or greyish-yellow. Length: 7½in to 8in. Immature birds are said to have less blue on the wing-coverts.
*Distribution:* The south bank of the lower Amazon from the Tapajóz to Pará and through the coastal forest belt to north-eastern Maranhão. It has been observed feeding on the seeds inside the fruit of the Mongúba tree *(Bombax monguba)*.
*Remarks:* Rarely imported. It was represented in the collection of the London Zoo as long ago as 1879. Reginald Phillipps had one in 1894 which lived for at least eight years. It was acquired by D. Seth-Smith who found it to be extremely fond of fruit, also soaked bread or biscuit which, if offered dry, would first be placed by the Tuipara in the nearest water dish. It was adept at mimicking the calls of other parrakeets. For some years this bird was kept with a Musky Lorikeet *(Glossopsittacus concinnus)* and during this time laid four eggs.

GOLDEN PARRAKEET *(B.j.chrysosema)*
*Description:* Dark green, lighter below. According to C. E. Hellmayr (19c) males have the crown washed with pale blue; in the female it is nearly uniformly green. The forehead and lores are yellow-orange and the chin is orange. Yellow is the colour of the primary-coverts, which distinguishes this parrakeet at a glance from *B.j.tuipara*. The tail feathers are green with a narrow yellow edge on the inner web, the central feathers being blue-tinged along the middle. Length: 8in.

*Distribution:* The Rio Madiera and its tributaries in the Brazilian states of Amazonas and Mato Grosso.

TUI PARRAKEET *(B.sanctithomae sanctithomae)*
*Description:* Mainly green, lighter, more yellowish on the underparts. The forehead and part of the crown are yellow and there is a yellow streak behind the eye in some specimens. It is often said that the female lacks the yellow streak but this is a geographical rather than a sexual distinction. The underside of the tail is yellowish-green. Yellowish-white is the colour of the iris. This species can be distinguished from other *Brotogeris* by the chestnut-coloured beak. Length: 7in.
*Distribution:* Eastern Ecuador and north-eastern Peru, east to western Brazil (Rio Solimoës, Rio Madiera). De Schauensee gives its distribution additionally as north-eastern Peru eastward to the middle Amazon, Northern Bolivia and the Amazonian region of Colombia.

This species may breed in termites' nests or in a hole in a tree. While collecting in Marañon, Goodfellow found a nest in a tree about 20ft from the ground. It contained five or six young, some almost ready to fledge, others only partly feathered. He took several and reared them on bananas and canary seed.
*Remarks:* Frequently imported. It has often been described as the least noisy of the genus but the single specimen I possessed was equally noisy. R. Phillipps wrote: 'I have kept the Tui for many years but have never been *bitten* by one yet. Moreover, I have never known a Tui hurt another bird – generally it is just the other way round, for it has neither the pluck nor the power to defend itself from the attacks of others.' Certainly I found my adult specimen rather nervous. If it was typical of its species it would be essential to obtain a hand-reared young bird for a pet.
*Breeding records:* I can find only one reference to the Tui breeding in confinement (see page 137).

SANTAREM PARRAKEET *(B.s.taka tsukasae)*
*Synonym:* Taka-Tsukasa Parrakeet
*Distribution:* Both banks of the lower Amazon from Obidos east to Santarem and the lower Tapajoz.

Genus: *Nannopsittaca*

The single representative of this genus is unknown to aviculture.

MOUNT RORAIMA PARRAKEET *(N.panychlora)*

*Description:* A small parrot, only 5½in in length, it is completely green, darker above, paler on the cheeks and breast. The tail is short and square. It has a tiny, delicate-looking beak, suggestive of a nectar-feeder.

*Distribution:* Known only from Guyana (Mount Roraima and Kamarang River) and from Mount Duida in Southern Venezuela.

Genus: *Touit*

Members of this genus, some of which are very beautiful, are, with a single exception, completely unknown to aviculture. These birds have prominent beaks which are stout and strongly curved. Their bodies are heavy and their tails short and slightly rounded. They are sexually dimorphic, the females having less colour on the wings and tail. When the range of these parrotlets is better understood it may be found that there are too many species in the present classification.

LILAC-TAILED PARROTLET *(Touit batavica)*

*Synonyms:* Black-winged Parrotlet, Scopoli's Parrotlet, Seven-coloured Parrotlet.

*Description:* This is an extremely beautiful parrot with a rather complicated colour scheme. The forehead is yellow and the crown green. The feathers of the nape are greenish-yellow tipped with black; this colour extended almost to the throat in some specimens examined. It is light bluish-green below and the under wing-coverts are bluish with a touch of pink on the inner edge of the wing. The back is brownish-black; the rump, tail-coverts, the flights and the tip of the tail are black. The rest of the tail is of exceptionally lovely shades from mauvish-pink to pinkish-mauve. The secondaries are yellow above, black and green below. Length: about 6in.

*Distribution:* Venezuela, Guyana and Surinam, also the islands of Trinidad and Tobago; possibly Cayenne. According to François Haverschmidt (18) it is an irregular wanderer in the coastal area. 'From the end of March till mid-April 1962 a flock frequented and roosted in a mango tree at Slootwijk (Commewijne district).' Their crops were found to be full of mango seeds. This species is very gregarious and lives in the tree tops.

*Remarks:* The only aviculturist I know of who has kept this species, which is almost unknown in aviculture, is H. Murray of Brentwood, Essex. He kindly supplied me with the following notes: 'The only thing about this bird that seems to be known for certain is that it breeds in the nest of tree termites. In Trinidad, where my birds came from, they say it feeds on a small red berry. It will not touch this berry in captivity. The large size and shape of the beak indicates specialised feeding.

'The first of these birds that I had, about the middle 1950s, lasted for some months and then gradually faded away. They had been fed on a diet of Spratts' CLO and Ostermilk. The second lot – two adults and two young – all caught together in a net at night, were fed the same way. They had to be force-fed for a long time in Trinidad. These did much better and I got them to take nectar and they did well for some months. Then Spratts stopped making CLO.

'I was forced to change the CLO but the birds developed enteritis and three died quickly. The last one lived for quite some time and seemed interested in an old log. Maybe they live on wood borers but mine would eat neither soaked seed, fruit nor mealworms.'

In 1970 a collector in Surinam apparently sent a dozen of these little parrots to the USA.

PURPLE GUIANA PARROTLET *(T.purpurata purpurata)*
*Description:* Dark green, lighter below and light yellowish-green on the flanks. The forehead and crown are pale brownish; the sides of the rump, and the upper tail-coverts are bright green. The scapulars are brown and the primary-coverts are black edged with green. The rump is cobalt. The two central tail feathers are green narrowly tipped with black, the outer ones being purple-maroon with black at the tip and outer web. The beak is lead coloured, yellowish at the tip. Length: 6½in.

The female is said to differ in having the scapulars of a paler shade of brown. There is a broad green band at the tip of the outer tail feathers, instead of purple-maroon, with no black on the outer edge, only at the tip.

*Distribution:* The Guianas and the Rio Negro region of north-western Brazil from the Içana and the Vaupés to Manaos. De Schauensee gives its range as southern Venezuela, the Guianas and north-western Brazil and, in Colombia, the tropical zone east of the Andes in Caqueta.

GREEN-BANDED PARROTLET *(T.p.viridiceps)*
*Synonym:* Chapman's Parrotlet
*Description:* It differs from *T.p.purpurata* in having the entire

crown, nape and the sides of the head green like the back. *Distribution:* Southern Venezuela to the Rio Guainia; also recorded from the Cerro Yapacana, Upper Orinoco.

BLACK-BACKED PARROTLET *(T.melanotus)*

*Synonym:* Wied's Parrotlet

*Description:* Mainly green, lighter on the cheeks, throat, flanks and under tail-coverts. The back and rump are brownish-black, also the primary coverts and secondaries; the primaries are black edged with green. The breast, abdomen, greater wing-coverts and inner webs of the flights are greenish-glaucous. The two central tail feathers are green, the outer ones red at the base with a broad, black band near the tip, which is green. The outer tail feathers are purple on the outer web. The bill is said to be dusky-yellowish, brownish-grey on the edges and at the tip. The iris is brownish-grey. Length: 6¼in.

The female's colouring is said to be slightly duller.

*Distribution:* South-eastern Brazil from Bahia to São Paulo.

HUET'S PARROTLET *(T.huetii)*

*Synonym:* Red-winged Parrotlet

*Description:* The male is dark green above, brighter on the wings, more brownish-green on the mantle and golden brownish-green on the crown; the forehead is black and the cheeks are cobalt. The under wing-coverts and the bend of the wing are scarlet and the shoulders and the inner edge of the wing are rich cobalt. The under parts are yellowish-green and the underside of the tail is bright yellow to lime green. The central tail feathers are rich dark green, the lateral ones being very beautifully marked with rich mauvish-pink and tipped with black. Length: 7in.

*Distribution:* Colombia, east of the eastern Andes, Venezuela, Guyana, eastern Ecuador, north-eastern Peru and Trinidad; possibly also Surinam and Cayenne. It is found in forested areas, and has been recorded in large flocks.

BLUE-FRONTED PARROTLET *(T.dilectissima dilectissima)*

*Synonym:* Mérida Parrotlet

*Description:* The male has the forehead blue, the crown bluish and the area above and below the eye scarlet; part of the cheeks, chin and throat are yellow. The upper and under wing-coverts and the bend of the wing are scarlet, the feathers tipped with yellow; some of the under wing-coverts and a patch on the side of the breast are brilliant crocus yellow. The underparts are lighter and more yellowish. The bill is yellowish at the tip, lead colour at the base. The iris is said to be pale yellowish-brown. Length: 6½in.

The female differs from the male in having only a small amount of red at the bend of the wing; the primary-coverts and the edge of the wing are black, the outer wing-coverts being green.

*Distribution:* Locally distributed from Mount Pirr in eastern Panama to the Andes of Mérida in western Venezuela.

COSTA RICAN PARROTLET *(T.d.costaricensis)*

*Synonym:* Red-fronted Parrotlet

*Description:* The forehead and part of the crown and a large spot below the eye are dull scarlet; the rest of the head, also the neck, is dull green, slightly tinged with blue below the ear-coverts and on the sides of the crown; lighter and more yellowish towards the throat which, with the chin, is yellow. There is more red on the under wing-coverts than in *T.d.dilectissima.*

The female has the edge of the wing and some of the lesser wing-coverts adjacent to the black shoulder red, the rest green. The yellow of the under wing-coverts is more extensive. Immature birds are said to resemble the female but have the red of the forehead mixed with green feathers.

*Distribution:* Costa Rica and western Panama. Slud (35) states: 'The Red-winged Parrotlet seems to have been taken only twice in Costa Rica (in 1910 near Puerto Limon and in 1922 at Santa Cruz on Turrialba Volcano). I met it twice in October 1953, at Matriculas de Pavones situated on a 3,000-foot forested ridge overlooking the Reventazon Valley and in plain sight of Turrialba Volcano. There is no other report.

'This little parrot, as represented by *costaricensis,* is undoubtedly rare in its range. It is probably a bird of the cool and wet lower middle altitudes; the Puerto Limon specimens may have been a wandering group taken in the foothill . . .

'The few birds that I have observed were in medium-sized trees at the forest border. They were with the barbet *Ebucco bourcierii* and the tanager *Buthraupis arcaei,* both indicators of cool, very wet portions of the hilly subtropical belt. Both sexes were present. The only sound I heard was a chatter. At the same locality I found four other parrots (*Aratinga finschi, Pyrrhura hoffmanni, Pyrrhura haematotis* and *Pionus senilis*) of which only the first and last were common.'

*Remarks:* Wetmore (43b) believes that the red forehead and the longer upper tail-coverts, also its wide geographic separation from *T.d.dilectissima*, are good reasons for making this a separate species.

## GOLDEN-TAILED PARROTLET *(T.surda)*

*Description:* Predominantly green, light green below and yellowish-green on the sides of the body. The feathers of the neck are narrowly edged with black and the forehead and part of the cheeks are yellowish. The flights are blackish-brown and the scapulars are brown, forming a conspicuous V shape. The two central tail feathers are green, tipped with black. The bill is yellowish. Length: 6¼in.

The female differs in having the two central tail feathers uniformly green; none of the tail feathers are tipped with black.

*Distribution:* Eastern Brazil in the states of Goyaz, Bahia, Rio de Janiero and São Paulo.

## SPOTTED-WINGED PARROTLET *(T.stictoptera)*

*Synonym:* Brown-shouldered Parrotlet

*Description:* Mainly green, the distinguishing feature being the orange greater upper wing-coverts. The remaining upper wing-coverts are brown with light tips. The inner webs of the outer tail feathers are reddish-brown near the base and golden yellow-brown below. Length: 7½in.

The female has the wing-coverts green with black centres. (It was formerly believed that the female was a distinct species – *T.emmae.*)

*Distribution:* Eastern Ecuador and Colombia; known definitely from Colombia only from the western slope of the Eastern Andes in the sub-tropical zone of Cundinamarca, from the upper tropical zone of the Macarena Mountains and the eastern slope of the Central Andes in Cauca.

CHAPTER 7

# SMALL PARROTS

THE genera Pionites, Pionopsitta and Pionus included in this chapter contain some of the most interesting of all small parrots. Unfortunately, more than half of the species are unknown to aviculture and only five or six are regularly imported.

## Genus: *Pionites*

Caiques are among the most intelligent and desirable of all parrots. In an aviary they are as playful and amusing as Lories, and as pets they are fascinating; so much so, in fact, that the most consistent breeder of these birds describes them as unique in their personality and temperament and in their response to care and training. Those who are interested in behaviour study will find Caiques of absorbing interest, as will those who like birds with strongly marked personalities.

For several reasons these birds are best kept in an aviary, being far too active to be caged for long. When several are housed together their activities will provide much amusement. I have even seen one Caique hanging from the aviary roof by one foot and swinging its mate with the other foot, like a trapeze artiste. As they are extremely messy feeders and flick particles of fruit in all directions, a cage and its surroundings are almost impossible to keep clean.

Like most small neo-tropical parrots, they are highly sociable – more so, in fact, than any bird I have ever kept, and so much so that if a single bird is housed only with large parrots, even Amazons, it will try to befriend them. I have seen a Black-headed Caique being fed by a Quaker Parrakeet in a mixed collection, and there is a record of a White-bellied Caique kept as a pet which made friends with a Lovebird. In my opinion, it is positively cruel to keep any but the very tamest Caique without a companion of its own kind. Having witnessed the frantic attempts of my Pallid Caique to reach another pair of Caiques, and its satisfaction when I gave way to its desire to be housed with them, I would never again consider keeping one of these birds as a pet unless it had been hand-reared.

Mrs Williams, the foremost breeder in the USA, has found that when they reach the age of about one and a half months, Caiques must be removed from their parents for hand-feeding. If this is not done they soon become hard to manage, independent and inclined to nip. I certainly found this to be true of my Pallid Caique, which took only two or three days to become finger-tame. Very quickly, however, it showed that it had a will of its own and would give a warning nip if it was not allowed its own way. Never have I seen such determination in a small bird!

This independence of spirit was also shown in a presumed female adult Black-headed Caique which, although not tame, was fearless enough to bite at my fingers. E. N. T. Vane recorded of his pair (*Foreign Birds*, vol. 22, 96) that the believed cock never missed a chance of grabbing his finger if he was at all incautious. If the other bird caught him at these tricks she would 'put him in his place and very smartly knocks him off the perch with severe loss of his dignity'. Unlike Amazons, breeding does not seem to affect the temperament – at least in Mrs Williams' and G. A. Smith's breeding males.

Due to their bold and fearless demeanour, Caiques manage to convey the impression of being larger than they actually are. If disturbed or alarmed they sway backwards and forwards in what is meant to be a menacing manner.

They are extremely destructive birds and can wreak terrible havoc in an aviary! Hard wood for chewing is essential, as their beaks quickly become overgrown if this is not provided. A rough piece of brick will serve the same purpose. Twigs from fruit trees should be provided regularly, daily if possible, and will reveal a fascinating side of Caique behaviour. An area of the branch is immediately stripped of bark and the body is rubbed, cat-like against it, first on one side, then on the other. So absorbed does the bird become in these vigorous, almost frantic, rubbing movements, that I am invariably reminded of a bird anting.

These movements are carried out equally enthusiastically on a twig completely stripped of bark, or on a dry but bark-covered one. If I held a twig vertically, my Pallid Caique would rub himself against it for minutes at a time, and would even sharpen the end to a point with his beak to obtain a more satisfying effect.

I have never witnessed similar behaviour in any other parrot.

The vocabulary of these birds is interesting when heard from a distance; it consists of metallic 'clinks' and 'yaps' and other penetrating noises, including a shrill whistling shriek which is often repeated seemingly endlessly. The noise made by a single bird kept indoors as a pet is just bearable, but that made by a pair is definitely not! A tame Caique, certainly a hand-reared one, is perhaps unrivalled by any other parrot as a pet, its endearing character compensating for its vociferous ways.

One reads in old avicultural literature that Caiques are sensitive to cold. This undoubtedly applies to newly imported young birds, which may even need heat if they are imported during the summer months. Acclimatised adults are perfectly hardy and may be wintered in an outdoor aviary provided they have a nest-box in which to roost.

*Breeding:* Caiques have been bred on regrettably few occasions and most of these have been in the USA. The most consistent breeder to date has undoubtedly been Mrs Williams of Florida. These small parrots perhaps need the stimulus provided by other birds of their own kind to induce breeding. It is interesting to note that Mrs Williams' Caiques did not breed until she introduced large flight cages in tiers with nest-boxes on the outside. She has bred Black-headeds to several generations, rearing 40 birds in 10 years, an unrivalled achievement.

Other aviculturists prepared to persevere with them could perhaps achieve similar success. Too few serious attempts are made to breed from such birds as Caiques, and not enough thought is given to the subject. Just what can be done by a determined aviculturist approaching the project in a sensible way was shown by G. A. Smith of Peterborough who had a chick from both his pairs of Caiques in the first year of trying.

Convinced that the first two Caiques he bought were not a true pair, he bought four more over a period of several months and placed them in compartments in an outdoor birdroom. After long periods spent observing their behaviour he found it difficult to distinguish a female from a submissive male. When one male was let out of its compartment it would try to attack another male through the wire but would not attack the Caiques which kept their plumage sleeked; in other words, those that did not look aggressive were not challenged. By introducing various birds to each other and studying their reactions a true pair of Pallid Caiques was found. When one which proved to be a hen was placed with two others which were thought to be cocks one of the latter tried to get close to the hen and, after some chortling and preening on both sides, the hen allowed one of the cocks to feed her.

The pair were left together and feeding took place regularly, usually by the cock, who made a sibilant call more often associated with the sounds that hens of some species – but not Caiques – make before or during copulation. (My male Red-capped Parrot *(Pionopsitta pileata)* makes a similar noise while feeding the hen.) It was found that hens feed cocks only under certain circumstances; if, for example, the cock's attention is distracted from the hen by some tempting item of food she may try to feed him to regain his attention.

The usual clutch laid by Caiques is three eggs, but may be two or four. Incubation lasts 26 or 28 days – probably the latter. Chicks fledge at the age of about 10 weeks.

*Feeding:* The food used by Mrs Williams to hand-rear her young Caiques is a mixture of baby cereal, preferably ready-cooked oatmeal, sunflower seed meal and a good grade of powdered milk. This is mixed with hot water to a fluid consistency and fed four times a day. Two drops of cod liver oil are given twice weekly, alternating with wheat germ oil. Adult birds also receive these preparations on the whole wheat bread provided.

Caiques are usually somewhat conservative feeders, often refusing absolutely all greenfood and being extremely particular in their choice of fruit. Apple (the pips are especially relished) and red currants appear to be the favourite fruits. Young or newly-imported birds may eat only banana but soon learn to sample apple. Grapes, orange and cherries were eaten by one of my Caiques and some will eat celery and carrot, but a recently obtained pair of Yellow-thighed will so far sample only apple and tinned paw-paw, and are among the very few parrots I have ever known to refuse cherries.

Boiled maize should be given to all young Caiques and any adult which will eat it. A newly-imported Pallid Caique in my possession would drink large quantities of nectar made for Lories with Benger's Food, condensed milk and honey, an excellent food for a young bird. Sweet fruit juices and nectar concoctions are enjoyed. Nectar made from rose-hip syrup and honey, and trifle sponge mashed in honey water, are the only foods for which my Caiques show real enthusiasm, with the notable exception of walnuts. These are relished above all but must be cracked before feeding.

The usual seeds should be provided but small seeds, with the exception of hemp, are often ignored. The preferred seeds are sunflower and spray millet, also peanuts. Birds from which it is hoped to breed should be encouraged to take sweetened bread and milk.

Caiques are immediately recognisable by their white breasts, a feature shared by no other parrot. They have always been regarded as two species; in my opinion they should be treated as one species. It is interesting to note that very young *leucogaster* Caiques have the crown black, thus their colouring more nearly resembles that of *melanocephala*, evidence of the very close relationship.

BLACK-HEADED CAIQUE *(P.melanocephala melanocephala)*
*Description:* The entire top of the head, also the beak and the feet are black; the throat and cheeks are yellow, merging into orange tips to some of the feathers and the under tail-coverts are yellow with an occasional orange feather. The underparts are white and provide a striking contrast to the dark green back, wings and tail. The iris is bright red. Length: 9in.

Slight colour variations seen in individuals, such as the brightness of the orange on the thighs, or the extent of the small area of green on the nape of the neck, are no indication of sex. Athough E. N. T. Vane recorded that the upper mandible of the cock of his pair was noticeably broader than that of the hen, Mrs Williams has not found this to be an indication of sex.
*Distribution:* Eastern Venezuela and the Guianas, southward to the Rio Negro and the Rio Branco, Brazil. Very little has been recorded about Caiques in the wild. According to Dorothy E. Snyder the Black-headed is widespread and fairly common in high forests and their edges in Guyana.
*Remarks:* A Black-headed Caique, owned by a dealer in foreign birds who lived in the Strand, London, was described as long ago as 1751. The London Zoo first exhibited this species in 1855. It is, with the Pallid, not imported in large numbers, but is fairly often available.
*Breeding records:* There is no record of the Black-headed successfully breeding in Britain but it (or the Pallid which, I believe, is more often available there) has been bred on a number of occasions in the USA, especially by Mrs Williams of Miami Beach, Florida, since about 1958. She has not found them at all prolific; from eight or

ten pairs only seven or eight young may be produced in one season. In 1971 only four young were bred (by two pairs). They nested as late as May but usually start breeding in January or February depending on the weather. Caiques like privacy and Mrs Williams has found that 'every change means a delay in mating'. The earliest age at which she has bred from them is four years and they have proved to be always single-brooded. The first time she was successful in breeding these birds, several pairs were housed in individual compartments of an outdoor aviary 20ft x 12ft x 8ft. Only strong 2in wood is used for the nest-boxes which measure 10in x 10in x 12in. Leaves, sand and fine twigs are used for nesting material.

In 1936 Lady Poltimore's Black-headed x White-bellied pair reared one youngster, after two years in which infertile eggs were laid. The complete clutch of four eggs was hatched but the two youngest chicks were not fed. The eldest of the remaining two was twice the size of its nest-mate, which died at the age of six or seven weeks. The survivor left the nest when 2½ months old. For some time it would not eat hard seed but lived on soaked biscuits, soaked sunflower and fruit. It was reared almost entirely on the first two foods with the addition of mealworms, of which the adults ate as many as they could. They relished fruit, including pear, apple, orange, grapes and ripe walnuts.

It is interesting to note that the young bird exactly resembled the male, the Black-headed Caique, except that it had green thighs, whereas the chick which had died before fledging resembled the hen. In 1958 the adult pair were still alive, had been in her possession for 28 years and were at least 34 years old. Mrs Williams has also found this species to be long-lived. Two of her original six are still alive and are at least 24 years old.

In 1971 F. Wait of Suffolk bred a hybrid between a Black-headed and a White-bellied Caique. It fledged after 71 days in the nest. A third bird, a hen White-bellied lived peacefully with the pair and was even allowed to enter the nest-box.

## PALLID CAIQUE *(P.m.pallida)*

*Description:* It differs from the nominate race in having the thighs, flanks and under tail-coverts bright lemon yellow.

An immature bird in my possession differs from adults in having the upper breast immediately below the throat of a dirty buff colour. Some of the white breast feathers are yellowish and a number of the yellow thigh feathers are tipped with green and show some orange in the centre. The green feathers of the wings have a distinctly blue tinge in places.

*Distribution:* Eastern Colombia south of Meta to eastern Peru. They are found in small flocks composed of a few pairs.

*Breeding records:* The first recorded breeding of the Pallid Caique in Britain – and, indeed, the first 'pure' Caique breeding – took place in 1971. The pair mentioned on page 180, belonging to G. A. Smith, laid the first of three eggs on May 28. A chick hatched on June 29; its down was white. The other eggs were fertile but the chicks had died, probably after the full incubation period.

The nest-box was examined regularly to record the growth of the baby Caique. At the age of 18 days it showed no trace of feather quill; at 27 days its beak was darkening and its eyes did not open until the 29th day, when its feet and beak were fairly dark. At 36 days the wing quills, also those of the crown, were prominent.

Its weight was recorded as follows: 32 days, 97 grams; 33 days, 100 grams; 38 days, 111 grams; 40 days, 115 grams; 41 days, 120 grams; 43 days, 125 grams; 46 days, 125.5 grams and 54 days 137 grams. At 43 days all the colours were discernible in the quills and 11 days later it was very well feathered. It left the nest at the age of 73 days.

WHITE-BELLIED CAIQUE *(P.leucogaster leucogaster)*

*Synonym:* White-breasted Caique

*Description:* The top of the head from the forehead to the nape of the neck, also part of the ear-coverts, are orange; the lores, side of the head and the fore part of the ear-coverts are yellow. The back, wings and tail are green and the whole of the lower parts are white, except the flanks and thighs which are green. The under tail-coverts are yellow and the underside of the tail is yellowish-grey. The bill and the small area of bare skin surounding the eye are pinkish-white. The iris is red. Length: about 9in.

*Distribution:* The valley of the lower Amazon: Para and north-east Mato Grosso.

*Remarks:* Irregularly imported in small numbers.

*Breeding records:* This Caique has yet to be bred in Britain. In the USA it was bred by Gilbert Lee in 1932; three young were hatched and reared. In 1934 one was bred at San Diego Zoo, another single chick being reared at Cincinnatti Zoo in 1969. In Tampa a *leucogaster* x *xanthomeria* pair had produced nine young by 1969.

YELLOW-THIGHED CAIQUE *(P.l.xanthomeria)*
*Description:* It differs from the nominate race in having the thighs and flanks yellow instead of green.

When in immature plumage a pair in my possession had the white of the breast replaced by pale buff and, as in immature *melanocephala*, a distinct blue tinge to the green of the wings. Very young birds have the crown black.
*Distribution:* Eastern Ecuador and eastern Peru to the Rio Machados and Rio Jururá in western Brazil; also recorded from Rio Beni Valley in northern Bolivia.

YELLOW-TAILED CAIQUE *(P.l.xanthurus)*
*Description:* According to Todd (39a), it differs in 'the colour of the tail, which is mostly yellow instead of green, the shafts of the feathers being white'.
*Distribution:* Originally described from specimens from Nova Olinda on the left bank of the Rio Parús in Brazil.
*Remarks:* By some oversight this sub-species was overlooked by Peters (29).

Genus: *Pionopsitta*

These small parrots are short and plump, aptly dubbed 'chunky parrots' by one aviculturist. Until 1969 the number of importations into Britain of any member of the genus could be counted on the fingers of one hand. They all related to the Red-capped of which quite a number have since been imported. It often happens that a species which has only rarely been available in the past suddenly appears on the market; sometimes it becomes a familiar bird to aviculturists, but in other cases the source of supply seems to dry up and the species again becomes rare. This happens frequently with South American birds – the Tanagers *(Tangara)* being a particularly good example.

A number of aviculturists seem to have found it difficult to establish newly-imported birds of this species, almost certainly because they have provided a diet which is deficient, especially in Vitamin A although in some cases, the birds were suffering from the incurable disease aspergillosis when received. My birds readily accept all fruit and greenfood offered, but I do not think that this has been the experience of others who perhaps have not provided enough variety in the diet. They relish figs, grapes, apple, etc, also raw young

29 The colours of the Bronze-winged Parrot *Pionus chalcopterus* must be seen in sunlight to be fully appreciated. Owner: author.

30 The red forehead of the male Red-capped Parrot *Pionopsitta pileata* distinguishes it from the female. Owner: author.

31 One of the best loved birds in the author's collection is this rare Purple-bellied Parrot *Triclaria malachitacea* from Brazil.

32 Two of the author's *Pionus* parrots—on the left a Massena's Parrot *P. seniloides* and right, a White-crowned Parrot *P. senilis*. One modern systematist has, confusingly, given the name White-capped Parrot to the former.

33 The Hawk-headed Parrot *Deroptyus accipitrinus* raises its bizarre headdress in aggression or display. This is one of the most fascinating of neo-tropical parrots. Owner: author.

34 Maximilian's Parrot *P. maximiliani* is one of the more quietly coloured members of the *Pionus* family. Owner: Christian Jensen.

35 An extremely rare bird in aviculture is the Short-tailed Parrot *Graydidascalus brachyurus*. This one belongs to the well known Danish aviculturist E. Nørgaard-Olesen.

carrots and boiled potato. All greenfood is eaten, even cabbage, to which most parrot-like birds are not very partial, also spinach beet, chickweed and grass with roots and earth attached. Autopsy has revealed that they have enormously long bowels which would indicate that their food needs a lot of digesting – possibly buds or fruit with hard pericarp, certainly not seed. My birds eat all the seeds offered, including canary, linseed, hemp, buckwheat and spray millet but sunflower is preferred to all others. Peanuts are also eaten. Rarely have I known parrots which will sample such a wide variety of foods.

Those whose Red-caps are less accommodating in this respect must give a vitamin additive. Mine are very fond of 'nectar' to which Abidec drops have been added. One of the favourite items in their diet is boiled maize which, I believe, should always be given to these birds and not only to newly imported ones. Plenty of cuttlefish bone and twigs from fruit trees should be available, as they tend to suffer from overgrown beaks.

Should the other and more colourful members of the genus ever become available they would almost certainly thrive on the same treatment. Red-capped Parrots do not appear to be completely hardy during their first winter and must be taken into heated quarters if they show any signs of discomfort in cold weather.

Very little is known about the other *Pionopsitta* but it would appear that, unlike *P.pileata,* most are *not* sexually dimorphic.

### RED-CAPPED PARROT *(P.pileata)*

*Synonym:* Pileated Parrot

*Description:* The male is green, darker above, and has the forehead, most of the crown, the lores and a narrow line below the eye, including part of the ear-coverts, scarlet. The bend of the wing, the carpal edge and the primary-coverts, are deep blue. The under wing-coverts are bluish-green and pale bluish. The beak is grey and whitish horn-coloured and the iris is brown. Length: 9in. Immature males have no red on the head, except a faint tinge on the ear-coverts. The red appears first on the forehead and crown. The two males in my possession, which are now in their third year, have the ear-coverts and the area below the eye only partly scarlet, so it appears that this is the last area to colour.

Females may be distinguished by the absence of red on the head. In some the forehead is bluish, yet neither of my adult hens show this colour. One skin which I have examined of a female received by the London Zoo in 1883 showed much deep blue on the head. Hens usually have the ear-coverts brownish-red and only a small amount of blue under the wings.

*Distribution:* South-eastern Brazil from southern Bahia to Rio Grande do Sul; Paraguay; Misiones and Corrientes in Argentina.

*Remarks:* The London Zoo first exhibited this species in 1877 and subsequently in 1883 and 1894 or 1895. In 1904 F. C. Thorpe of Hull imported several. In 1923, when H. Astley received two pairs, he commented that he believed that none had been imported since 1905. Those that reached Britain in 1969 were probably the first since 1923.

Russ described this species as 'Beloved, because beautiful, pleasing, gentle, and peaceable, vigorous, and enduring' and Astley wrote of the first one he owned as 'one of the gentlest and sweetest tempered parrots I ever saw'. It is difficult to add to testimonials such as these! Many are naturally fearless and I have sometimes almost to push mine off the food containers before I can remove them for refilling. Astley wrote that his bird would allow him to hold it and stroke it without showing any wish to bite. Even when I have had to catch mine they remained quiet in my hand and also made no attempt to bite.

The cocks warble in a manner which is reminiscent of Budgerigars, and it was not until I had had mine for almost two years that I discovered that their voices can be far from inoffensive. In breeding condition the call of the male can be described as a loud, plaintive mewing noise, which carries a considerable distance and is repeated several times.

They are very sociable birds and preen each other constantly. I doubt whether a single pair would go to nest; they probably need the stimulus of the presence of at least one other pair. At the time of writing the cock of one of my pairs has been feeding the hen for about six weeks and the pair have explored various nest-boxes. This species has yet to be bred in confinement but in view of the fact that there are a number of pairs in Britain and on the Continent it may not be long before the first breeding occurs.*

These birds seem to thrive in a small aviary – in fact, a large aviary would be quite unnecessary. They enjoy bathing and being sprayed.

* At the time of going to press one of my hens was incubating eggs.

BROWN-HOODED PARROT *(P.haematotis haematotis)*
*Synonym:* Red-eared Parrot
*Description:* The feathers of the crown are greyish-brown with a narrow brownish-red edge, becoming golden-olive on the hind-neck and the upper part of the mantle. The cheeks and throat are blackish-brown with a reddish tinge on the cheeks. The ear-coverts are red. The lores, and sometimes the chin, are white. There is a scarlet patch on the sides of the breast and a blue patch below the bend of the wing, the primary-coverts and the primaries being black with a tinge of deep blue. The under wing-coverts are pale bluish-green. The tail is olive green, tipped with blue, with deep blue on the outer edge of the outer feathers and red on the inner webs. The underside of the tail is light bluish-green. The iris is greenish-yellow to yellow and the beak yellowish-white to pinkish grey-white. Wetmore (43b) described the female as 'usually somewhat duller in color'. Immature birds are said to lack the brownish-red edges to the feathers of the crown, and the reddish tinge on the cheeks. Length: 9in.
*Distribution:* Southern Mexico (from the state of Vera Cruz), south to western Panama. Paul Slud (35) states that this parrot is found in the humid life zones from sea level to 10,000ft. In Costa Rica it is uncommon in some places, very common to abundant in others. It is more numerous on the Caribbean than the Pacific side, yet scarce in the extreme south-east. It usually occurs in well-wooded areas and along woodland borders and adjacent tree-scattered clearings and plantations. Groups of several to a dozen individuals are usually seen, flying rapidly. It is apparently easily overlooked as it feeds quietly in the tree-tops. Wetmore saw the Brown-hooded Parrot feeding on figs in company with other parrots and with toucans.

RED-NECKLACED PARROT *(P.h.coccinicollaris)*
*Description:* It differs from *P.h.haematotis* in having a rose-red collar below the dark grey of the throat. According to Salvadori the feathers of the crown are never edged with brownish-red but with olive brown. The latter feature is consistent but the black on the throat is seen only in some specimens. In the skin specimens examined the cheeks and lores were dull dark greyish with some white on the throat and two or three white-tipped red feathers on the ear-coverts. One specimen from Chiriqui had a brilliant scarlet patch on the ear-coverts. It may be that the extent of the scarlet on the ear-coverts

is, as in *P.pileata*, an indication of age. Length: about 8½in.
*Distribution:* Panama from the Canal Zone eastwards and north west Colombia from the Pacific coast eastward to Bolívar.

BEAUTIFUL PARROT *(P.h.pulchra)*
*Description:* The forehead and crown are dark brown and the feathers of the nape are edged with golden-olive. There is a band of the latter colour nearly 1in in width on the mantle, extending to the upper breast to form a wide collar. The ear-coverts are deep brick-red and the lores and throat are buffish and pinkish. The bend of the wing is golden-orange and there is bluish-black along the edge of the wing. The under wing-coverts are a mixture of blue and green and the flights are bluish-black. There are several red and yellow feathers on the centre of the edge of the wing. The underside of the flights and tail are a greyish-dusky colour and greenish; the tail is tipped blue with scarlet or dusky scarlet on the inner webs. The body colour is dark green above, light green below. The iris is light grey or light brown; the bill has been described as yellowish horn-coloured and greyish-white to white. Length: 9½in.
*Distribution:* The tropical zone of the Pacific coast of Colombia, from the Baudó Mountains southward, and Ecuador from the Rio Atrato almost to the Peruvian border.
*Remarks:* One of the skins in the British Museum is labelled 'E. J. Brook's Trustees'; it was collected in 1914 by Goodfellow, but whether it reached Brook alive I do not know.

CAICA PARROT *(P.caica)*
*Synonym:* Hooded Parrot
*Description:* The head is brownish-black and the throat and forepart of the neck are greenish-bronze. There is a collar about ¾in wide (only ½in in one skin examined and as much as 1½in in another) of bronzy-orange feathers tipped with brown. The body colour is dark green above, bluish-green below. There is some blue just below the bend of the wing and along the edge of the wing. The flights are dusky on the inner edge, blue edged green on the outer edge. The under wing-coverts are bluish-green. The tail is tipped with blue with bright yellow on the inner webs; the underside is yellowish-green. The iris is hazel and the bill pale brown. Length: 8½in to 9in. Immature birds are said to be green on the crown with olive-green cheeks and an olive-brown collar around the neck.
*Distribution:* Eastern Venezuela, north-eastern Brazil and the

Guianas, where it is said to be widespread but not common in the forests of the interior, where it lives in small flocks.

BARRABAND'S PARROT *(P.barrabandi barrabandi)*
*Description:* This is one of the loveliest members of the genus. It has the head black except for a large conspicuous patch of golden-orange on the cheeks and ear-coverts. The upper parts are dark green except for the tail which is tipped with dark blue, with yellow on the inner webs. The primaries, secondaries and wing-coverts are black, some being tinged with blue. The upper breast is golden-olive merging into green and strongly tinged with blue on the lower breast. The thighs are yellow and the under wing-coverts and the carpal edge of the wing are scarlet with a conspicuous patch of golden-orange at the bend of the wing. The iris is brown and the bill blackish. Length: about 10in, the largest of the genus.

Immature birds have the orange of the cheeks replaced by the same colour as the upper breast, ie, golden-olive. There is only a small amount of golden-orange at the bend of the wing. A skin of an adult bird examined had no orange at the bend of the wing and little on the thighs. Another labelled as a female and collected in Marabitanas, Brazil, had a mixture of red and gold on the bend of the wing and on the cheeks.
*Distribution:* Eastern Ecuador, extreme southern Venezuela and the upper Rio Negro of north-western Brazil. It is said to be rare and locally distributed. According to Dr João Moojen (28) 'It is only in the early morning that they perch high in the dead branches and stay quiet and immobile, once in a while emitting a high whistling call. Too shy to attack crops, they eat mostly the sapucara (*lecythis*) nuts or the ingá fruit.'

*P.b.aurantiigena* (Gyldenstolpe)
*Description:* It differs from the nominate race in having the cheeks, cubital edge of the wing and thighs bright orange instead of pale yellow to orange, and the bases of the feathers scarlet.
*Distribution:* Western Brazil, south of the Amazon, extending southward to northern Mato Grosso and eastern Peru south of the Rio Marañon.

SAFFRON-HEADED PARROT *(P.pyrilia)*
*Synonym:* Bonaparte's Parrot
*Description:* The head, throat and the lesser wing-coverts are golden-

yellow, the ear-coverts with a red tinge and the bases of the wing-coverts red. The nape, part of the throat and the upper breast are olive. There is much blue and black in the wings, and all the under wing-coverts, the bend of the wing and the sides of the breast are scarlet. The tail is broadly tipped with blue, with yellow on the inner webs. The bill has been described as horn-white and as light grey-yellow; the iris is dark brown. Length: 8½in to 9in – the smallest of the genus. Immature birds have the head green and the throat olive. The small upper wing-coverts are green instead of yellow and there are a few red feathers on the edge of the wing.
*Distribution:* Northern Colombia in the valleys of the Tuyra, Atrato, Cauca and Magdalena, southward to about 5°N; western Venezuela; possibly eastern Panama.
*Remarks:* Placed by Chapman in the monotypic genus *Pyrilia* because of the uniform golden-yellow head, the bare orbital and loral region and small size. Its body colouring, however, indicates its close relationship with *barrabandi, caica* etc.

The following *Pionopsitta* were considered as members of the separate genus *Hapalopsittaca* by Peters. Subsequently they have been included with the *Pionopsitta* by some authors.

BLACK-EARED PARROT *(P.melanotis melanotis)*
*Description:* The head, throat and mantle are dull slate-bluish and the area surrounding the eyes is yellowish-green. The ear-coverts are black and there is a large patch of that colour on the upper part of the wing. The tip of the wide, tapering tail is blue, also the underside of the tail and wings. The lower parts are light green, darker on the upper breast. The flights are dark grey, bluish on the outer edge. Length: 10in, including the 3½in tail.
*Distribution:* The highlands of Bolivia.

PERUVIAN BLACK-EARED PARROT *(P.m.peruviana)*
*Distribution:* The temperate zone of central Peru.

LITTLE AMAZONIAN PARROT *(P.amazonina amazonina)*
*Synonym:* Bogota Parrot
*Description:* The forehead, part of the crown and the cheeks are dull red. The plumage is greener than in *P.a.fuertesi*, olivaceous only on the breast. The lores are yellowish and the crown and ear-coverts have yellow-orange shaft streaks (reminiscent of the streaks seen on

the ear-coverts of lorikeets of the genus *Trichoglossus*). The remainder of the plumage is as described for *P.a.fuertesi*. Length: about 9½in. In immature birds the yellow streaks of the ear-coverts are scarcely visible; the face is a duller shade of red, and there are only a few pale red feathers at the edge of the wing.
*Distribution:* Subtropical and temperate zones of the western slope of the eastern Andes of Colombia.

FUERTES'S PARROT *(P.a.fuertesi)*
*Description:* The forehead, part of the crown and the sides of the head are greenish-yellow; the hind part of the crown is blue. The body is mainly olive-green, bluer on the wings and yellower on the upper tail-coverts. The tail is crimson-maroon at the base, blue at the tip. In the male the shoulders are crimson, the remiges rich blue. The female is said to differ in having the shoulders crimson-maroon only. Length: 10in. (NB. It is difficult to see why Peters considered this as a separate species when it so closely resembles *P.a.amazonina*.)
*Distribution:* The temperate zone of the central Andes of Colombia in Caldas.

PRINCESS THERESE'S PARROT *(P.a.theresae)*
*Distribution:* Known only from the Andes of Mérida in western Venezuela, where it inhabits the subtropical or temperate zones.

RED-FACED PARROT *(P.a.pyrrhops)*
*Description:* The forehead, cheeks, lores and chin are red merging into pale green or yellow on the crown, bluish on the nape. The ear-coverts are light green with some streaks of yellow. The upper parts are dark green with a large scarlet patch at the bend of the wing, scarlet at the edge of the wing and on the under wing-coverts. The primary-coverts and the outer webs of the primaries are blue, the underside of the flights and tail being pale blue. The tail is tipped with blue. Length: about 9in.
*Distribution:* The Andes of Ecuador and Santa Nita.

Genus: *Gypopsitta*

The single member of this genus is perhaps nothing more than the representative of *Pionopsitta barrabandi* in the southern lower Amazon.

VULTURINE PARROT *(G.vulturina)*
*Synonym:* Vulture-headed Parrot
*Description:* This species is placed in a separate genus because its

head is naked but for a fine covering of black hairs over the black skin and white hairs on the whitish skin of the forehead and lores. The head is surounded by a broad band formed by yellow feathers tipped with black. Its colouring greatly resembles that of *P.barrabandi.* The nape is blackish and the throat olive-yellow with the feathers edged with black. The thighs are yellow and red and the upper wing-coverts are orange; the carpal edge of the wing and the whole of the under wing-coverts are red. There are blue and black on the wings and the tail is green, tipped with blue, the inner webs being yellow. The iris is orange and the beak blackish, yellow at the base. On examination of a number of skins C. E. Hallmayr (19a) found that the only sexual difference was the greater amount of red on the thighs of the male.

Immature birds have only the forehead and lores naked, the rest of the head being covered with short green feathers which extend to the hind-neck. There is more green on the remainder of the plumage than in adults.

*Distribution:* South of the Lower Amazon and east of the Rio Madeira, southwards at least to the Sierra do Cachimbo between the upper Rio Xingú and Rio Tapajóz. Jürgen Haffer (16) states: 'All regional handbooks including Phelps and Phelps (1958) and de Schauensee (1966) inform wrongly that *P.vulturina* is also found north of the Amazon in Guyana and South Venezuela. This information dates back to Berlepsch and Hartert (1902) who named wrongly in error two examples of *Deroptyus accipitrinus* from the lower Rio Caura in southern Venezuela as *G.vulturina* which Hellmayr (19c) corrected in a footnote. Hellmayr's remark, however, has unfortunately been overlooked.' There is no proof that this species is found north of the Amazon.

*Remarks:* I can trace no records of this species being imported into Britain. About 1919, when Goodfellow was collecting in Ecuador, he obtained a Vulturine Parrot from the Indians. He kept it for 'many months' and it was very tame but it died while he was detained in Ecuador due to the outbreak of war. He wrote that it was not at all noisy and that it was very intelligent.

## Genus: *Graydidascalus*

### SHORT-TAILED PARROT *(G.brachyurus)*

*Description:* It is mainly green, paler and more yellowish on the underparts with the feathers of the secondaries and the greater wing-coverts edged with yellowish-green. There is a dark red patch on the top of the shoulder and some red at the base of the very short tail. The beak is black and the iris red. Length: about 9in.

The sexes are usually stated to be alike. Of the three skins in the British Museum all have red in the tail but only one, labelled as a male, has the reddish-brown on the shoulders.

*Distribution:* Tropical zone in south-eastern Colombia from Caquetá southward to eastern Ecuador, eastern Peru and Brazil from the Rio Juruá and Solimoës down the Amazon Valley to its mouth, and north to the coast of Amapá.

Little has been recorded about this species. Emil Goeldi (*Ibis*, 1897, 162) saw 'a flight of some 20 individuals perched (October 30) on a siriúba'. Walter Goodfellow (*Ibis*, 1902, 219) 'once came upon a large flock of these parrots, when they were congregating at sunset in the high trees along the river banks for the night'.

*Remarks:* As far as I know the Short-tailed Parrot has not been imported into Britain for many years. There is, however, a pair in the collection of E. Norgaard-Olesen, near Esjberg in Denmark. This species was exhibited at the London Zoo as long ago as 1894. Astley obtained one in 1910 which was extremely tame and allowed itself to be stroked and handled. He wrote 'A gentler bird I never saw, and its looking like a pygmy Amazon gives it some fascination all of its own.'

Single specimens were exhibited in 1914 by Mrs B. J. Moore and in 1937 or 1938 by a Miss Henderson. Chapman received three in 1925 and one on another occasion. Maud Knobel noted of the three imported by Chapman that their beaks and mouths were large in relation to their size and that the tongue was 'unlike that of any other parrot. Instead of being round it is flat and large, flesh-colour in appearance with a black edge. One cannot help wondering what these small Parrots feed on in their wild state for they do not seem constructed to crack small seeds, but certain it is that they belong to a genus entirely by themselves.'

*G.b.insulsus*

*Description:* It supposedly differs from the nominate race in being smaller but with a proportionately larger and heavier bill. Gyldenstolpe, (15b), who studied a large number of skins, did not believe this sub-species to be valid.

*Distribution:* Brazil, south of the Amazon.

## Genus: *Pionus*

The Pionus are among the most engaging and neglected of neotropical parrots. Of the eight recognised species only the Blue-headed is frequently available, the remainder being irregularly or very rarely imported. They are compact birds, 9in to 11in in length with short, square tails and red under tail-coverts. Some have most unusual colour schemes and the colouring of two species is more falcon-like than parrot-like. The plumage of immature birds is greener and less colourful, and it is usually several years before full adult plumage is obtained. Adults of the same species show considerable variation in the plumage.

*As Pets Pionus* Parrots are ideal, especially for children or those who are nervous of the larger birds such as Amazons. Unlike the latter, which are suitable only for those with much patience and a real understanding of parrots, they are quiet and normally very gentle. There are exceptions, of course, one being a pet Dusky that I know of, but a harmless jab at one's hand is their usual method of showing disapproval. Almost all the Blue-headed Parrots imported are very young and hand-tame – 'ready-made' pets at a very reasonable price.

Walter Goodfellow, one of the great collectors of the early years of the century, discovered what amusing pets *Pionus* parrots made during his stay in Quito, Ecuador. He was able to collect several species from the nest and hand-rear them, including four Blue-headed, a number of Bronze-winged, a pair of Massena's and two Coral-billed. They were all very tame and were allowed the freedom of a glass-covered corridor and two rooms. Some of them could talk, each knew its name and had a very distinct personality. The Massena's slept in a basket with a pair of Black-headed Caiques, and one of the Bronze-winged would visit a store-room and watch for rats.

In my experience, when one of these birds is kept as a pet it enjoys the company of another *Pionus*, regardless of the species. A companion does not prevent it from becoming very tame, although naturally the tamest birds are usually those which are completely devoted to their owners. A young White-crowned (*P.senilis*) in my possession was rather subdued until it was let out of its cage at the same time as a Massena's Parrot. The two while housed indoors became firm friends, and the White-crowned would plainly solicit preening by bowing its head and remaining motionless. They would spend hours preening each other, on occasions reaching a complete deadlock, heads bowed and touching. The Massena's always gave in first and began to preen its companion, although it was the dominant bird in other ways.

When given the freedom of a room these birds spend most of their time on the top of the cage and are quick to learn to go in and out. Mine have proved surprisingly obedient, and return inside the cage when told to do so. This is in direct contrast to Amazons who have a very decided will of their own and whose favourite pastimes consist of destroying furniture, doors and floor-boards!

*As aviary birds* they have been sadly neglected, so much so, that the Blue-headed is the only species which has been bred on more than one or two occasions. Few serious attempts have been made to breed from the other members of the family, but they should not prove any more difficult to rear. Here, then, is an incentive to the aviculturist: a group of small, attractive parrots, which are no problem to house and ideal for built-up areas, and for which there are scarcely any breeding records. Unfortunately, they are rather difficult to sex because, in addition to the usual problem of the plumage being alike in cock and hen, both sexes have very flat heads. Little is known about the breeding behaviour of these birds; anyone who could add to the existing information would make a most useful contribution to aviculture.

Their flight is swift and strong and they would undoubtedly appreciate a long aviary; this is not a necessity, however, and pairs seem quite contented in 15ft flights.

*Pionus* appreciate a varied diet, being particularly fond of fruit and greenfood; some individuals show little interest in seed with the exception of sunflower and spray millet. They are frequently addicted to the last two items, also to peanuts and boiled maize. Almost all fruits and vegetables are eaten including apple, orange, grapes, cherries, carrot, cucumber, spinach beet, cabbage, chickweed, dandelion leaves and grass with earth and roots attached. Cheddar cheese is a great favourite of most of my *Pionus*.

These birds greatly appreciate being sprayed, opening their wings and ruffling their feathers to allow the water to penetrate every part of their plumage. A shower of rain is also enjoyed to the full.

BLUE-HEADED PARROT *(P.menstruus menstruus)*
*Synonyms:* Blue hooded Parrot, Red-vented Parrot
*Description:* The head, neck and upper part of the breast are rich

dark blue. The ear-coverts are blackish; the feathers of the throat are pink at the base and on the outer edge in some feathers, producing an irregular pink patch. The lower breast feathers are green tinged with brown and edged with blue. The wings are dark green with a bronze patch on the shoulders. Red is the colour of the under tail-coverts, which are tipped with green. The central tail feathers are green, the outer webs blue on the outer feathers, with a red-patch at the base. The bill is dark grey with a noticeable pink spot on either side of the top of the upper mandible. Length: about 11in, but this widespread species shows considerable variation, birds from Ecuador and Peru being among the largest. Coloration is equally variable. Wetmore found that specimens from northern Colombia differed in the depth of blue on the head, in the darker green on the back and the amount of red below the throat, also in their smaller size. Those from southern Colombia agree in colour but are larger. Friedmann thought that examples from Upper Amazonia (eastward to Santarém) are brighter, with more extensive blue on the breast and upper abdomen than birds from Guyana.

Immature birds are greener on the head, neck and upper breast, usually with some pink on the forehead.

*Distribution:* The greater part of tropical South America: Venezuela, Peru, Bolivia, Mato Grosso and the southern affluents of the Amazon eastward at least to the Rio Capim. It is also found in Trinidad where, according to G. A. C. Herklots (20) its numbers are increasing. It feeds on the seeds of the teak tree, which has been extensively planted in the south and centre of the island. It nests in holes in dead trees and lays four eggs. Slud (35) records that in Costa Rica it occurs in small groups in tree-scattered clearings and openings and in shaded cocao plantations – but not inside woods, although it is said to be a common forest species in Surinam, where it is known to feed in the tree-tops, mainly on the seeds of the possun tree *(Hura crepitans)*.

*Remarks:* Goodfellow aptly summed up the attributes of this species as a pet 'I think this is one of the most delightful of all parrots to keep, if hand-reared, especially for a lady or an invalid, as they are not a bit noisy and so docile and affectionate.'

*Breeding records:* The first recorded breeding in Britain took place in 1902 in the aviaries of the Rev. B. Hemsworth in Yorkshire. Two young were reared. In the USA it was bred by Mrs Ferne Hubbell of San Diego in 1958. Three young were hatched but only one survived and this was partly hand-reared. It was described as having 'very little blue on the head or neck; just a few pink feathers under the tail'. In Australia, Sir Edward Hallstrom bred the Blue-headed Parrot during the same year.

*P.m.rubrigularis*
*Description:* Said to differ in the depth of blue on head and breast, in darker green of the back, in the amount of red below the throat and in its average smaller size.
*Distribution:* Costa Rica to western Ecuador.

In 1937 Dr J. M. Derschied bought a pair of *P.cobaltinus* from a Brussels dealer, identifying them from the one skin known to science, which was in the British Museum. They were considerably smaller than *P.menstruus* and of a dull cobalt blue, decidedly more blue than that of the head and neck of *P.menstruus*. This colour extended to the under tail-coverts instead of giving way to green from the breast downwards. The green of the wings was brighter and more yellowish. These birds were presented to the Duke of Bedford. It was thought that an identical specimen was received by E. J. Brook during the First World War, collected by Goodfellow. Two *P.menstruus* presented to the London Zoo in 1963 were described by J. J. Yealland as being 'smaller and more slim, of a paler blue with paler ear-coverts and no trace of red on the throat. They may be what Massena and Souance called *Pionus cobaltinus* and although the original description mentions a red front, the Type may presumably have been an immature* bird!'

SORDID PARROT (*P.sordidus sordidus*)
*Description:* The head is a metallic green, each feather being broadly edged with dark blackish-blue. The lower part of the cheeks is bronzy-green, the chin and throat being blue or tinged with blue. The underparts are a light olive-green and the under tail-coverts are red. (In one skin, in the British Museum, labelled as a male, the upper parts, including the nape, are golden-bronze and the underparts are yellowish-olive.) The plumage is olive-green above and the first primary is edged with blue. The central tail feathers are green, the outer ones blue on the outer webs, red at the base. The bill is red with a tinge of yellow near the base. Length: about 11in.

* It was.

*Distribution:* The subtropical zone of the mountains of Venezuela.*
*Remarks:* Rarely imported and likely to be incorrectly identified as the Coral-billed sub-species. Walter Duncan of Dumfries received a pair as 'Coral-bills' in 1966, one of which died during the following year. In March 1971 he informed me that the other 'has only now assumed its full adult plumage'. He believed that the name of this species is inapt. '*P.sordidus sordidus* is a lovely bird and the breast plumage is like a dove-grey veil thrown over a green undercoat. An artist visitor recently admired it more than any other bird in my aviary and would have bought it but I could not recommend it as a pet.'

COLOMBIAN SORDID PARROT *(P.s.saturatus)*
*Distribution:* The subtropical and tropical zones of the Santa Marta Mountains in Colombia.*

CORAL-BILLED PARROT *(P.sordidus corallinus)*
*Synonym:* Coralline Parrot
*Description:* It differs from *P.s.sordidus* in being dark green above with the feathers of the head and neck edged with dark blue and those of the mantle edged with dusky-bluish. The feathers of the cheeks are faintly edged with blue; the forehead is dark blue. The breast is a darker shade of olive green than in the nominate race and the upper breast feathers are broadly edged with blue. The bill is coral-red and the iris is brown. Length: about 11½in.

According to Salvadori (32) immature birds have a few reddish feathers on the forehead and brighter blue on the lower throat.
*Distribution:* The subtropical zone of the Andes, eastern Ecuador, northern Peru and possibly Bolivia.*
*Remarks:* Seldom imported into Britain, although a few specimens have been received by a London dealer during recent years. Walter Duncan of Dumfries informed me that a specimen in his collection 'is a very silent bird except when being handled when he screams "blue murder". He is a clamberer and a sitter-about, not a great flyer, so of recent years he has been housed in a 6ft x 6ft flight as he does not make much use of a larger one. This bird likes nuts and adores apple of which he gobbles up all he can get.'

* De Schauensee (33b) gives the distribution of *P.sordidus* as follows: 'Tropical and subtropical zone. The mountains of Venezuela north of the Orinoco; Colombia in the Santa Marta Mts., the Perijá Mts. and the eastern Andes; eastern and western Ecuador; eastern Peru. Northern Bolivia in Chochabamba and Santa Cruz.'

ECUADORIAN SORDID PARROT *(P.s.mindoensis)*
*Distribution:* The subtropical zone of western Ecuador.*

*P.s.antelius* (Todd)
*Description:* Its general coloration is paler and more yellowish-green with little or no bluish tinge; the breast is without any purplish-pink suffusion, the rest of the underparts being dark citrine with the paler edges to the feathers slightly smaller.
*Distribution:* Venezuela, south of Cumanacoa.*

*P.s.pansi* (Alvedo and Gines)

MAXIMILIAN'S PARROT *(P.maximiliani maximiliani)*
*Description:* The feathers of the head are green, very narrowly edged with dark grey. The forehead and lores are nearly black and the feathers of the cheeks are green edged with bluish-grey. The chin and a band across the throat are dull purplish-blue, and the feathers of the hind neck have whitish streaks (only visible when ruffled). The mantle and the upper part of the wings are bronzy-olive, the bronze being most pronounced on the shoulders. The primaries, secondaries and the tail are olive-green with a bronze tinge, the tail with a patch of red on the inner webs of the feathers, the outer webs being edged with blue. The underparts are green and the under tail-coverts are red, the longest with yellowish-green edges. The bill is blackish. Length: about 11in. There is a prominent area of white skin surrounding the eye. Immature birds are much greener on the head with the forehead reddish and less blue on the throat.
*Distribution:* Eastern and south-eastern Brazil in the states of Piauhy, Bahia and Rio de Janiero.
*Remarks:* Infrequently imported but not rare. Almost nothing seems to have been recorded about this parrot in confinement.
*Breeding records:* The only breeding of which I know occurred in Beira Moz Zoo in 1970. Two young were reared.

SIY PARROT *(P.m.siy)*
*Description:* Differs from *P.m.maximiliani* in having the feathers of the crown from the forehead green, with a dark edge so that only the lores are black. The chin and a band across the throat are

* See footnote * on previous page.

vinous-red instead of blue and the green of the body is of a more olive shade.
*Distribution:* Eastern Bolivia; western and southern Brazil in the states of Mato Grosso, São Paulo, Paraná, Santa Catherina and Rio Grande do Sul; Paraguay, northern Argentina in the provinces of Formosa and Chaco.

## YELLOW-BILLED PARROT *(P.m.lacerus)*

*Synonym:* Tucuman Parrot
*Description:* There is only one skin in the British Museum (a male, collected in Salta). It is of a more olive shade above, especially on the tail-coverts and rump, than *P.m.maximiliani.* The upper breast is also a slightly different shade – more mauvish. Hartert and Venturi (17) also noted these characteristics. Length: 11½in.
*Distribution:* North-western Argentina in the provinces of Salta and Tucumán.
*Remarks:* A Yellow-billed Parrot was exhibited at the Crystal Palace Show in 1927 by C. T. Maxwell and at Paignton Zoo in the same year.

## RESTLESS PARROT *(P.tumultuosus)*

*Synonym:* Tschudi's Parrot
*Description:* This is, perhaps, the most striking and beautiful of the light-coloured members of the genus. Its most arresting feature is the delicate shade of pinkish-maroon of the crown and forehead. The centre of each feather is white, which can only be seen when the feathers are parted. There are a few flecks of white showing on the nape of the neck where the colour shades into blackish-green and the dark green on the remainder of the upper parts, including the rump and tail. (One of the skins examined was distinctly blue on the back of the head.) The cheeks, throat and upper breast are an unusual mixture of pinkish-maroon, white and dark blue (in the less typically coloured specimen dark blue only) and the upper breast feathers are edged with greyish-pink and dark blue. The underparts are green, being a lighter shade on the lower breast, and the under tail-coverts are red, edged with yellowish-green. The tail is green above, with a red patch near the base, the underside being the same shade of pinkish-maroon as the head, except the terminal band. The bill is yellow and the iris is brown. Length: about 10½in.
*Distribution:* Peru and Bolivia.
*Remarks:* I can find no record of this very beautiful parrot being

kept in confinement. In 1969 a dealer told me that he had received in a consignment a parrot with a pink head which was probably of this species, but it was most unfortunately dead on arrival. I have only seen skins: in life it must be superb.

MASSENA'S PARROT *(P.seniloides)*

*Synonym:* Grey-headed Parrot

*Description:* The feathers of the crown are dark grey (with white bases which are normally hidden). There is a little pink on the forehead and, in some specimens, two or three white feathers. The feathers of the lores, cheeks and throat are edged with dark grey, the centres being white or pinkish white. The large feathers of the nape are buffish-white in some birds and the ear-coverts are dark grey. The whole of the upper parts, including the tail, are dark green. The upper breast is dark vinous and some of the feathers below the throat show salmon-coloured centres. The abdomen is also vinous and the under tail-coverts are pinkish-red. There is a reddish patch at the base of the tail. The area of bare skin surrounding the eye is much less prominent than in most *Pionus* parrots. The bill is pale yellow. Length: about 10½in.

The colour of individuals varies considerably, especially on the lower parts. The upper breast feathers vary from dark mauvish-blue to vinous with pink centres. In some specimens the vinous-tinged feathers extend right through to the red of the vent. Undoubtedly age has a bearing on this colour, immature birds being much greener on the underparts. Young birds have the cheeks and part of the head green and white, with only a small amount of vinous on the breast. There is no buffish-white on the neck and the feathers of the crown are faintly edged with orange.

Salvadori noted that specimens from Venezuela and Ecuador differed from those from Colombia in never having the feathers of the crown white with red edges; such feathers occurred only on the forehead, the rest of the feathers of the crown being dark grey and white. Chapman (10a) also noted this feature but later (10b) contradicted this, attributing the white, rose-tinged forecrown 'to age and not environment'. One of my birds, however, which is at least six years old, does not have the forecrown white, only the forehead.

*Distribution:* Subtropical and humid temperate zones of the central and eastern Andes of Colombia and the Andes of Ecuador; north-western Venezuela in Táchira and Mérida.

*Remarks:* This species has been imported into Britain only rarely. It was represented in the collection brought from Ecuador by Goodfellow for E. J. Brook in 1915. To my knowledge only three have been imported in recent years, two of which are in my collection. One was extremely nervous at first and usually behaved like a wild-caught adult, although it was in immature plumage when imported. The other is a most delightful bird. It was fairly young, although not tame, when obtained, but soon allowed me to rub its head. It took a year for it to become completely confident: one day, after weeks of hesitation, it landed on my shoulder when let out of its cage. After that it climbed over me nearly every day without a moment's hesitation. This bird seems to have a penchant for getting into mischief, no doubt due to its fearlessness and great curiosity. It sometimes gets involved in a scrap with my Yellow-fronted Amazon, an inveterate coward almost twice the size of the Massena's. The Amazon uses her beak and lashes her feet in battle, but the Massena's is not impressed and often sends the Amazon rushing to me for protection!

The Massena's is such an engaging little parrot that its misdemeanours (which included eating the spines of my three volumes of Greene's *Parrots* – a rather expensive meal) are easy to overlook. It is not the mismarked monstrosity that the late Duke of Bedford would have one believe. His description of 'the untidy-looking *Pionus seniloides* which has the appearance of a bird making a half-hearted effort at albinism or suffering from weak feather growth' was entirely unjustified.

I have found this species to be noisier than other *Pionus* parrots; it possesses a loud and often persistent call note.

Possibly *P.seniloides* should be treated as a sub-species of *P. tumultuosus*; de Schauensee inclined towards this view.

## WHITE-CROWNED PARROT *(P.senilis senilis)*

*Synonym:* White-capped Parrot

*Description:* The forehead and a semi-circular patch covering half of the crown is white, this being its most striking feature. The rest of the head appears dark blue, darkest on the ear-coverts, the feathers being white at the base, green in the centre and blue at the edges. There is a white patch covering the chin and throat and, in some specimens, a few coral-pink feathers on the throat. The upper breast is dark mauvish-blue with brownish-green centres to the feathers; the lower breast is a greenish shade of blue. The under tail-coverts are pinkish-red, each feather being tipped with yellowish-green; the thighs are green. The mantle, rump and lower back are dark green and all the wing-coverts are bronze. The secondaries are dark green and the primaries are brilliant blue – very attractive when the wings are spread. The tail is green, bluish at the tip and on the outer webs of the outer feathers, with a reddish patch near the base of the tail. The bill is pale yellow and the iris is brown. Length: about $9\frac{1}{2}$in. The appearance of this parrot is, in my opinion, rather spoiled by the area of dull pink skin surrounding the eye. According to Wetmore (43b) females are duller. Immature birds are much less colourful, having less white on the crown, and the rest of the head dull bluish-green or olive-green, the ear-coverts bluish and the throat buff-coloured. The upper breast is dull greyish-blue, the rest of the lower parts being dull green faintly washed with blue.

*Distribution:* Southern Mexico in the states of Oaxaca and Vera Cruz; Guatemala. Blake gives its distribution in Mexico as the lowlands of the south-east from San Luis Potosí and southern Tamaulipas southward, including the Yucatan Peninsula.

*Remarks:* Rarely imported. London Zoo received specimens as long ago as 1862 and 1867. Greene (1884) wrote that he had seen a *Pionus senilis* which 'could whisper "Pretty Polly" in a very small voice', offered for sale at £2. This species has been imported into Britain on several occasions during the past few years. A young bird in my possession is very quiet and quite tame and fearless. It allows itself to be handled but dislikes close attention from strangers. If annoyed it gives the typical threat display: holding the carpals away from the body, puffing out the cheek feathers and spreading the tail.

*Breeding records:* A pair in the possession of the Duke of Bedford in 1933 'nested as soon as they were turned out and the hen hardly left the nest for weeks'. The one egg failed to hatch; a second clutch was laid and one chick was hatched but was killed by the cock when one week old. The following year a chick was hand-reared by J. J. Yealland from the age of four days. The rearing food was a mixture of soaked peanuts, soaked and shelled sunflower, brown bread, sweet apple, lettuce, dandelion, sowthistle, egg yolk, malt, Marmite and 'lorikeet' food. The mixture was warmed in the mouth before being given to the baby parrot, which took the food from the mouth. This remains the only record of the White-crowned Parrot breeding in captivity.

SOUTHERN WHITE-CROWNED PARROT *(P.s.decoloratus)*
*Description:* It supposedly differs slightly from the nominate race in its shade of colour. Wetmore (43b), however, treated it as being synonymous with *P.senilis*, believing light or dark colouring to be due to age and not to geographical variation.
*Distribution:* British Honduras and adjacent parts of Yucatan south to western Panama. Paul Slud found it to be abundant over much of Costa Rica in the humid life zones. It ranges from the lowlands to the slopes of the lower subtropical belt, above which it decreases rapidly in numbers. It usually inhabits semi-open areas such as those which have been partially deforested for plantations and field crops, alternating with stands of trees, blocks of woodland, wooded borders and slopes and open woodland, occasionally well inside forests. A few to several dozen are the numbers usually seen together. This species is apparently very noisy on the wing and has a rapid, twisting flight. In trees it is usually silent, except immature birds which keep up a ' distinctive dithering chatter '.

BRONZE-WINGED PARROT *(P.chalcopterus chalcopterus)*
*Description:* This is undoubtedly one of the most beautiful of South American parrots, although its beauty is often not immediately obvious. It must be seen in sunlight for its colours to be fully appreciated. The head, underparts and thighs are very dark, dull blue, with the exception of a small patch covering the throat and part of the upper breast. The throat is white and the feathers below are salmon-coloured or broadly edged with white. The mantle is also dull dark blue; the wings are bronze-brown, lighter on the shoulders and brilliant deep blue on the primaries. The upper side of the tail is dark bronzy-blue and brilliant deep blue, the underside being shiny blue of a richer shade than the body; the under tail-coverts are scarlet. The most beautiful feature is hidden until the wings are opened: the undersides are rich, bright skyblue. The rump is rich, deep blue. An unusual feature – the deep pink colouring of the bare skin surrounding the eye – is more reminiscent of a Bataleur Eagle than of a parrot! The beak is pale yellow and the iris is dark brown. Length: 10½in.

Immature birds have the head, back, scapulars and upper tail-coverts greenish and the feathers of the underparts brown, edged with dark green or blue. The upper wing-coverts are brown with lighter tips and green edges.

*Distribution:* North-western Venezuela in the Sierra de Perija, the upper tropical and subtropical zones of Colombia in the eastern, central and western Andes to north-western Peru.
*Remarks:* Formerly rarely imported, quite a number of consignments of this species have reached Britain during the past few years. Bronze-wings are well worth a place in any collection, where their unusual colours will provide a contrast to that of any other parrot. To appreciate to the full the beauty of their flight an aviary at least 15ft long is required; the bright skyblue of the under wing-coverts is then seen. Their vocal efforts are neither loud nor harsh but consist of a strange rasping noise. Unlike my other *Pionus*, the Bronze-wings will eat any small seeds offered – white millet, canary, hemp, linseed, etc.
*Breeding records:* I cannot trace any records of successful breeding. Eggs were laid by one of five birds living in a community aviary owned by Dr and Mrs Swaenpoel of Belgium during the winter of 1969-70. The hen of a supposed pair in a separate aviary also laid. These birds had been bought four years previously when they were very young. As *Pionus* usually take about four years to attain full adult plumage it may be that they are not sexually mature until that age. In 1971 two eggs were laid by one hen. One egg, which contained an almost fully formed chick was punctured; the other hatched but the chick died at 15 days, when it weighed nearly 80 grams. Its crop contained whole sunflower seed which was, perhaps, the cause of its death, as 15 days would appear to be an early age for it to have received whole sunflower. A second hen laid during July.

*P.chalcopterus cyanescens*
*Distribution:* Colombia, in the upper tropical part of Nariño.

DUSKY PARROT *(P.fuscus)*
*Synonyms:* Little Dusky Parrot, Violaceous Parrot, Violet Parrot
*Description:* The feathers of the crown and lores are bluish-black and the ear-coverts are black surrounded by very prominent buff streaks. The feathers of the chin, throat and lower cheeks are broadly edged with buff. Fine, hair like red feathers surround the cere. The feathers of the sides of the upper breast are dark brown edged with buff and the upper breast is mauvish-vinous, becoming a deeper, more reddish-vinous on the lower breast or even scarlet, as in two newly imported Duskies which I once saw. The thighs are dark brown

with vinous edges to the feathers and the wings are black, the feathers being faintly edged with dark brown. The under wing-coverts are a deep, rich blue and the under tail-coverts are scarlet. The flight feathers are a beautiful shade of violet and the secondaries are greenish. The rump and the middle of the tail are black, the terminal band of the tail being deep violet. The upper mandible is black with a yellow patch on either side of the base; the lower mandible is yellowish with a black tip. The bare skin surrounding the eye is blue and the iris is brown. Length: about 9½in.

*Distribution:* Venezuela, from the Caura River, east over the Guianas and south to the Amazon valley from the Rio Madiera to Pará and extending into northern Maranhão. In Colombia it is found in the upper tropical zone of the Peruja Mountains. In Guyana and Surinam it is said to be moderately common in forest areas.

*Remarks:* Russ described it as 'very rare' and it is still a rarity today. Chester and Amsterdam zoos have exhibited this species during recent years. One owned by Mrs Duncan of Dumfriesshire attacks her, yet her husband can safely handle it. Another belonging to F. Keen of Middlesex showed its dislike of his wife by attacking her ankles, yet it quickly became tame and refrained from this practice. It is one of the most delightfully tame parrots that I have seen, being as lively, fearless and friendly as a Budgerigar. It allowed itself to be handled for me to measure it, and permitted its owner to spread out its wings to reveal the richness of its colouring.

This is perhaps the most sought-after of the genus and is often considered to be the most beautiful.

CHAPTER 8

# AMAZON PARROTS

WITH the exception of the African Grey *(Psittacus erithacus)* 'Amazons' are the best known of the true short-tailed parrots. Most of them are of heavy build, varying in size from 10in to 17in. The colours of the head and, to a lesser degree, those of the wings and tail are the features that distinguish the various forms. Species have been rather generously bestowed on this genus; Peters recognised 25. Further study will undoubtedly show that the number could be reduced to perhaps 20 at the most.

The beak colour and that of the feet vary from almost white through every shade of horn to black. Some have well-developed eyelashes and these are most conspicuous in such species as the Blue-front because, like the beak and feet, they are black.

This is a group about which it is difficult to generalise. Perhaps in no other genus of neo-tropical parrots is the personality of the individual so strongly marked. Affectionate, unreliable, intelligent, demanding, mischievous, strong-willed, noisy, even dangerous: Amazons show all these traits and many more. Sydney Porter, who perhaps knew and understood more about these birds than anyone and hand reared many young Amazons taken from their nests in the wild, remarked that as they grew their personalities emerged as distinctly as children's.

*As pets.* Some Amazons make extremely good pets while others are quite unsuitable. Only young birds should be obtained for this purpose. They can be distinguished by the colour of the iris, which is a less definite colour. In adult Yellow-fronts, for example, the iris is orange with an inner circle of yellow; in young birds it is brownish. The plumage usually lacks the definite colours of the adult, especially on the head. Yellow-front babies have such a small area of yellow on the head that a ½p piece could cover it and Blue-fronts have perhaps only a small patch of blue on the forehead and very little yellow. In recently-fledged Yellow-fronts and other species with horn-coloured beaks the tip is still black.

It is interesting to note that, for some reason, some Amazons bred in captivity show almost adult plumage on fledging. Aviary-bred Yellow-fronts and Yellow-cheeks, to give two examples, have left the nest in plumage which resembles that of the adults except for its softer shades, yet their imported equivalents show the usual immature markings.

Young Amazons look most appealing and are usually tame and gentle, but their temperament bears no resemblance to that of a fit adult bird. For this reason I believe that children should never be allowed to have Amazons as pets. There are plenty of small parrots, such as *Brotogeris* and *Pionus*, which are ideal for children; Amazons are not. When they become sexually mature at about four years old they may, especially males, become very dangerous to handle and could seriously injure a child. In any case, children do not have the patience a pet Amazon requires. These birds are always liable to bite without warning or explanation, often being provoked by quick movements.

The most important aspect of the care of a newly-imported young Amazon is feeding. It is a regrettable fact that some newly-imported parrots die of starvation, due to ignorance on the part of their owner or dealer. It cannot be emphasised too strongly that few are able to eat hard seed. If they are not provided with soft food they will starve rather than eat seed and other items they may not recognise as food. It is, therefore, absolutely essential to provide nourishing soft foods. Nothing can compare in this respect with a baby food such as Farex to which sugar has been added and enough water to make the consistency smooth, but not sloppy or too firm. I have found that Amazons will take this without hesitation. Other beneficial food such as Bemax, glucose and vitamin drops can be added to the Farex. Boiled maize should also be given to young birds.

It may be some months before they take hard seed. Those that are slow in this respect will learn much faster if they can watch another parrot eating hard seed. A young Yellow-fronted Amazon I know of was obtained from a dealer in such poor condition that for months its life hung in the balance. During this time it was fed on hard-boiled egg and bread and milk and stubbornly refused all other foods. Not until a Yellow-cheeked Amazon was placed in a cage close by did it begin to eat hard seed. It then absolutely refused its former diet.

*Screaming:* Most Amazons, if they are fit, will indulge in regular periods of screaming which can be very frustrating for the owner. Music is especially likely to set off this annoying habit, so the only answer may be to remove the offender from the room while the record player or radio plays. Screaming induced by other reasons may stop if the bird is distracted by giving it a titbit, something to play with, or a twig to destroy. When all else fails the cage should be covered. To prevent parrots from disturbing the whole household by screaming in the early morning the curtains should be left closed all night.

*As aviary birds.* In the past the 'Green Parrot' or 'Amazon Green', as it was called, was almost invariably kept as a pet, its potential as an aviary bird being completely ignored. This state of affairs has only recently been remedied and the Yellow-front, now the most commonly imported member of the family, was bred in Britain for the first time as recently as 1967.

In an aviary Amazons' periods of screaming are usually confined to predictable sessions, especially for about half an hour in the early morning. If other parrots in a collection become unduly noisy for some reason Amazons are certain to join in. The harsh far-carrying shrieks and yells of a pair are good cause for annoyance on the part of near-neighbours, so this aspect must be considered carefully before these birds are bought.

Most Amazons spend more time climbing than flying and some seldom bother to fly, making a large aviary unnecessary. The majority will do well in an aviary 12ft or 14ft in length.

*Breeding.* The *albifrons* are the only members of the genus that are sexually dimorphic (the female lacks the red wing speculum), although in the *autumnalis* superspecies the male is often more colourful on the head. In the other birds the eternal problem of sexing is present. It is an undoubted fact that *some* hen Amazons display in an identical manner to the male, ie, they dilate the pupil, throw the carpal edge of the wing into prominence, spread the tail and sway from side to side, waving the head sideways at the same time.

Clifford Smith of Yorkshire, currently the most successful breeder of Amazons in Britain, who regularly breeds Yellow-fronts and has bred Double Yellow-heads and Vinaceous Amazons, informs me that the hens of his pairs display in identical fashion to the cocks. Boosey noted this when he bred Blue-fronts. Two other aviculturists with pairs of Amazons which they have seen mating but which have not produced eggs, have told me that they have never seen the hens

O

display. All one can safely assume is that display is no indication of sex. I believe the shape of the head is a fairly consistent feature in these birds, that of the cock having more height above the eye, although it is flatter and extends further back before dropping away to the neck. In hens the head is rounder, with little height above the eye, and drops away more steeply behind the eye.

Amazons take several years to reach maturity and their first breeding attempt often results in clear eggs. Vane's Yellow-cheeked Amazons first attempted to breed when three years old, but it would seem that four or five years is a more usual age. The Blue-fronts bred at Keston Foreign Bird Farm in 1940 and 1941 made no effort to breed until they were four years old and one first bred successfully in 1950. It was four years before four young Cuban Amazons at Keston showed any desire to nest.

The number of eggs laid varies between two and five. Incubation normally lasts 25 or 26 days and is carried out by the hen only. Boosey recorded that a cock Blue-front assisted in incubation (or did it just sit by the hen in the nest?) but this must have been an unusual occurrence.

It is well known that Amazons are the most treacherous of birds during breeding operations. The wise owner will therefore ensure that breeding pairs are placed in aviaries where they can be fed from outside. If the aviary is entered the intruder will almost certainly be attacked if the birds are nesting. Ex-pets are the worst offenders since they are quite fearless. While many parrots will tolerate nest inspection it would be foolhardy in the extreme to even contemplate it where Amazons are concerned.

If and when the young hatch they are fed by both parents and brooded by the hen at night until about three weeks before they fledge, usually at about 74 days old. Extras in the way of food that can be provided during the rearing period include cooked vegetables, boiled fish and bread and milk.

*Feeding.* Sunflower, also hemp, are the only seeds that most Amazons eat readily. All the usual seeds should be offered at first, especially to young birds, but it must be remembered that seeds form a fairly small part of their diet and that fruit, greenfood and protein-rich foods such as meat and cheese play an important part in it. These birds are passionately fond of meat; the way they devour it makes one wonder whether in the wild some small carrion is eaten. It may, however, be that the average parrot is so starved of protein that its system recognises the need for it. Writers of many years ago invariably stressed that meat was harmful and should never be given to parrots; this is quite incorrect. Several years ago I was looking after two cats while their owners were on holiday. I cooked some liver for them and placed a dish of this, to me, revolting mixture of liver, blood and gravy on the floor. At the time I had a Salvin's Amazon as a pet who, on glimpsing the dish of liver, something probably outside its range of experience (since I rarely eat meat), made a bee-line across the floor towards it and started to devour the contents as though they alone could save it from starvation! My present pet, a Yellow-fronted Amazon, enjoys nothing better than removing the meat from chicken bones and crunching up the bones.

The average Amazon eats seed not because it likes it (with the exception of sunflower) but because it is offered little else. Some fruit or greenfood must be provided daily. Apple and grapes are among the most suitable, but almost any fruit can be tried. A clod of grass with earth and roots attatched will provide much amusement, especially for birds that have to be left alone for long periods.

Biscuit and sponge cake are eagerly eaten by Amazons and can be offered regularly. They can also be given household scraps such as boiled potato.

## YELLOW-BILLED AMAZON PARROT *(A.collaria)*

*Synonym:* Red-throated Amazon.

*Description:* The forehead and lores are white, the white extending below the eye to the ear-coverts, which are dark bluish-green. Part of the cheeks, the throat and sometimes a wide collar extending around the neck, are dull pink. The feathers of the crown and nape are distinctly edged with black. There is some dark blue in the flights, the tail-coverts are yellowish-green and there is a band of the same colour at the tip of the tail, with yellow and pink at the base of the tail. The remainder of the plumage is green, brighter on the breast. The bill is pale yellow. Length: about 11½in.

This small Amazon, of rather slender build, could not be confused with any other species. Its colouring is very much duller than that of the Cuban Amazon. Sydney Porter noted that some specimens, which could have been males, had a few bright orange feathers at the bend of the wing.

*Distribution:* Jamaica.

According to Gosse (14) it feeds on fruit, even opening oranges for the pips, and cashew nuts for the kernels. He stated that it nests in tall trees, often hollow bread-nut trees: 'often the capacious and comfortable cavity chiselled out by the Woodpecker. Four eggs are usually laid; and when the green feathers begin to clothe the callow heads of the promising family they are too often taken by some daring youth, who, having watched the parent to her hole, climbs the giddy elevation. He feeds the young with ripe plantain or banana till they approach maturity, and their appetites can digest plainer food; for when grown they will eat almost anything.'

James Bond (6) states that it inhabits the forested hills and mountains but is rare in the Blue Mountains. It is apparently more widespread than *A.agilis,* the Black-billed Amazon.

In 1930, Porter judged it to be fairly plentiful by the numbers offered for sale in the Jamaican markets. On a later visit he bought three from natives. These birds greatly relished green peppers so hot that the merest taste would blister a human tongue. He also obtained two chicks only a few weeks old which were excessively fat and felt like 'downy bags of liquid'. The natives told him that the parents starve the young Amazons so that they are able to fly when they leave the nest. They were reared on a mixture of crushed biscuit, banana and paw-paw.

*Remarks:* A hundred years ago this species appears to have been not uncommon in confinement but it is now very rare. Greene wrote that it was 'met with occasionally in the dealers' shops on the continent of Europe, as well as in this country, where it is priced at from fifteen to twenty shillings'. In 1912, W. A. Harding described his Yellow-billed Amazon which was 'able to say a word or two and made an affectionate pet'. Whitley owned one in 1930. Its skin is in the British Museum, together with two received by the London Zoo in 1880. One lived for eight months, the other just over three years. Such short life-spans were common in captive Amazons of 100 years ago. Their requirements were not understood and they were subjected to the cruelty of having water permanently withheld.

The quietly-coloured Yellow-billed Amazon would be easily overlooked but I can recall having seen only three, one of which was exhibited at Rode Tropical Birds Gardens (labelled as a Cuban Amazon).

CUBAN AMAZON PARROT *(A.leucocephala leucocephala)*

*Description:* The forehead and crown are white, also a line below the eye. The hind neck – or even the whole of the back of the head – is blue. The dark green feathers of the entire upper parts are edged with black, also those of the head and neck (in which the black borders are particularly pronounced). The cheeks, lores and the upper parts of the breast are an extremely beautiful shade of rose-red; the ear-coverts are dark grey. The breast feathers are heavily edged with black, some being tinged with blue. There is a patch of vinous-red on the centre of the abdomen. The primaries are bright light blue on the outer webs, black on the inner webs. The tail-coverts are light green and on all but the four central tail feathers there is a large patch of cherry-red on both webs, also yellow in some specimens. Length: about 13in.

*Distribution:* Cuba and the Isle of Pines. According to James Bond (6), it inhabits remote woodlands in Cuba, in mountainous and low country. Elsewhere it is found in dense scrubby woods near sea level. In the *Red Book* it is stated that this species 'has now doubtless withdrawn, with the felling of woodlands, from a wide original range, but is still common in wilder districts of Cuba and the Isle of Pines'.

This Amazon has always suffered at the hands of Man. For generations the easily-located nests situated in palm trees were divided up among the natives, who hand-reared the young birds for shipping to Europe. Their flesh was considered to be good eating.

*Remarks:* Like all island Amazons, the Cuban is now very rare in aviculture but was formerly more frequently imported. Butler described it as 'not rare' and many years ago Canon Dutton believed that 'unless specimens be clever, £1 is ample at any time. They might be bought much cheaper'.

In 1970 there were a number in zoos, including 12 in nine zoos in the USSR, 13 in the USA (including nine in a private collection), eight in Germany, including six in East Berlin Zoo, 12 in Havana, four in Brazil, two in Puerto Rico and one in Wassenaar Zoo, Holland.

This is one of the most desirable of the Amazons. E. J. Boosey wrote of his (AM, vol. 60, 168): 'They are delightful aviary birds, being strong flyers and altogether very lively and active. They are also very vocal, uttering both morning and evening a wonderful medley of typically Amazonian cries. These, however, while very attractive when heard from a distance out of doors might prove rather deafening indoors, and this is one reason why I think these Amazons more suited to aviary than cage life.' Boosey described the display of the Cuban in which the male thrusts forward and slightly lowers his wings to bring the vivid blue of the flights into prominence.

Velma McDaniels' observations agreed with those of Boosey in that this Amazon enjoys flying, not climbing. At five months old her young ones had started to talk.

The Duke of Bedford recorded a strange friendship between a Cuban Amazon and an Adelaide Parrakeet (*Platycercus elegans adelaidae*). A young bird of the latter species which was bred at liberty and living free paired with a Cuban Amazon and nested in an oak tree. The Duke of Bedford made the surprising observation (AM, Third Series, vol. VII, 331): 'Unfortunately the parrot died or was killed before she had a chance of hatching the eggs.' He cannot surely have believed that the eggs from such a distant inter-generic cross would have been fertile!

The most recent reference I can find to this species in Britain is about one belonging to Mrs D. Webb of Bishop's Stortford. She wrote (*Birds Illustrated*, September 1963) that its diet consisted of sunflower seed, orange, apple, carrot, green peas and cabbage. It plucked itself slightly on the breast. Boosey's birds were fed on sunflower, peanuts, canary seed, groats and hemp and cubes of stale bread soaked in slightly sweetened diluted milk. They were very fond of apple and spinach beet. While rearing young the adults were provided with such extras as boiled potato and scrambled egg.

*Breeding Records:* The first recorded breeding of this species took place at the Keston Foreign Bird Farm in 1956. Two young were reared and the Avicultural Society medal was awarded. Boosey recorded in *Foreign Birds* (vol. 24, 182): 'The two young ones were splendid specimens, but their parents were very excited and over-possessive when they first left the nest; to such an extent that, in excess of fussing round them and preening them they managed to pluck the head of the first one which emerged almost bare, and to a lesser degree they did the same thing to the second one when it left the nest.'

In the USA Velma McDaniels bred the Cuban Amazon in 1960. Young hatched in 1959 died at the age of three weeks, so in 1960 they were reared by hand from the time they were three days old.

A hybrid between the Cuban Amazon and the Blue-fronted is said to have been reared by an Eclectus in Holland in 1885.

## BAHAMAS AMAZON PARROT *(A.l.bahamensis)*

*Description:* An altogether more striking bird than the Cuban

Amazon, from which it differs in having the colours generally brighter and the feathers more heavily edged with black, especially on the head. The under parts are green with a few scattered red feathers; the red on the throat is brighter and more extensive. The tail is entirely green, except the two outer feathers which are edged with blue and have a small area of red. It is slightly larger than the Cuban, ie, about 13in.

*Distribution:* Bahama Islands: Inagua, Acklin, Fortune, Abaco and Long Islands. In 1903, J. L. Bonhote reported (*Ibis*): 'They are now becoming very scarce, and are exterminated in most of their former haunts – viz. Abaco – and Long Island. A few may possibly still be found on Inagua; but I only know of their existence on an island the name of which I think it inadvisable to divulge.'

The *Red Book* gives the following information: 'No Bahama parrot has been seen in historical times on New Providence, or on Crooked Island, where bones have been found in a cave with associated Amerindian culture of about 3,000 to 1,500 years ago. On Abaco it was common in the 1930s, still in fair numbers around the south of the island in the 'forties, and perhaps hanging on in the 'fifties; but it has been lately sighted only once. On Acklin, where it was common in the 'thirties and held to be fairly common in the 'forties, it is now believed to be extinct. Only on Great Inagua does it still survive in any strength. The last remnant of the race is found in the northern part of this rather large and still relatively wild island . . . but though it is protected by law, the law is hard to enforce.'

*Remarks:* A rarity even in the early years of the century, it is never again likely to be available to aviculture.

J. L. Bonhote collected several of these handsome Amazons, the skins of which are in the British Museum. They are conspicuous for their superb condition; Bonhote must have been one of the few of his era to understand the requirements of these birds. He wrote of them (AM, New Series, vol. II, 1904, 240): 'The Bahama Amazon seems to have a great disinclination for flying, and even when in an aviary with full use of its wings it always prefers climbing. Presumably it is for this reason that we find these birds differentiated from their allies in islands but a few miles apart. . . .

'To my way of thinking there is only one satisfactory way of keeping Parrots, and that is to allow them to roam at will round a West Indian garden. Two that I brought over spent six months in that manner and were a delight to the eye as they climbed about among the thick foliage of the Bougainer Uia [*sic*] or sat preening themselves near the blossoms of the pink oleander, while I even learnt to appreciate (at a distance) the matutinal screams with which they welcomed the rising sun. As soon as they heard the clatter of plates denoting a meal they would solemnly stalk into the dining-room, climb on to the back of a chair and worry their nearest neighbour until they received their meal of bread, potato, or banana after which they would retire to the garden and patiently await their next meal.

'This was their only food and they seemed to thrive. When spring came round and the sapodillas began to open they betook themselves to the sapodilla tree and wrought untold havoc amongst the fruit, throwing down what they had no use for.'

*Breeding records:* When Bonhote brought his Bahama Amazons to England he kept them in adjoining aviaries. After about five years two birds were seen continually feeding each other though the wire so they were placed in the same aviary. During the following year the hen laid three eggs 'very similar in shape and texture to pigeons' eggs'. When the hen stopped visiting the nest it was found that one chick had hatched and died.

## CAYMAN ISLAND AMAZON PARROT *(A.l.caymanensis)*

*Synonym:* Grand Cayman Amazon

*Description:* Various authors have given means of identifying it from *A.l.leucocephala,* such as 'the pinkish-red tinge to the breast', 'forehead dull yellowish white, white not reaching to the eye', (incorrect – it reaches to the middle of the eye), etc. Porter described his birds as having 'the white on the forehead more restricted and being mixed with pink, black and yellow'. The examination of skins of both sub-species showed that there is considerable variation among individuals but both sub-species are basically so alike that no consistent distinguishing feature could be seen. It is slightly smaller, ie, about 12in.

*Distribution:* Grand Cayman Island, West Indies. In 1930 Sydney Porter thought that this Amazon was in danger of extinction because it had the smallest range of any parrot. It inhabited an area which suffered terrible hurricanes which took a great toll of bird life. The *Red Book* states that the Grand Cayman (*A.l.caymanensis*) and *A.l. hesterna* are 'restricted but not uncommon in their surviving range'.

*Remarks:* Imported into Britain on a few isolated occasions until about 1930. At the present time there is a pair in Washington Zoo.

Porter described (AM, Fifth Series, vol. 1 (1936), 7) his specimen as 'Extremely intelligent and inquisitive this Parrot reminds me more of a dog than a bird. As soon as the aviary door is opened in the morning, it will fly out into the birdroom, flying back and forwards until it is tired, when it returns to the aviary. Sometimes it will go round the other cages and aviaries, pulling out wires and knocking down pots and tins, for no matter how firmly a pot is fastened it will pull it out and haul it to the ground. If another aviary door be open, it will enter and make a short tour of inspection.

'It is the only species of "Amazon" which I possess which bathes freely. The other birds like to be sprayed, but this one loves to roll in the water pot and get thoroughly soaked. This bird is extremely fond of elder-berries, when I first had it, it would screech terribly if thwarted of anything, but now it seldom ever uses its voice.'

## CAYMAN BRAC AMAZON PARROT *(A.l.hesterna)*

*Synonym:* Little Cayman Amazon

*Description:* Said to be slightly smaller than *A.l.caymanensis*.

*Distribution:* The islands of Little Cayman and Cayman Brac in the West Indies. The *Red Book* states that it is restricted but not uncommon on Cayman Brac although very rare on Little Cayman Island.

## SALLE'S AMAZON PARROT *(A.ventralis)*

*Synonyms:* Hispaniolan Amazon, San Domingo Amazon

*Description:* The forehead and lores are white, the crown and the upper part of the cheeks are dull blue and there is a prominent patch of black on the ear-coverts. All the feathers of the head and mantle are distinctly, although narrowly, edged with black, also those of the breast. There is a patch of vinous-red on the abdomen and the thighs are bluish. The bastard-wing and primary-coverts are blue and this colour is particularly conspicuous on the outer webs of the flights. The tail is green, with blue on the outer webs of the outer feathers, yellow on the inner webs and red at the base. The bill is yellowish and the iris reddish. Length: about 12in.

*Distribution:* The islands of Hispaniola (San Domingo), Gonave and Grande Cayemite. According to James Bond (6), this species is still common in forested areas. Writing in the *Ibis* in 1897, Dr C. Christy observed that 'This Parrot is common in San Domingo. Round

Sanchez it was to be met with at every turn, flying out of its nesting hole in some old palm-tree or in small parties overhead, waking the echoes with their screeches.

'I can testify from personal experience that the flesh of this Parrot is very good eating, and it is much esteemed by the natives, whom I often met coming home with a string of half a dozen or more shot with their old muzzle-loaders.'

*Remarks:* A rare species in aviculture. In 1970 I saw single specimens in two zoos in Holland: Amsterdam and Tilburg. H. Murray had a pair for several years. In 1964 the hen laid three eggs which failed to hatch. He wrote of his pair (*Cage and Aviary Birds*, August 5, 1971): 'These Parrots settled down to eat seed, nuts, fruit, and to drink nectar. They were the only Amazons I know that would consume mealworms. They had about a dozen each of these daily all the time I had them, and they never had a day's illness . . .

'In temperament as well as in plumage, they differed from the general run of Amazons. Most have the curiosity and love of play of a puppy or a small child, a cheerful extrovertness, but these Salle's were of a rather sullen disposition.'

In 1936 Sydney Porter recorded that although this Amazon was far from common in the wild the natives kept specimens as pets, usually housing them in converted petrol tins and feeding them on mango skins and stale bread or sweet potato. They could be bought for as little as a dollar each and Porter bought three.

*Breeding records:* A pair in Jersey Zoo hatched one chick in May 1971 which was on the point of leaving the nest when the breeding was reported to me in July. On fledging it differed from its parents in its duller colours and yellow forehead.

YELLOW-LORED AMAZON PARROT *(A. (albifrons) xanthlora)*

*Description:* This species must, in my opinion, be considered as a member of the *Albifrons* group, from which it differs only in the blue crown, yellow lores and heavier scalloping. The forehead and part of the crown are white; the area surrounding the eyes (except in front) and the upper part of the cheeks are bright red. The ear coverts are black. The smaller upper wing-coverts along the cubital edge and the primary-coverts are scarlet in the male. The first primary is black, the next four being green at the bases and blue towards the tips; the inner primaries and secondaries are mainly deep blue. The two central tail feathers of the short square tail are tipped with yellowish-green, and the lateral ones are yellowish-green with crimson bases. The remainder of the plumage is deep green, heavily scalloped with black on the neck, mantle and upper breast. The beak is yellow. Length: about 10in, including the 3in tail.

The female is less colourful. According to Blake the crown is essentially blue, not white, there is less black on the ear-coverts and little or no red on the head or wings, which are green instead.

*Distribution:* Yucatán, especially in the eastern and central parts; Cozumel Island; formerly found in British Honduras.

*Remarks:* Rarely imported (or rarely identified) in Britain; apparently more frequently available in the USA.

SPECTACLED AMAZON PARROT *(A.albifrons albifrons)*

*Synonyms:* White-fronted Amazon, White-browed Amazon

*Description:* Differs from *A.a.nana* (see page 220) only in being slightly larger.

*Distribution:* The arid tropical zone of the Pacific coast from Sinaloa in Mexico to north-western Guatemala.

*Remarks:* Little appears to have been recorded about this species in confinement. G. A. Smith (pers. comm.) noted of his pair: 'In all the true breeding pairs of Amazons that I've yet seen one obvious difference between the sexes is the larger, bulkier, male compared with the slighter built female. In Spectacled Amazons this size difference is perhaps more pronounced, also the male has a great splash of red in the open wing – not apparent when closed. The hen has no red or just a few token feathers. What is most noticeable is the voice – no screaming or shrieking. Not that they are quiet; they emit Jackdaw-like " chacks " and ricochet-like " chows ".'

*Breeding records:* The Spectacled Amazon does not appear to have been bred in Britain. In the USA David West informed A. A. Prestwich in 1949 that 'Putman and Mrs Gilmer recently reared young'. In the same year V. Wright reported that his pair, which had bred previously, were incubating. In 1922 N. Taka-Tsukasa recorded that he had bred ' White-fronted Amazons ' in his outdoor aviaries in Japan.

SONORA WHITE-FRONTED AMAZON PARROT *(A.a.saltuensis)*

*Description:* It differs from *A.a.nana* in the more extensive blue on the head (mauvish rather than dark blue) which extends right down the nape of the neck. There is a bluish tinge to the breast, the feathers of which are not edged with black. Length: 9½in.

*Distribution:* North-western Mexico in the state of Sonora. Blake gives its distribution as southern Sonora, Sinaloa, and western Durango.

LESSER WHITE-FRONTED AMAZON PARROT *(A.a.nana)*

*Description:* It differs from *A. (a) xantholora* in having the lores red and, in the male, the whole of the area surrounding the eye red. In the female the red orbital ring is usually less well defined. The crown is white (with a small area of pale yellow in some specimens) followed by bluish-green. The ear-coverts are green. The wings are as described for *A. (a) xantholora* and the remainder of the plumage is green with narrow dusky edges to the feathers of the neck and upper breast. The beak is yellow and the iris is yellowish-white. Length: 9½in to 10in.

Females usually show scarcely any white on the forehead, have less red around the eye, and lack the red in the wing, or have very little. Immature males have less white on the forehead.

*Distribution:* South-eastern Mexico in the states of Chiapas and Yucatan, south-eastern Guatemala and British Honduras to Honduras, western Nicaragua and western Costa Rica.

According to Paul Slud (35) '. . . it is plentiful upward into the subtropical belt on the deforested slopes of the Guanacaste Cordillera. Its numbers become greatly reduced south of the head of the Gulf of Nicoya, and it does not seem to have been reported even as a straggler on the central plateau on the southern shore of Lake Nicaragua . . .

'The bird frequents open and semi-open country with scattered trees and stands of open woodland characteristic of the scrubby Guanacaste ranch lands. It occurs in twos and threes, also in larger groups, sometimes in large flocks. Its shallow wing beats, not fluttering above the horizontal, are typical of *Amazona*, but its continually veering flight, like that of an *Aratinga*, is not.'

*Remarks:* Most of the few White-fronted Amazons imported into Britain probably belong to this sub-species.

BLACK-BILLED AMAZON PARROT *(A.agilis)*

*Synonyms:* Active Amazon, All Green Amazon

*Description:* This small Amazon is all green, of a rich shade not found in any other Amazon, described by Porter as 'a rich dark shining laurel green'. The colour is darker, more bluish on the top of the head and the feathers of the neck are faintly edged with black. The ear-coverts are blackish. The primaries are mainly black, the secondaries blue, there is a scarlet patch on the lower edge of the wing on the first four primary-coverts and the inner webs of the lateral tail feathers are also scarlet. The underside of the tail is yellowish-green. The beak is greyish-black. Length: $10\frac{1}{2}$in. Immature birds are said to be of a less rich shade of green, and to lack the red on the primary-coverts which are green.

It is interesting to note that Porter described the hen of his young pair as lacking the red in the wing, yet I can find no other reference to this sexual difference.

I find this species reminiscent, in shape and size, of the *Pionus* parrots; it further resembles them in its dark ear-coverts, a feature found only in the 'island' Amazons.

*Distribution:* Jamaica. Gosse (quoted by Butler) described how: 'Flocks varying from half a dozen to twenty or thirty fly hither and thither over the forest, screeching as they go, and all alight together on some tree covered with berries. Here they feast, but with caution; on a slight alarm one screams, and the whole flock is on the wing, vociferous if not musical, and brilliant if not beautiful, particularly when the sun shines on their green backs and crimsoned wings. They generally prefer lofty trees, except when, in June, the ripe yellow plantain tempts them to descend, or when the black berry shines upon the pimento. Of the latter the flocks devour an immense quantity, and the former they destroy by cutting it to pieces with their powerful beaks, to get at the seeds.'

After Sydney Porter's visit to Jamaica, he reported (AM, Fifth Series, vol. 1 (1936) 73-79) this species had become so rare that he thought it to be the rarest of all Amazons, not even excluding the Imperial and Guilding's. It apparently moved about in certain restricted forested parts of the island at different times of the year, breeding in the deepest recess of the mountain forests. It had disappeared completely from the southern part of the island.

James Bond states that it is still found in the forested hills, but is absent from the eastern part of the island (Blue Mountains and John Crow Mountains). Its distribution sometimes overlaps with that of the Yellow-billed Amazon, which usually occurs at higher elevations.

The *Red Book* gives the information that it is 'less common and widespread than the yellow-billed parrot, and does not range so high in the mountains, being absent from the eastern (Blue Mountain) end of the island where the yellow-bill is common in some places. Neither species appears to be in danger of extinction'.

*Remarks:* Extremely rare in confinement. The London Zoo first exhibited this species in 1873 and is one of the very few of the world's zoos to have one at the time of writing. There is one in Kingston, Jamaica, and another in San Diego. Few have reached Britain. Sydney Porter was fortunate in obtaining a true pair, in perfect condition, just before he left Jamaica. They were only six to eight weeks old and very tame. They proved to be delightful birds and full of character. On seeing the syringe with which they were fed the hen would go into paroxysms of rage if she was not fed first, going instantly to the cage floor and proceeding to tear the paper to shreds with cries of rage! Porter observed: 'The cock is a good-tempered and lovable bird, while the hen is quick-tempered, peevish, and always ready to give a nasty nip. In fact, both seem to exhibit typically masculine and feminine traits.' On their arrival in England they were placed in a large aviary with 13 other Amazons, including an adult Active brought back from Jamaica.

PUERTO RICO AMAZON PARROT *(A.vittata vittata)*
*Synonym:* Red-fronted Amazon
*Description:* There is a narrow band of red on the forehead and an occasional red feather on the ear-coverts and cheeks. The throat is pinkish. Most of the feathers are edged with black, especially on the head, neck and upper breast, less conspicuously on the lower parts and mantle. The outer webs of the flight feathers are blue, also those of the tail feathers, which are yellowish at the tip, with a patch of red at the base (in some specimens). The bill is yellowish and the iris yellow. Length: about 12in.
*Distribution:* Puerto Rico. This is one of the most threatened of the island Amazons and hovers near the brink of extinction, yet as recently as the beginning of the century it was described as 'common'. Wetmore (43c) found it to be almost entirely frugivorous, feeding on wild figs and almost any other fruit in season. As late as 1903 children were kept from school to drive these birds out of the corn fields. In 1967 it was estimated that its numbers were reduced to 150. All those remaining are found in a reserve in the Lunquillo Forest, which has been set aside in an attempt to save this parrot.

The *Red Book* states: 'By 1931 it was a relict in the Sierra Lunquillo alone, where it survives in what is fortunately, now, the Lunquillo National Forest – comprising some 5,600 acres of the 8,500 acres (at most) of climax forest left in the whole of Puerto Rico. Its status here was still "present and safe" in 1943; and in 1958-60

several estimates by José Rodriguez Vidal and other experts estimated the world population of the species, all in the National Forest, at not more than 200. In the habitat available, this may prove to be a viable population – saved beyond doubt by forest dedication and protective legislation. Unfortunately, the Hispaniolan parrot has recently been introduced in Puerto Rico. Competition may result, further depleting the population of the indigenous species, already harassed by egg-eating margays, smallish tree-climbing wild cats introduced from Central America.'
*Remarks:* Always rare in confinement (although several specimens were exhibited at the London Zoo in the 19th century), it is never again likely to be seen in aviaries, with the exception of two birds in the zoo in Mayaguez in Puerto Rico.

CULEBRA AMAZON PARROT *(A.v.gracilipes)*
Extinct
*Description:* Similar to *A.v.vittata* but smaller.
*Distribution:* Formerly found on Culebra Island, east of Puerto Rico.
*Remarks:* According to the *Red Book*, although this form was common in 1899 it was extinct by 1912, even before it was formally named in 1915, and is known to science by only three specimens.

PRETRE'S AMAZON PARROT *(A.pretrei pretrei)*
*Description:* This is a most attractively marked Amazon. It is dark red on the forehead, the lores, area surrounding the eye, shoulders, outer edge of the wing, primary-coverts and the thighs (the latter a mixture of red and yellow feathers). It is mid-green, darker above (except on the head and neck), each feather edged with black, more heavily on the upper parts. There is no red wing speculum; the flights are rich cobalt and brownish-black. The outer tail feathers have yellowish tips and there is a small amount of vinous near the base of the tail. The iris is yellow, also the bill which has some orange-red near the base of the upper mandible. Length: 13in.

Some skin specimens examined, which were presumably immature birds and not females, showed less red, especially on the wings.
*Distribution:* Southern Brazil in the states of São Paulo and Rio Grande do Sul; Uruguay.
*Remarks:* Extremely rare in confinement. It was first imported in 1883 into Germany and was exhibited at the London Zoo in 1889. Whitley exhibited one at Paignton, but it seems to have become unknown to aviculture during recent years.

## TUCUMAN AMAZON PARROT *(A.p.tucumana)*

*Description:* It differs from *A.p.pretrei* in being green instead of red at the bend of the wing and on the metacarpal edge, on the lores and in the region behind the eye; ie, only the forehead and the primary-coverts are red. The thighs are yellow and red. The iris is orange. Length: 13in.
*Distribution:* North-western Argentina in the provinces of Jujuy, Salta and Tucumán. De Schauensee states that it is found additionally in south-eastern Bolivia in Chuquisaca and Tarija. It inhabits alder forest.
*Remarks:* There is a single bird of this species in Jersey Zoo.

## GREEN-CHEEKED AMAZON PARROT *(A. (autumnalis) viridigenalis)*

*Synonyms:* Mexican Red-headed Parrot, Red-crowned Parrot
*Description:* One of the most attractive of the Amazons, it has the forehead, crown and lores crimson, with the bases of the feathers yellow. The cheeks are very bright green. There is a small patch of blue or lilac behind the eye and the feathers of the hind-neck are tipped with lilac and black, those of the upper breast with black only. The primaries are blue-black and there is a large patch of red on the secondaries, which are blue and green. A broad, yellowish-green band tips the tail; there is no red at the base. The rest of the plumage is green, lighter below. The bill is pale horn colour and the iris yellow. Length: 13in. Immature birds have the red on the head restricted to the forehead, the crown being green or mixed with red feathers.

Karl Plath recorded (AM vol. 51, 55) owning a Green-cheeked Amazon with yellow shoulders and wondered ‘ if it could be a hybrid ’. This is most unlikely; the male of the pair at Birdland also shows this feature.
*Distribution:* North-eastern Mexico in the states of Nuevo Leon, Tamaulipas, San Luis Potosi and Vera Cruz. According to Blake (5), it is usually found at moderate elevations and is common in north-eastern Mexico. It is noisily conspicuous and not likely to be overlooked by the most casual observer.
*Remarks:* As is the case with most Amazons from Central America, this species is better known in the USA, where it is popular as a pet, than it is in Europe. It is seldom seen in Britain.
*Breeding records:* Whitley bred a hybrid between this species and

*A.albifrons* in 1934. The pair at Birdland, Bourton-on-the-Water, regularly have eggs but fail to incubate properly, doubtless because of the close proximity of the public.

FINSCH'S AMAZON PARROT *(A. (autumnalis) finschi)*
*Synonym:* Lilac-crowned Amazon
*Description:* The forehead and lores are deep maroon and the crown and the outer edges of the cheeks are lilac with a few green feathers interspersed. The feathers of the neck and breast are edged with black. The wings and tail are as described for *A. (a) viridigenalis.* Length: about 12in; its build is slim. The iris is orange.
*Distribution:* Southern Sinaloa and Durango south to Oaxaca. It is found in wooded foothills and mountains up to about 7,000ft.

In *Two Bird Lovers in Mexico*, C. W. Beebe described how, in 1904, near Barranca Vueltran 'Several times during our stay we saw a beautiful sunset flight of Finsch Amazon Parrots. A flock of two hundred or more, massed together as closely as possible, appeared high in air, alternately soaring and fluttering. Then the entire flock swung earthward in a magnificent loop, from wall to wall of the *barranca*, the delicate lavender edgings of the feathers showing plainly as they swept past with a loud whirr of wings, each little foot clenched tightly close to the tail feathers. Upward they went, swinging together with a grace and unison, of which one never gets a hint from caged specimens.' Beebe described this species as 'common' in the *barrancas* and in the low region about Colima.
*Remarks:* Rarely imported into Britain, but apparently better known in the USA where it is quite often imported.
*Breeding Records:* It has been bred in the USA on a number of occasions since 1951. In that year it was bred at San Diego Zoo. The incubation period was 28 days. At the age of five days the chick was removed from the nest and reared by hand as the parents had stopped feeding it. Of its development, Kenton Lint wrote (AM vol. 58, 24): 'The eyes were not fully opened until the eleventh day. When thirteen days old, feather tracts were in evidence for the first time on the wings and on the back. On the seventeenth day pin feathers showed for the first time.

'For a period of three months this baby was hand fed with a spoon on our regular Wheat-heart cereal formula used for all of the young Parrots, Cockatoos and Macaws that are raised by hand. At the age of four months he was eating well, and independent in the matter of feeding.'

The interesting fact about this breeding is that it took place when the parents were only three years old. They were obtained as young birds.

In 1954 Mrs F. Hubbell of San Diego recorded that she had bred two Finsch's Amazons that year. They left the nest after eight weeks. This parrot has been bred on other occasions in the USA. In 1970, R. Nelson of Coquille, Oregon, informed me that he had a 2½-year-old pair which was aviary-bred.

*A. (a.) woodi*
*Description:* It differs from Finsch's Amazon in having the green of the plumage less yellow. The red band on the forehead is narrower and more restricted and somewhat duller. It is slightly larger.
*Distribution:* South-eastern Sonora and south-western Chihuahua south to Babizos in the mountains of east-central Sinaloa.

## YELLOW-CHEEKED AMAZON PARROT *(A.autumnalis autumnalis)*

*Synonyms:* Primrose-cheeked Amazon, Scarlet-lored Amazon
*Description:* Few Amazons have a prettier arrangement of head colours. The forehead, part of the crown, the lores and the lower part of the cheeks are scarlet. The feathers of the upper part of the cheeks are orange-yellow with red bases, those of the crown and the nape of the neck being lilac towards the tip, with dusky edges. The wing speculum is scarlet and the primaries are blue-black and green. The tail is green with a yellowish-green band at the tip with blue on the outer edges. The bill is light horn-colour, dusky at the tip of the upper mandible. Length: 13½in.

Immature birds are generally described as having only a small amount of yellow on the cheeks, this area being mainly green; the red on the forehead is restricted and the feathers of the hind-neck lack the lilac tips. This feature distinguishes them from adults of *salvini*. Vane, however, described the plumage of the young bird reared by his Grey Parrot as being identical with that of the adults. Its eyes were dark. The iris of the cock was bright golden, that of the hen being dark brown.

The eyes of the Yellow-cheeked Amazon are one of its most striking features and were very accurately observed by Sydney Porter (AM, Fifth Series (1930), vol. VIII, 10): 'They are very large for the size of the Parrot, and are surrounded by a ring of pure white skin and set off by black eyelashes which give the bird a very soft and gentle expression.' He considered this species as 'the most beautiful of the Amazon Parrots'.

*Distribution:* South-eastern Mexico and northern Central America from extreme southern Tamaulipas, Puebla and Oaxaca south through eastern Guatemala, British Honduras and Honduras south to the Segovia River; Ruatan Island.

*Remarks:* Although this species is well-known in the USA it is unfortunately seldom seen in Britain. A single specimen has been in the possession of the London Zoo for several years.

Porter wrote of his: 'Though rather reserved the bird is not at all lacking in intellect; it has very little to do with other Parrots in the same aviary, but will savagely resent any attack made on it by another bird.' Vane found that his pair were quarrelsome with the birds in adjoining flights, as some young King Parrakeets (*Alisterus scapularis*) found to their cost.

*Breeding records:* In 1956 E. N. T. Vane recorded of his pair (*Foreign Birds*, vol 22, 95): 'Yellow-cheeked Amazons again had fertile eggs which failed to hatch. They talk a good deal, and are too interested in everything that goes on. When breeding the cock is very aggressive, and swears at anyone and anything. This brings the hen off to see what all the bother is about, and the result is perfect young, dead-in-shell. They have hatched on previous attempts. He is a real brute to his hen, and often knocks her about, but she seems to take this as some sign of affection, and puts up with his tantrums.'

This pair started laying when they were about three years old and laid fertile eggs for some years without ever hatching them. In 1956 a Grey Parrot in Vane's possession laid two clutches of eggs in an 18in square parrot cage. The following year the laying of her eggs coincided with laying by the Yellow-cheeked Amazon. The latter pair were housed in an 18ft flight with a nest-box outside the flight, covered with asbestos to prevent them gnawing their way through. However, during seven seasons they made no attempt to gnaw it. The two Amazon's eggs were removed and given to the Grey, who incubated them on the thickly-sanded floor of the cage. A third egg was removed from the Amazons on June 16. About June 19 the Grey started to soak her breast and thigh feathers every morning. When Vane floated the eggs in a bowl of warm water one sank and two floated. On June 23 one egg began to chip and a young bird could be heard squeaking inside. Shortly before mid-day the chick hatched, assisted by its foster mother, who very carefully cut the top out in a small circle, so that the young one wriggled through a hole leaving the shell in two clean pieces. One of the other eggs was infertile, the other being addled in the early stages of incubation. The fertile egg was incubated for 25 or 26 days.

The chick was brooded very closely, although the Grey made no attempt to brood it during the first 24 hours when she repeatedly cleaned it. She moved it about by lifting it by the head. The usual seeds were supplied, also bread and milk to which Abidec had been added, soaked brown bread, sprouted seeds and greenfood.

The unique account of the rearing of this youngster is of such interest as to be worth quoting in full (AM vol. 63 1957, 187): 'The first feed was given on the second day. The young bird was lifted bodily by the head, and the point of the parent's upper mandible was then gently inserted into the small gap of the youngster's mandibles right at the rear. . . . She then trickled liquid down her tongue into the opposite side of the baby's mandibles. Once the young bird started feeding thus, this procedure was no longer necessary and as soon as the mother clucked the young one instinctively raised its head and gaped ready to accept its food. Taking the tips of the mandibles in her beak the mother then applied the usual pumping action or regurgitation and one could actually watch the young one's crop fill out. At this stage feeding was carried out with unfailing punctuality every two hours. The consistency of the crop milk was about the same as that of ordinary milk. For practically the whole of the first two weeks the Grey brooded continuously, but thereafter left the nest for longer and longer periods. Feeding intervals were slowly increased in frequency, but decreased in bulk. During this time, too, the consistency of the food was also thickened. By this time the young bird was becoming very intelligent and knew full well that every time mother had something to eat it would get a taste, and it was not backward in asking for its share.

'At about ten days, the eyes began to open, and quills began to appear. At this stage we were a little apprehensive that the difference in colour might upset the mother. We need not have concerned ourselves, however, as "Polly" was a most attentive and competent parent. The floor of the cage became littered with seed husks, but no attempt was made to clean it out for the first month as I was away at the time, and no one else dared put a hand inside the cage. This applied whether she had a youngster or not. At a month old the squab resembled nothing more than a dirty looking pin-cushion, and was extremely awkward-looking and ugly, but "Polly" thought it was the loveliest thing that ever happened, and she spent hours cleaning it.

'The young one grew rapidly, and as the feathers opened out the young bird was deliberately taught to preen itself and was always in spotless condition. The plumage was complete at seven weeks, exactly similar to the adult bird's, except that the flight and tail feathers were not fully developed. The young bird was just over eight weeks old when it first succeeded in climbing on to the central perch – an age at which it would normally have reached the stage of peeping out of the nest hole. Its bill was blackish on the upper mandible, yellowish at the edges and towards the point. The eye was dark and the feet grey. On its breast it has a few yellowish feathers. The fact that its plumage is similar to the adult was interesting, as according to some accounts many Amazons are reputed to be all green when immature, and to assume full colour when a year or more has passed.'

## SALVIN'S AMAZON PARROT *(A.a.salvini)*

*Description:* It differs from *A.a.autumnalis* in having the cheeks and ear-coverts bright green; the red of the lores does not extend below the eye. Some specimens from Costa Rica and Nicaragua have a distinct but small area of yellow on the lower part of the lores. Immature birds have less red on the forehead. Length: 14in.

*Distribution:* Eastern Nicaragua and eastern and south-western Costa Rica to northern Colombia; Pearl Islands.

Paul Slud states that this species occurs in extensively forested and partially deforested regions, plantations and clearings with trees. Birds departing from and returning to their roosting site fly in loose flocks, individual pairs well separated from one another. Wetmore states (43b) that they feed on figs and other fruits, occasionally with macaws.

*Remarks:* During recent years the Salvin's has been imported into Britain frequently and has been available at most times. It is an attractive bird but cannot rival the beauty of the Yellow-cheeked Amazon. Unfortunately, like the latter it has one very great drawback: its vocal powers. It is one of the noisiest of a noisy family. On one occasion a passer by knocked at my door believing that the loud yelping noises issuing from my garden were being made by an ill-treated puppy; a Salvin's Amazon was the culprit.

This bird once lived in the bar of a well-known public house in the London area, where he was named " Crispy " due to his addiction for crisps! He was then taken into the home of one of the employees and, finally, passed to me as a biter, being unsafe for a home with young children. He was very quick to make friends and for some time proved an ideal pet, discounting his regular periods of yelling and shrieking. Nearly two years later I bought from a consignment as it arrived at a dealer's premises a Salvin's I believed to be a hen, which had irregular patches of yellow in its plumage. This was probably due to a dietary deficiency and a year later, after a second moult, all traces of yellow had disappeared from the plumage.

I wondered what the male Salvin's reaction would be to a probable female of his own species. The hen provided an amusing incident when they were introduced – she took one look at him and gave an exaggerated wolf-whistle. This apparently good omen was a false one. For over a year the two Salvin's were given the freedom of a room with a Panama Yellow-fronted Amazon; the two birds became inseparable and would have nothing to do with the original Salvin's. This resulted in unfortunate repercussions about two months later. The original Salvin's was so jealous of the other two Amazons that he began to attack me in precisely the same way that the cock of a breeding pair will attack an intruder in its domain. He was particularly dangerous when he descended to the floor where he would rush after me (cackling with glee!) and attack my ankles. These attacks became so serious that I did not dare to wear any lighter footwear than fashion boots, as he would sink his beak in and hang on for grim life. Normally a very lovable – and rather a cowardly – bird who could be intimidated by a raised voice he was transformed into a feathered demon who did not hesitate to fly at my face (on one occasion narrowly missing an eye) using beak and claws in the attack. Such behaviour from an Amazon in breeding condition is to be expected, which is why owners of nesting pairs avoid entering the aviary. Eventually I was able to house the Salvin's in an outside aviary and the two birds quickly became friendly towards each other. The probable hen has spent much time inside the nest-box during the past three summers but as yet no eggs have been laid.

## LILACINE AMAZON PARROT *(A.a.lilacina)*

*Synonym:* Lesson's Amazon

*Description:* It differs from *A.a.salvini* in the colour of the cheeks which are pale yellowish lime-green, in having the lavender feathers of the crown (not the nape) edged with pale reddish and in having a narrow crimson streak above the eye. In the only adult specimen

I have seen the nape feathers were heavily edged with black. Length: 13in. The beak is black – another distinguishing feature.

In 1934 Andrew Wilson described an abnormal bird of this species in his possession, whose general colour was green, heavily mingled with yellow feathers (a common aberration). Of interest, however, was the brick-red crown and the neck feathers which were blackish, with no suggestion of lilac.

*Distribution:* The tropical zone of western Ecuador.

*Remarks:* A rarely imported sub-species, although probably few would identify it correctly. On following up a dealer's advertisement for a 'Golden-cheeked Amazon' I discovered that the bird advertised was, in fact, a most attractive young Lilacine.

In 1920 a Liverpool dealer, who in a period of 40 years had handled probably more Amazons than anyone else, failed to recognise one he received. It must therefore have been very rare in the trade then.

While in Ecuador, Goodfellow collected a single specimen before 1915 for E. J. Brook. It delighted in sitting on its owner's knee or shoulder and gently nibbling at his ear until its head was scratched.

DIADEMED AMAZON PARROT *(A.a.diadema)*

*Description:* Its plumage differs little from that of *A.a.salvini* but it can be distinguished at a glance by the small – almost hair-like – red feathers which cover the cere and nostrils. In the Salvin's the nostrils are uncovered. (This fact was made known by Herbert Whitley and illustrated by his photographs (AM Fourth Series, vol. VII (1934), 305.) On examination of the two skins in the British Museum (one of which was the bird in Whitley's collection), the only difference I noted in the plumage in comparison with *A.a.salvini* is the break in the crown colouring, the centre of the crown being green and the surrounding feathers dark green edged with lilac. In *A.a. salvini* all the feathers of the crown are edged with lilac. Length: about 14in.

*Distribution:* North-western Brazil from the Solimoẽs eastward to the Barra do Rio Negro.

*Remarks:* Very rarely imported. I once saw one in a consignment of Salvin's which passed unnoticed by the dealer; undoubtedly it is imported, unrecognised, from time to time. Miss Maud Knobel owned two, one of which went to the London Zoo where it lived until about 1966.

## DUFRESNE'S AMAZON PARROT *(A.dufresniana dufresniana)*

*Description:* There is a narrow band of colour varying from gold to orange on the forehead and lores. The crown is yellowish-green or green, the cheeks being mauve and the throat bluish or green, and the breast bluish. There is a patch of colour varying from fiery orange to yellow on the wing and the flights are dark blue. The remainder of the plumage is dark green with the exception of the outer tail feathers which are edged with mauve, the tip of the tail being greenish-yellow. The bill is dusky, with red at the base of the upper mandible. The iris is red. Length: 14in.

I have never seen this species alive, but judging by the skins it must be an extremely beautiful bird.

*Distribution:* Guyana, Surinam and Cayenne. In Guyana this species is said to be restricted to the cooler, elevated forests of the interior and is not common. Haverschmidt (18) described it as 'less numerous than *A.farinosa* and occurring in small flocks' in Surinam.

*Remarks:* This species is now almost unknown to aviculture. It has been exhibited at London and Paignton Zoos, but has always been rare in confinement. E. McLoughlin while in Guyana cared for a Dufresne's for a month. He described it as being extremely quiet and gentle and noticed that it appeared to suffer more than other species from the coastal heat. In 1971 a single Dufresne's Amazon was imported into Britain.

## RED-TOPPED AMAZON PARROT *(A.d.rhodocorytha)*

*Synonyms:* Red-browed Amazon, Red-capped Amazon, Red-crowned Amazon.

*Description:* It differs from *A.d.dufresniana* in the following respects: there is less mauve on the cheeks which vary from skyblue to a mauvish-blue; the feathers of the crown are green edged with dark red; the forehead is scarlet, mixed more or less with yellow (probably less in females which, judging by the six skins examined, are less brightly coloured, especially on the head); the speculum is red (not orange) and the tail green, lighter at the tip, with a red patch towards the inner web of all but the upper three tail feathers. Length: 14in.

Immature birds have a much smaller amount of red, lighter in shade, on the tail. The feathers of the crown are only slightly tinged with red and there is less red on the wing.

*Distribution:* South-eastern Brazil from southern Bahia to Rio de Janiero.

36 The Salvin's Amazon *Amazona autumnalis salvini* is regularly imported into Britain. This one was kept as a pet by the author for several years before it was provided with a mate.

37 Rare in aviculture is the Rothschild's Amazon *Amazona barbadensis rothschildi* not, as the scientific name suggests, from Barbados, but from the islands of Bonaire and Blanquilla off the coast of Venezuela. Owner: London Zoo.

38 The Green-cheeked Amazon Parrot *Amazona autumnalis viridigenalis* is also known as the Mexican Redhead and is particularly popular as a pet in the USA. Owner: Roy Nord.

39 The Lilacine Amazon Parrot *Amazona autumnalis lilacina* differs from the Salvin's Amazon in the pale lime green colour of the cheeks. Owner: Mrs N. Howard.

40 The magnificent Guilding's Amazon Parrot *Amazona guildingii* is one of the island species whose numbers have always been alarmingly low. When this bird was imported in 1971 it was the first Guilding's Amazon to be seen in Europe for many years. Owner: A. V. Marques.

41 The Double Yellow-headed Amazon Parrot *Amazona ochrocephala oratrix* is the largest of the Amazons normally available. This one was photographed in Cologne Zoo.

42 One of the most familiar of all parrots is the Panama Yellow-fronted Amazon *Amazona ochrocephala panamensis*. It is frequently kept as a pet. Owner: author.

*Remarks:* This attractive bird is, unfortunately, rarely imported. The only specimen I have seen was a pet bird belonging to a family in Paris. One reached the London Zoo in 1879 but lived only one month.

RED-TAILED AMAZON PARROT *(A.brasiliensis)*
*Synonyms:* Blue-faced Amazon, Brazilian Green Amazon
*Description:* The whole of the top of the head, including the lores, is an unusual shade of pinkish-red; this feature alone distinguishes it from all other Amazons. The cheeks, throat, ear-coverts and upper breast are dull greyish-blue, dusky on or behind the ear-coverts. The metacarpal edge of the wing is red and the wing feathers have pale or yellowish-green edges. The primaries are black and deep blue and the under tail-coverts are yellowish-green. There is no red wing speculum. The tail is most unusual and has a band of yellow at the tip, followed by another of carmine red, with purplish-blue towards the base. The bill is a pale horn-colour, dusky at the tip of the upper mandible. Length: about 14in.

Salvadori (32) described a female with less pinkish-red on the head the feathers being yellowish-green edged with red, in that area. The pinkish-red was nearly confined to the lores and forehead. The feathers of the cheeks were dusky-green with purple-blue tips.
*Distribution:* southern Brazil from São Paulo to Rio Grande do Sul.
*Remarks:* This beautiful and unusual Amazon is almost unknown to aviculture and is also rare in skin collections. It was exhibited at the London Zoo in the 19th century and there was one in England in 1916. Probably the only one imported in recent years is that which was owned by P. H. Maxwell of London from 1958 to January 1968. (There is an excellent coloured photograph of this bird, AM vol. 66, 1.) He obtained it from a woman whose son brought it back from Brazil. It was a clever mimic and talker.

BOUQUET'S AMAZON PARROT *(A.arausiaca)*
*Synonyms:* Blue-faced Amazon, Lesser Dominican Amazon, Red-necked Amazon
*Description:* The forehead, part of the crown, lores, part of the cheeks and the throat are violet-blue (which colour usually fades to a dull blue in skins and, apparently, in birds in aviaries). The middle of the lower throat or even the whole of the upper breast is red, with a few yellow feathers in some specimens. Most of the green feathers are edged with black. The red wing speculum is present and the

primary-coverts are very dark green, almost black; the primaries are black and deep blue, tinged with green. The upper and under tail-coverts are yellowish-green and there is a broad greenish-yellow band at the tip of the tail. There is red at the base of the first four tail feathers and the outer ones are edged with blue. The bill is a light horn-colour with the base of the upper mandible yellowish. Length: about 16in.

While in Dominica Sydney Porter saw birds which had neither red nor yellow on the upper breast, and some which had a few feathers only of either colour. Others had the whole of the upper breast either red or yellow, so the amount of colour in this area probably increases with age. In Porter's pair the male was very much larger than the female and nearly as large as a small Imperial Amazon. He reported that a lutino had been seen in the wild (and shot and eaten).

*Distribution:* Dominica, West Indies.

Sydney Porter wrote (AM Fifth Series, vol. VIII (1930), 36) '. . . while the Imperial Parrot keeps to the most inaccessible parts of the mountain forests of Dominica, this bird at certain seasons of the year comes down into open country – in fact, right down to the sea coast – in search of certain fruits, and is consequently much better known than the other bird, and this would give the stranger the impression that it is the commoner of the two. It is certainly easier to capture or, rather shoot, but in a few years I am sure that it will pass away for ever.'

*Remarks:* Always an extreme rarity in aviculture, it is unknown at the present time. *The International Zoo Year Book* lists, in error, a male and two females in Jersey Zoo; the species exhibited there is *A.ventralis*.

Sydney Porter obtained a pair in Dominica (before 1930). The birds had been in the possession of a native for 12 months. The man had shot 30 birds before he wounded two so slightly that they lived. In Dominica they are, or were, killed for making soup, the flesh usually being too dry and insipid for roasting, although on occasions even white people bought them for eating. Shooting was the only method the natives knew of obtaining them. Porter did his utmost to have the precarious population of Bouquet's Amazons protected.

Before leaving Dominica he managed to obtain three more birds, one of the original pair having escaped. Two were terribly wounded and tied up with rope, but they quickly recovered. Great difficulty was experienced in weaning them from a diet of sugar-cane, so a hundredweight of this food was put in cold storage on the boat at Barbados on the way home. Fortunately, soon after setting sail they began to feed on soft fruits smuggled from the dining saloon.

One of the hens died soon after reaching Britain, due to the gun-shot wound received in Dominica, and another died from a diseased spleen. The older bird Porter described as a magnificent specimen and the most intelligent parrot he had ever had. 'When one enters the aviary he is always ready for a game. Hanging from a slender branch by one foot, he will seize hold of one's nose, ear or hair, with the other foot and kiss one's lips. He loves to tease the other parrots especially a large hen of his own species, but he is never malicious, though sometimes when excited he will give an extra hard nip . . .

'I believe Bouquet's Parrot is the most delicate, in spite of its large size, of all the Amazon Parrots, and needs to be kept in a high temperature or it will soon go wrong. When the thermometer falls below 70 degrees the birds appear dull and lifeless, but when it reaches 80 or over they soon regain their *joie de vivre*.

'For food they require an abundance of fresh ripe fruit, such as pears, apples, grapes, etc.; they are very fond of hawthorn-berries and also elderberries; I also give them ordinary Parrot mixture.'

Excluding Porter's birds, probably less than half a dozen specimens have ever been imported into Britain, including one received by the London Zoo in 1900, a pair collected by W. A. Harding in the early years of the century and one bought by Spedan Lewis in 1929.

## FESTIVE AMAZON PARROT *(A.festiva festiva)*

*Synonym:* Red-backed Amazon Parrot

*Description:* There is a narrow line of maroon from the frontal edge to the eyes; the rest of the forehead is green and there is a bluish tinge on the crown and below the maroon stripe, with a dark blue streak above the eye. The cheeks are green and there is a small patch of blue on the throat. There is no red wing speculum but the lower back and rump are crimson, the feathers being yellow at the base (this colour is not seen unless the feathers are parted). The remainder of the plumage is mid-green, slightly darker above, with the edges of the outer tail feathers bluish and the tip of the tail yellowish-green. The iris is yellow-orange and the beak is black. Length: about 14in.

*Distribution:* Eastern Ecuador and eastern Peru to the Rio Negro, upper Rio Branco and the lower Madeira. It has been recorded in Guyana on two or three occasions only.

*Remarks:* This Amazon is one of the less often imported species although it cannot be described as rare. Little seems to have been recorded about its habits.

*Breeding records:* I can trace no breeding records for this species except the hybrid cross between a cock and a Yellow-billed (*A.collaria*) hen. The three youngsters all took after the cock in appearance.

## BODIN'S AMAZON PARROT *(A.f.bodini)*

*Description:* It may be distinguished from *A.f.festiva* by the crown, which is a mixture of red, green and blue, by the bluish-green or blue cheeks and the red rather than maroon forehead; also by the bluish, rather than rich dark blue, flights. It is a slightly lighter green below and darker, more olive, above. Bates and Busenbark (2) state that the rump is green but this is definitely incorrect. Salvadori (32), however, described such a bird under the name of *Chrysotis chloronata*, from two *adult* skins, one having been collected in Yquitos (upper Amazons). It is likely, however, that these green-rumped birds were not fully adult and that this is nothing more than the juvenile plumage.

It is interesting to note that Hopkinson (AM Fourth Series, vol. V (1927), 321) described 'a red-backed Amazon' midway between *festiva* and *bodini*; it has no blue cheeks and no black scallop-edges to the nape feathers, and is exactly as depicted in one of the two plates Reichenow gives of *bodini*, explaining that the first was incorrectly coloured. Whether this was so or not, there are now three red-backed birds to be seen at Paignton in Herbert Whitley's collection, each equally distinct from the other, and exactly representing the three plates in Reichenow.'

*Distribution:* Middle Orinoco River in Venezuela eastward to the Barima River, north-western Guyana.

*Remarks:* Seldom imported or correctly identified.

Sydney Porter bought one in Trinidad which he described (AM, 1930, 9) as 'a sweet, gentle little creature, perhaps the tamest Parrot I have ever possessed, delighting to come on one's shoulder, nestling up against one's neck, and gently playing with one's ear. She, for it is a hen, never in moments of excitement gives one a good nip like most other Parrots do. She is very fond of being put out in the garden on warm days, when she will imitate all manner of animals – cats, dogs, fowls, etc. – and holds long unintelligible conversations with herself.

'The chief beauty of this bird lies in the lovely crimson back, which can only be seen when it flies. Though the bird is often out in the garden all day it never wanders away. It is very fond of bathing in the wet foliage or of rolling over in the grass during a shower.'

YELLOW-FACED AMAZON PARROT *(A.xanthops)*
*Synonym:* Yellow-bellied Amazon, Yellow-crowned Amazon
*Description:* I have seen neither a living specimen nor an adult skin so will quote Salvadori (32): '*Adult.* Green, the feathers with darker edges; under surface and upper tail-coverts yellowish-green; head yellow, a broad band across the abdomen yellow; on the sides an orange-red spot; primary-coverts green; outer webs of the primaries bluish-green; central tail feathers green, the lateral ones with the apical half greenish-yellow and the basal half orange-red; the outer tail-feathers green on the outer web: bill dusky yellow.' Length: $10\frac{1}{2}$in.

Immature birds have much less yellow on the head, usually confined to forehead, lores, the area surrounding the eye and the ear-coverts. The remainder of the head is light green, each feather, also those of the neck and breast, being tipped with dark green. The upper parts are olive green.
*Distribution:* Eastern and central Brazil in the states of Mato Grosso, Goyaz, southern Piauhy, Bahia, Minas Geraës and northern São Paulo.
*Remarks:* Extremely rare in aviculture. Single specimens have been exhibited by Herbert Whitley (1927), London Zoo (1937) and Hagenbeck's at Stellingen.

YELLOW SHOULDERED AMAZON PARROT *(A.barbadensis barbadensis)*
*Description:* The forehead is white, merging into yellow on the crown, the lores and the area surrounding the eyes. (Some specimens show a pronounced pinkish tinge on the bases of the yellow feathers of the crown.) There is a distinct bluish tinge where the yellow feathers meet the green ones, especially at the side of the lower mandible. The upper parts are dark green, the feathers of the mantle and upper breast being heavily edged with black. The feathers of the lower parts are less distinctly edged with black. (In one skin specimen examined, labelled as a male, the feathers of the underparts were edged with very rich light blue; in fact, the areas which are bluish in normal specimens were pronounced and its colours were altogether brighter.) The area surrounding the vent is bluish. The

shoulders are very bright yellow, with a larger area of colour than is found in most other Amazons; the thighs are also yellow. Bright blue is the colour of the flights and the red wing speculum is present. There is a patch of red near the base of the tail and a broad yellow band near the tip. The beak and cere are almost white and the iris is orange with an inner ring of yellow. Length: 13in.
*Distribution:* The island of Aruba, off the coast of Venezuela, also sporadically along the littoral coast, particularly in the semi-arid regions of the Paraguana Peninsula. (Erroneously named *barbadensis* and attributed to Trinidad.) In the early years of this century this species was described as not rare in the wild, but shy and not easily obtained in any numbers. Its population, however, decreased rapidly, probably due to the disappearance of suitable habitat through the extension of the oil-refinery industry. In 1955 K. H. Voous listed it as extinct, as he had been unable to trace it on the island, but two specimens were observed in or before 1957.
*Remarks:* Needless to say this species is a great rarity in aviculture. Probably most of those said to be *A.b.barbadensis,* including the single specimen at London Zoo at the present time, the pair kept for several years by Mrs Howard of Wolverhampton and the female obtained by P. H. Maxwell in 1950, are actually *A.b.rothschildi.*

ROTHSCHILD'S AMAZON PARROT *(A.b.rothschildi)*
*Description:* The yellow on the head and shoulders is generally more restricted than in *A.b.barbadensis* and the cheeks and the throat are largely glaucous green. The yellow at the bend of the wing is said to be deeper in colour and often flecked with red.
*Distribution:* The islands of Bonaire and Blanquilla, off the coast of Venezuela, where it apparently breeds on rocks as well as in hollow trees.
*Remarks:* See under *A.b.barbadensis.*

BLUE-FRONTED AMAZON PARROT *(A.aestiva aestiva)*
*Description:* The forehead and lores are blue; the crown, the area surrounding the eyes, sometimes part of the cheeks, the throat and, in some individuals, even part of the upper breast, also the thighs, are yellow. The primaries are blue and black with a prominent red speculum. The bend of the wing is red, or red and yellow (see page 239). There is a broad yellowish-green band at the tip of the tail and a red patch at the base of the lateral feathers. Many of the feathers, especially those of the neck and upper breast, have black

edges. The beak and cere are black; the eye-lashes are more prominent than in most Amazons, perhaps because they too are black. Length: 14in to 15in.

E. J. Boosey, the first and, to date, the most consistent breeder of Blue-fronts in Britain, believed that these birds could be sexed by the colour at the bend of the wing. He observed (AM vol. 55, 113): 'During the display, however, the wings are slightly lowered and thrust forward by both sexes, thereby bringing these patches of colour into prominence. At present we have eight Blue-fronted Amazons at Keston, and in each case the colour patches are either pure crimson or crimson at the back shading through orange into bright yellow in front.

'In both the nesting pairs the cocks have precisely the same tri-coloured wing patches, while in the hens they are pure crimson.' This is by no means a consistent feature, however; I have seen the cock of a proved breeding pair with red only at the bend of the wing, also presumed but not proved cocks with this feature. Autopsies carried out on six young birds showed the following colour patterns:

| Sex | wing butts | colour of face | width of lower mandible | wing length |
|---|---|---|---|---|
| Male | red – very little yellow | mostly yellow – little blue | 20mm | 22.2cm |
| Male | yellow | mostly yellow – little blue | 21mm | 22.2cm |
| Male | yellow, red sprinkled | very yellow – little blue | 21mm | 21cm |
| Female | red, very little yellow | mostly yellow – little blue | 19mm | 20.8cm |
| Female | yellow, red sprinkled | mostly yellow – little blue | 19mm | 21.2cm |

Several lutino Blue-fronts have been recorded. The Duke of Bedford secured one in 1925. He described it as having the areas which are green in a normal bird of a deep golden-yellow, the normally blue areas replaced by white, and the red retained. The eye was pink and the beak and feet cream-coloured. This bird was believed to be a hen and was provided with several mates, but never attempted to breed.

A coloured plate in Bates and Busenbark's *Parrots and Related Birds* shows a mutant Blue front which is mainly yellowish olive-green, with pale blue on the head and the usual red at the bend of the wing.

*Distribution:* Brazil, from Piauhy and Pernambuco to Rio Grande do Sul.

*Remarks:* Until comparatively recently this was the most commonly imported of all true parrots, reaching Britain in immense numbers. In 1924, for example, Chapman's received one importation consisting of 573 Blue-fronts! For several centuries this must have been the best known of all parrots. In recent years, however, the numbers reaching Britain have decreased to a fraction of their former number.

It is seldom kept as an aviary bird; its talents as a talker, mimic and general entertainer are too well known. With the exception of the African Grey no parrot has more often been kept as a pet in Britain. It is apparently much less common in the USA. Countless amusing stories have been told illustrating the intelligence and powers of mimicry of this species.

*Breeding records:* The first recorded breeding took place in the 1880s in France. A Monsieur Renouard bred three young from a pair brought by him from Buenos Aires. The eggs were said to have taken 30 days to hatch and the young remained in the nest for 62 days.

In Britain the Avicultural Society's medal for the first breeding was awarded for the rearing of five young at the Keston Foreign Bird Farm in 1939. In 1940 four more were reared, and in 1941 one only. From 1943 onwards it was attempted to breed second generation Blue-fronts, but this was not achieved until 1950. A hen from the original brood was paired with an unrelated cock and four young were reared. The aviary used was about 15ft long and the nest chosen was of the grandfather clock type. While the young were in the nest the diet was supplemented with such extras as boiled carrots and potatoes, scrambled egg and boiled white fish. Although the colouring of each young bird differed considerably, they all had pure red shoulder patches.

Boosey found that his young birds made no attempt to nest until they were four years old. On one occasion the cock is said to have shared in the incubation. In Boosey's experience males of this species quickly take to a newly introduced female and do not even need to be caged within sight of their prospective mate. One cock in his possession, however, was not so reliable and scalped and killed the hen.

I can find records of only two other aviculturists breeding this Amazon, probably because pairs are seldom kept in aviaries. In 1939, a pair owned by G. D. Smith of Aberdeen hatched two chicks from four eggs but they were killed at the age of 14 days. In 1941 one young Amazon was reared, partly by hand, and the following year one died at the age of 18 days. The remarkable thing about these breedings is that they all took place in the sawdust on the bottom of an ordinary parrot cage. In 1945 two young were reared by the parents and this feat was repeated in 1946.

W. H. Rose reported (AM, vol. 64, 35) that he had bred one young Blue-front, 11 weeks old at the time of writing. 'It is remarkably well feathered and quite able to fly. It shows the red wing butts and blue forehead – but the yellow is quite pale in comparison with the adults.' Three eggs were laid but two were broken during incubation.

The Blue-front has hybridised with several other species including the Yellow-cheeked, Festive, Spectacled and probably with the Double Yellow-headed.

## YELLOW-WINGED AMAZON PARROT *(A.a.xanthopteryx)*

*Description:* It differs from the nominate race in the colour of the frontal edge of the wing and the shoulder which is yellow (not red). Only the rear shoulder-coverts are predominantly red, more or less mixed with yellow. The red is seen only when the wings are lifted. The shade of blue on the forehead is usually a lighter, more turquoise, colour and often the underparts are a much yellower green. In a number of birds I have seen which appear to belong to this race the yellow on the head is confined to the area surrounding the eye. In immature birds there is no yellow at all on the head. (This resulted in one aviculturist buying such a bird as a 'rare Amazon', as he was unable to identify it.)

*Distribution:* Bolivia, southern Mato Grosso, Paraguay and northern Argentina south to Tucumán, Cordoba and the north-western part of Buenos Aires province.

## ORANGE-WINGED AMAZON PARROT *(A. (aestiva) amazonica)*

*Description:* This parrot is frequently mistaken for the Blue fronted Amazon which is considerably larger and has a slightly different arrangement of blue and yellow on the face. In the Orange-winged the forehead, lores and a stripe above the eye are blue. The crown is yellow, also the cheeks, which are usually of a deeper shade; the ear coverts are green. The wing speculum is orange-red and the primaries are black, deep blue and green. The rest of the plumage is green, paler below, with the feathers of the hind-neck edged with blackish. Part of the tail-coverts and the tip of the tail are yellowish-green; there is an orange-red patch at the base of the tail. The bill is a pale horn-colour but dark at the tip. The iris is orange. Length: about 13in; build very slim.

Like the Blue-front, it shows an enormous amount of variation in the blue and yellow on the head, in the shade of blue and in the colour of the wing speculum.

In 1960 I saw a pure yellow Orange-winged Amazon at Paignton Zoo, but neither I nor the Zoo staff can now recall whether it was pink-eyed. It was collected by a Zoo expedition and lived at Paignton for several years, but never attempted to breed.

*Distribution:* Northern Colombia from the lower Magdelana Valley eastward through Venezuela and the Guianas to eastern Brazil, and south through eastern Ecuador and Amazonian Peru to Mato Grosso and Paraná.

This species has apparently adapted itself well to changes brought about by agricultural development in Guyana. It is a common bird in inhabited areas, where it feeds on cultivated fruits such as mangoes. It nests in a variety of trees, sometimes in the vicinity of quite heavily-populated areas. One nest was located by an ornithologist in a dead greenheart tree at a height of about 50ft. When the tree was felled it was found that the nest cavity, situated 5ft below the entrance hole, contained three young, two of which were ready to fly – the third being much smaller.

Included in the diet of the Orange-winged are the seeds and part of the blossoms of the swamp immortelle and the seeds of a legume encased in large flat pods. Out of the breeding season it may be found in small groups or large flocks. Individuals return to the same roost every evening, these roosts sometimes containing thousands of birds.

*Remarks:* This must be one of the most consistently imported into Europe of all Amazons. It does not now appear to be imported in such large numbers as formerly but is usually available – often advertised under the mistaken identity of the Blue-front. Orange-wings make good pets (except for the usual habit of screaming) and because of their small size are particularly suitable for this purpose.

*Breeding records:* Apart from a vague record of *Psittacus amazonicus* bred in Rome in 1801, I can trace only one breeding record: that of the three bred in Tampa USA, in 1970. I know of two aviculturists whose pairs have produced eggs, but not young.

TOBAGO ORANGE-WINGED AMAZON PARROT *(A. (aestiva) tobagensis)*

Differs almost imperceptibly from *amazonica.*

*Distribution:* The islands of Trinidad and Tobago. It is still common in the wild and communal roosts are used by hundreds of birds. In Trinidad the mangrove swamps were its habitat many years ago but the introduced bamboos are now favoured roosting sites. The nest is usually a hole in a rotten palm tree, often the tall moriche palm. Even these, however, do not give protection from the local people, who value these birds as pets; they cannot reach the nesting holes, so cut the trees down to remove the young.

An Argentine ornithologist who has studied the behaviour of this species in Trinidad has discovered that it has well-marked local dialects, depending on the communal roost to which it belongs. Each roost gathers its birds from a definite area. As the young birds probably learn their calls from the adult members of the community the dialects persist and maintain their fixed boundaries.

*A. (a.) micra* (Griscom and Greenway)

*Description:* Said to be smaller than *A. (a) amazonica* and with a more slender bill.

YELLOW-FRONTED AMAZON PARROT *(A. ochrocephala ochrocephala)*

*Synonym:* Yellow-headed Amazon, Single Yellow-headed Amazon

*Description: There is a narrow band of pale green on the frontal edge of the forehead,* the crown is yellow and the rest of the head is green. The hairs covering the cere are black. The upper surface is a medium shade of green, the feathers of the neck and mantle being faintly edged with black and those of the wings with pale yellowish-green. The lower parts are yellowish-green, also the upper tail-coverts. There is a red wing speculum and a small amount of red at the bend of the wing, also a red patch at the base of the tail. A broad yellowish-green band decorates the tip of the tail. The beak is dark grey, except the base of the upper mandible, which is light horn. The iris is orange-red with an inner ring of yellow. The skins examined measured between 14in and 15in.

Immature birds show less yellow on the crown, sometimes none at all, and less red at the bend of the wing and on the tail.

E. J. Brook possessed a specimen which was almost a pure lutino.

*Distribution:* Colombia (east of the base of the Eastern Andes),

Venezuela and the Guianas, south to the Rio Branco and the middle Amazon.

In the wild this species has been observed feeding on the seeds of the manicole palm and the swamp immortelle, also the fruit of the Jamoon plum. It is seldom seen near the coast, preferring more elevated altitudes in wooded areas. In Venezuela it is apparently found more often in dry woods (while the Orange-winged Amazon prefers wet woods) and nests in termites' nests. The usual clutch is two eggs.

*Remarks:* Fairly frequently imported, but not in such large numbers as *A.o.panamensis*. Both are normally sold as pets, which is one reason why no breeding successes for either were recorded in Britain until as recently as 1967.

As pets I would recommend them more highly than any other Amazons. They are amusing clowns who love attention and delight in entertaining. They like to be handled and will become ridiculously tame but when adult often allow only their owner to handle them. If allowed the freedom of the house, as my Panama was for a time, they will follow their owner everywhere – or occupy themselves in mischievous deeds of destruction! Mine will often sit for long periods on a window sill, surveying the world outside, for, like most Amazons she is very interested in what is going on around her. If a stranger speaks to her she will fan her tail, dilate her pupils and wave her head to and fro in display, whistling and cooing and revelling in attention. Should anyone be unwise enough to attempt to touch her however, they will almost certainly be bitten. Like many Amazons, in temperament she is completely unreliable and unpredictable and has bitten me on many occasions, although never seriously. I have never attempted to teach her to talk but she has picked up the phrases 'Come on', 'Hello', and 'Bye-bye'. She enjoys whistling and will hold a whistling match with anyone as long as they have the patience to continue, never tiring of this pastime. She is a never-ending source of amusement to everyone who meets her because of her extraordinary human-like laughter. Sometimes she laughs quite unprompted at amusing situations, so that one is almost tempted to believe that she has a sense of humour. The sound of laughter never fails to send her off into shrieks of wicked, hysterical laughter which causes even more amusement to the one who induced it, often resulting in the person becoming quite helpless with mirth. Sometimes she yells and shouts at the top of her voice, reminding one of a child which is purposely being naughty and noisy.

*Breeding records:* Clifford Smith of Yorkshire was the first aviculturist to breed this species in Britain and I can trace no other record of it having been bred anywhere else in the world previously He obtained two birds from separate sources in 1961. They were identical in appearance and both displayed at times, walking along the perch with head thrust forward and wings partially spread. They were housed in an aviary 10ft long, 5ft wide and 6ft high with a shelter 5ft x 4ft attached. From 1962 to 1965 no interest at all was shown in the nesting facilities provided.

In 1966 two nest-boxes were offered, one being a grandfather clock type of nest, 5ft high and 10in square. It had a 4in diameter entrance hole 6in from the top and a wire ladder inside leading to the turf and peat filling which occupied a depth to about 12in below the entrance hole. A natural hollow log 15in in diameter with 2in thick walls and bark attached was positioned on a 4ft solid log, as it was only 2ft high. In early June the hen began to take an interest in the log, eventually disappearing inside for long periods. She laid two eggs and incubated them for about five weeks, without result.

In 1967 the same nesting facilities were available; this time, however, the box was selected. On July 11 a young bird was heard in the nest. On September 23 the first youngster fledged, to be followed a week later, by a second. Both resembled the adults except for the slightly duller shade of green and the black edges to the feathers of the mantle, which were possibly even more clearly defined than in the adults. Their beaks were dull black, without any trace of horn colour and their eyes were black with a faint suggestion of grey irides, which soon became more pronounced.

While the young were being reared both parents visited the nest and the hen brooded the young until three weeks before they fledged. They were reared on soaked and dry canary seed, millet, hemp, safflower, sunflower and wheat; dry seed was not eaten until the last week of rearing. Although fruit was available none was consumed during the rearing period. Chickweed and groundsel were provided daily and dandelion roots and leaves were given twice weekly.

In 1967 three eggs were laid and two young were reared by the same pair. In 1968 and 1969 the clutch consisted of two eggs, the number of chicks reared being one and two respectively. In 1970 two chicks were hatched and reared.

From these results the incubation period was found to be approximately 25 days and the average period the young remained in the nest was 74 days, with a further 20 days from fledging to complete independence.

In Hamilton Zoo, Bermuda, one *Amazona ochrocephala* was bred in 1970.

## PANAMA YELLOW-FRONTED AMAZON PARROT
*(A.o.panamensis)*

*Description:* It differs from the nominate race in the following respects: (a) the forehead is yellow (not green), (b) a distinct bluish sheen follows the yellow of the crown (a consistent feature – but occasionally also present in *ochrocephala*); (c) the hairs surrounding the nostrils are yellow or of a light colour (not black); (d) the black edges to the feathers of the nape are probably less often present or are less well defined; (e) the beak is horn- and lead-coloured and normally lacks the pinkish spot sometimes seen on the upper mandible of *ochrocephala*; (f) smaller size: ie, about 12in.

There is a very beautiful blue specimen of the Panama Yellow-front at Wassenaar Zoo. It is of the same shade of blue throughout as the blue mutation of the Ringneck Parrakeet (*Psittacula krameri*) except for the forehead, where white replaces the normally yellow area. It was bought from a Dutch dealer who expected to receive a Hyacinthine Macaw!

*Distribution:* Panama and the tropical lowlands of northern Colombia east to the Santa Marta region. Wetmore (43b) observed this species in flocks of from 20 to 40 individuals, feeding and roosting together but mixing only casually with other large parrots. 'Though smaller in body, the Yellow-head is louder in voice, so that though in fewer numbers its raucous notes contribute largely to the morning and evening chorus near parrot roosts.'

*Remarks:* See under Yellow-fronted Amazon.

*Breeding records:* Mrs E. Davis was reported as having bred one Panama Amazon in the USA in 1945. No details were given. In Denmark two young were bred in 1963 and three in the following year.

## MARAJO YELLOW-HEADED AMAZON PARROT
*(A.o.xantholaema)*

*Description:* It is said to differ from *A.o.ochrocephala* in having an extensive area of yellow on the side of the head.

*Distribution:* The island of Marajo at the mouth of the Amazon.

*A.o.parvipes* (Monroe and Howell, 1966)
*Description:* It differs from *A.o.auropalliata* (see below) in its smaller size (and notably smaller feet), in the presence of red at the bend of the wing and in the generally paler bill.
*Distribution:* The lowland pine regions of Islas de la Bahia (Roatan, Barbareta and Guanaja) and the Mosquita in eastern Honduras and north-eastern Nicaragua. (Those from the lower Sula Valley in north central Honduras from Lake Yoyoa northwards are tentatively referred to this sub-species.)

*A.o.belizensis* (Monroe and Howell, 1966)
*Description:* It differs from *A.o.magna* (see page 249) in its smaller size and the smaller amount of yellow on the head, this colour usually being confined to the forehead and crown, lores and auriculars.
*Distribution:* The lowland pine savanna and adjacent areas of British Honduras.

YELLOW-NAPED AMAZON PARROT *(A.o.auropalliata)*
*Synonym:* Golden-naped Amazon
*Description:* Adult birds have a large yellow patch on the nape of the neck (sometimes, apparently, also on the crown). The red wing speculum is present and there is a red patch at the base of the tail. The primaries are black and green and there is some blue in the secondaries. The rest of the plumage is green, lighter on the upper tail-coverts and underparts, and yellowish-green at the tip of the tail. The larger wing-coverts have paler yellowish edges and the outer tail feathers are edged with blue. The cere, the hairs around the nostrils and the beak are black. The iris is orange. Length: about 14in.

Immature birds have no yellow on the nape (or crown) or two or three yellow feathers only, making identification difficult.
*Distribution:* Southern Mexico from extreme eastern Oaxaca through Chiapas and the Pacific slope of Central America to north-western Costa Rica, extending into the Caribbean lowlands of northern Honduras east to the Ulua Valley.

Slud (35) observed this species in Costa Rica and found it to occur singly, in twos or threes or in larger groups, often close to settlements. It usually keeps high in the trees, taking off silently. He described its cries as 'rather deep, not raucous, very human-sounding calls that bring to mind a person trying to imitate a parrot.' It is found in dry forested lowlands, also in scrubby cattle lands which alternate with marshy lagoon type of country. It appears to be fairly common and often feeds in cornfields.

*Remarks:* This species has never been readily available in Europe but is much better known in the USA, where it is considered to be one of the most talented talkers and a very desirable pet. Nineteenth-century writers also gave glowing accounts of the accomplishments and trustworthy temperament of the Yellow-naped. Now it is rarely seen in Britain but has been exhibited at the London Zoo.

*Breeding records:* In 1948 Sir Edward Hallstrom reported breeding this species. In the USA it is believed to have hybridised with the Blue-fronted Amazon.

DOUBLE YELLOW-HEADED AMAZON PARROT *(A.o.oratrix)*

*Synonyms:* Levaillant's Amazon, Mexican Yellow-headed Amazon

*Description:* This is a large and very handsome parrot. The entire head and neck and part of the mantle are yellow in adult birds, darker on the mantle and much lighter, almost cream on the head. The metacarpal edge of the wing and the thighs are also yellow. The bend of the wing is red, sometimes with a few yellow feathers, and there is also a red wing speculum; the primaries are black and green. It is dark green above, paler and with a bluish tinge below, and yellowish-green on the upper wing-coverts. There is a broad band of greenish-yellow at the tip of the tail, blue on the outer edges and a patch of red at the base of the tail. The bill is yellowish-white. Orange is the colour of the iris, which has an inner ring of yellow. Length: about 15in.

Immature birds have much less yellow on the head, this being confined mainly to the forehead, crown and lores in very young birds, when they may almost resemble adults of *panamensis* in this respect. According to Blake (5) immature birds have the head wholly green and lack the red (and yellow) in the wings.

*Distribution:* Mexico in the states of Puebla, Mexico, Guanajuato, Colima, Guerrero and Yucatan; British Honduras. (Erroneously attributed to Honduras and Ruatan Island.)

*Remarks:* This Amazon is seldom seen in Europe and, like the Yellow-naped, is much better known in the USA, where it is very popular as a pet. Some individuals are extremely talented talkers. There is a record of one which could sing parts of Italian operas in a soprano voice, also the Italian song 'Canta Carmel'. It was a clever mimic, imitating a child crying and calling for its mother.

An American kept a pet Double Yellow-headed at liberty. It would fly from its owner's house, situated on the top of a hill, until it was lost from view, returning daily, entering its cage only for food and water and sleeping among the wide leaves of a maple tree.

*Breeding records:* In 1970 three were bred in Houston Zoo and one in Tampa, USA. The first breeder in Britain was Clifford Smith of Yorkshire. In 1969 two clear eggs were laid; in 1970 four eggs were laid, resulting in two young reared, which fledged at the age of eight weeks. This pair reared young again in 1971 and 1972.

*A.o.magna* (Monroe and Howell, 1966)

*Description:* It differs from *A.o.oratrix* in its decidedly larger size and from *A.o.tresmariae*, which it resembles in size, in lacking any bluish caste to the green plumage.

*Distribution:* The Atlantic slope of Mexico from central Tamaulipas and extreme south-eastern San Luis Potosí south through Vera Cruz to eastern Tabasco.

## TRES MARIAS AMAZON PARROT *(A.o.tresmariae)*

*Description:* It differs from *A.o.ochrocephala* in its light grass green back, more bluish-green underparts and the much greater extension of yellow on the neck. The black edging to the feathers of the back, breast, etc., are very indistinct or missing. Length: about 15in.

*Distribution:* Tres Marias Islands, off the west coast of Mexico.

*Remarks:* Rare in aviculture, due to its limited range.

## NATTERER'S AMAZON PARROT *(A.o.nattori)*

*Description:* According to Hellmayr (19c) it is not related to *A. farinosa* (with which Finsch compared it in the original description) but ' belongs to the group of *A.aestiva* and *A.ochrocephala* '. He states that ' It resembles these two species in having the edge of the wing and a large wing-speculum bright red, and the base of the inner web of the outer rectrices pale red, but differs from *A.ochrocephala*, with which it agrees in the absence of yellow on the sides of the head, by having a broad, bluish frontal band (instead of a narrow, green edge), and by the sides of the head, throat, and under parts being decidedly bluish-green (not pure green or yellowish-green).' The iris is said to be orange.

*Distribution:* Peters gives its range as eastern Ecuador and eastern Peru to north-western Mato Grosso. Monroe and Howell (27) studied 31 skins which showed that it has a much wider range which included

Brazil: Rio Madiera, São Paulo de Olivenca on the Rio Solimoẽs, Obidos, Santarem, Rio Tapajoz, Para; Peru: the mouths of the Rio Curaray and Rio Urubamba, and Sarayacu, Rio Ucayali and Oroso on the Amazon; Bolivia; Yungas and Rurrenabaque.

MERCENARY AMAZON PARROT *(A.mercenaria mercenaria)*
*Synonym:* Tschudi's Amazon, Scaly-naped Parrot
*Description:* The head is completely green, except on the edges of the feathers of the crown and hind neck, which are edged with black. The forehead, cheeks, upper tail-coverts and the underside of the tail are a lighter shade of green than the rest of the body. The carpal edge of the wing is yellow, tinged with red and the red wing speculum is present. The flight feathers are blue and black. The tail is the most colourful part of this Amazon: the central feathers are green with yellowish-green tips and the lateral ones are red between the yellowish tips and green bases, with some dark purple on the outer webs. In the second and third tail feathers the red extends to the base; the outer feathers are edged with blue. The bill is dusky with the base of the upper mandible yellowish. Length: about 13in. Some birds, probably immature, lack the red wing speculum.
*Distribution:* Western South America from north-western Venezuela to Ecuador and northern Bolivia.
*Remarks:* Very rare in aviculture. Many years ago Taczanswski wrote that although it was common and found in great numbers in Peru it was quiet while feeding and the natives could not discover its nesting places.

GREY-NAPED AMAZON PARROT *(A.m.canipalliata)*
*Synonym:* Colombian Amazon Parrot
*Distribution:* The tropical to upper temperate zones of the Eastern, Central and Western Andes of Colombia; Santa Marta Mountains.

MEALY AMAZON PARROT *(A.farinosa farinosa)*
*Description:* This large Amazon has yellow on the crown; the amount and even the position of this patch of colour varies considerably, but age probably has a bearing on the extent and I have seen specimens with the yellow extended to the forehead. In some birds the yellow feathers are tipped with red. There is an indistinct grey patch on the hind neck, whose feathers, with those of the mantle, are broadly edged with very dark brown or black. The carpal edge of the wing and the speculum are red; the primaries are black, blue and green

and there is a broad yellowish-green band at the tip of the tail. The upper parts are green with a greyish mealy appearance, the colour below being a lighter green. The bill is a pale horn-colour. Brown is the colour of the iris and the white area of skin surrounding the eye is rather prominent. Length about 15in to 16in. Immature birds have less yellow on the head – perhaps only two or three yellow feathers.
*Distribution:* Eastern Venezuela (Caura-Orinoco region), Guyana east to Surinam, southward to Peru, northern Mato Grosso and the lower Amazon. It inhabits lowland forests and coastal river areas.

A nest of this species was found at the back of a coastal sugar estate in the trunk of a cabbage palm, the entrance being through the decayed summit. The nest was many feet below, about 10ft above the ground. It contained three nestlings, one of which was much smaller than the other two.
*Remarks:* Not very frequently imported into Britain. It has no bright colours, yet makes an attractive aviary bird – for those without neighbours. The volume of its voice is truly formidable, even for an Amazon. This fact, and its size, would discourage those requiring a pet Amazon.

PLAIN-COLOURED AMAZON PARROT *(A.f.inornata)*
*Description:* It differs from *A.f.farinosa* in usually lacking the yellow on the head. It is a darker green, especially on the forehead and underparts, with a darker blue on the hind neck. The carpal edge of the wing is partly or entirely red. These features are not always constant and there is some doubt as to the validity of this sub-species. Length: about 15in.
*Distribution:* Panama, from Veragua eastward, and north-western South America south to Ecuador and east to Lake Maracaibo and the Caura River in Venezuela.

It feeds on figs and other fruit and if given the opportunity will raid cornfields.
*Remarks:* Probably imported a little more often than *A.f.farinosa.*

*A.f.chapmani*
*Distribution:* East of the Andes in Putumayo and Vaupés, in Colombia.

COSTA RICAN AMAZON PARROT *(A.f.virenticeps)*
*Synonym:* Green-headed Amazon
*Description:* It differs from *A.f.guatemalae* (see below) in having

the head mainly green, the forehead, crown and lores only being tinged with blue, and can be distinguished from *inornata* in having little or no red on the edge of the wing. It is said to be more yellowish-green, especially below. Length: about 14in.
*Distribution:* Nicaragua, Costa Rica and western Panama (east to Chiriquí and Bocas del Toro). It is common locally. According to Slud (35), it is most numerous in heavily wooded regions, but is not a true forest inhabitant as it prefers forest borders and nearby clearings and plantations with tall trees. It occurs in groups consisting mainly of pairs.
*Remarks:* Rare in Europe.

### BLUE-CROWNED AMAZON PARROT *(A.f.guatemalae)*

*Synonym:* Guatemalan Amazon
*Description:* It differs from *A.f.farinosa* in having the whole of the top of the head from the forehead to the nape blue, lighter on the crown and merging into darker greyish-blue on the nape and mantle. The bill is black with a yellow spot near the base of the upper mandible. The iris is reddish-brown. Length: about 15in. Some specimens show a little red on the inner webs of the tail feathers.
*Distribution:* Southern Mexico from the states of Oaxaca, Mexico and Vera Cruz south through Guatemala to the Ulua Valley in Honduras. Hugh C. Land (25) records that it is fairly common in the tree tops in humid forest. It is a very noisy bird and its calls carry for a mile or more. Sometimes 100 birds congregate to roost and create a tremendous din.
*Remarks:* It is rarely seen in Europe but is apparently quite well-known in the USA, where it is considered to make quite a good talker.

### VINACEOUS AMAZON PARROT *(A.vinacea)*

*Description:* This is one of the most distinct and colourful of the imported Amazons. Adult birds have the forehead, chin and lores red, with the upper mandible of the same shade except the tip, which is horn-coloured. The elongated feathers of the hind neck, which can be raised, are green with a bluish-grey band near the black edges. The upper breast, often also the abdomen, is purplish-vinous, sometimes with bluish-green or green on the abdomen. The carpal edge of the wing is red and the red wing speculum is present. The primaries are black, blue and green. The tail is green, yellowish-green at the tip, with a red patch near the base of the lateral feathers, the outer one with a purplish-red patch. The iris is orange-red. Length: about 14in.

Immature birds have less vinous on the breast, a duller shade of red on the forehead and yellow, instead of red, on the carpal edge of the wing. Females are generally described as being less brightly coloured, but it may be that immature birds have been mistaken for females. I know of two true pairs of this species, one of which is owned by Clifford Smith, who tells me that the two birds are identical in colouring and can be distinguished only by the smaller head of the hen, while in H. Murray's pair the shoulders of the cock are red, those of the hen being pale yellow. In the hen of the latter pair the vinous of the breast extends even further down the abdomen than it does in the cock.

*Distribution:* South-eastern Brazil from Bahia to Rio Grande do Sol; Paraguay; Misiones. Many years ago this species was described as being found in very large numbers feeding in orange groves in Misiones. One nest was found in a huge murta tree; the nesting cavity was situated about 6ft below the entrance.

*Remarks:* This is one of the most desirable of the Amazons available in Europe but is imported irregularly and in very small numbers. Little seems to have been recorded about it as an aviary bird but it is said to make a very good pet. Miss Maud Knobel described a young one which was received by Chapman's in 1923. She bought it although it was in poor health, being affected by the cold and unsuitable food. For the first three or four days she kept it very warm and fed it on sponge-cake and banana only. It then sampled canary seed, maize and peanuts. After a fortnight its health and temper had improved beyond recognition and it soon became very affectionate, lively and talkative. It enjoyed running about on the floor, squealing with delight when it found a dark corner.

Sydney Porter also thought highly of this species. He wrote of his Vinaceous: 'A quiet, gentle creature, my bird seems to have no vices, delights in being spoken to and taken notice of, it whistles but seems to make no other noises. It is the gentlest of my Parrots and never resents the attacks of other birds.'

Lest anyone should get the mistaken impression that this is a quiet species, I should add that it is just as noisy as other Amazons.

*Breeding records:* During 1970 and 1971 both the hens of the pairs mentioned above laid eggs – one hen on the aviary floor and the other hen from the perch! However, Clifford Smith was successful in breeding two chicks in 1971, a first success with this species.

## GUILDING'S AMAZON PARROT *(A.guildingii)*

*Synonym:* St Vincent Amazon

*Description:* Next to the Imperial this is the largest and the most magnificent of the Amazons, immediately identified by the orange wing speculum and the band of bright yellow at the end of the tail. It takes several years to attain full adult plumage. When mature the crown is white with a yellow patch on the hind part, the rest of the crown feathers being tipped with lilac; the lores and the feathers below the eyes are white. Those of the sides of the head and the throat are blue with yellowish-green bases, the lower part of the neck, breast, thighs, shoulders and lower edge of the wing being tinged with green. The feathers below are tawny brown, also green on the abdomen with black edges. The upper tail-coverts are rich, golden-brown and the under tail-coverts are golden-yellow tinged with green. The wings are most colourful; when opened they reveal bronzy-green on the upper part, an orange speculum on the secondaries and bands of yellow, blue and black on the primaries. The tail is orange and green at the base, with a broad band of yellow at the tip. The iris is orange with an inner circle of yellow and the bill is whitish. Length: 16in to 18in.

Immature birds are much less colourful and have less blue on the head.

*Distribution:* The island of St Vincent in the Lesser Antilles. A precarious population of this beautiful parrot survives, despite the natural hazards provided by hurricanes and volcanoes and the fact that the natives shoot them if the opportunity arises.

The population of this parrot was terribly reduced at the time of the great hurricane in 1898, before which it was still common. In that storm many were destroyed or disabled and caught by the natives. For days afterwards they were found in the smaller towns in a more or less helpless condition and starving. Two were even picked up dead on the shores of St Lucia. Before the species had recovered from the effects of the hurricane, the volcano erupted, killing many of them and laying waste the part of the island which suited them best. As these birds are very slow breeders, laying only one or two eggs, their numbers have never recovered from these setbacks.

In 1959 Keith Frost wrote (AM vol. 65, 85): 'For the past five or six years I have been visiting St Vincent once yearly and on almost every occasion I have seen them in the mountains. They are by no means as rare as the *imperialis* but, nevertheless, a specimen can be obtained occasionally for about £3 to £4. Like *imperialis,* they lay two eggs and once a year only. Unfortunately, instead of increasing they are becoming less and less. I hate to think what will be their lot in about 20 years. Unless drastic measures are taken against the natives who destroy them whenever the opportunity arises the bird will be extinct before the Great Imperial.'

*Remarks:* The Guilding's Amazons known to have been brought into Britain number well under 10. In 1851, when the Earl of Derby's collection was dispersed, one was sold for £4! The London Zoo obtained one in 1874 and in 1902 there were three in Britain – one at London Zoo, one in the possession of Canon Dutton and another owned by a woman. The Duke of Bedford later owned a pair, the hen of which died in 1930. I believe the last of that era seen was the one still at London Zoo in 1937. Of recent years it seemed highly improbable that another would ever be seen in Europe and a living specimen was more than I, for one, ever dreamed of seeing.

In May 1971, however, A. V. Marques of Bedfordshire, obtained a young Guilding's from the USA. Although not fully coloured, it is as exquisite as the skins of this species have led me to believe. The delicate blue of the head, the bronze and tawny shades of the body and the gold of the wings combine to produce the superlative. Moreover, it is hand-reared with a most delightful temperament.

There are two or three more in the USA at the time of writing, including one bought in St Vincent by a woman tourist who was completely unaware of its rarity and was undoubtedly attracted by its bright colours! In 1970 it was reported that there was also one in Hamilton, Bermuda, probably the one owned by K. Frost.

The Duke of Bedford found that all the large Amazons from the islands were unsuited to cage life but were 'Hardy and enduring aviary birds'. One female Guilding's spent over 25 years in captivity, 10 of them in an outdoor aviary. 'Her mate is much younger and is unfortunately disfigured by a blind and damaged eye. In spite of this defect he is the most uproariously cheerful bird in my collection. At first very friendly, though latterly somewhat inclined to be treacherous, he has always been completely fearless. He says a few words distinctly and carries on long conversations in double Dutch. He chortles and guffaws in most human fashion and uses laughter to express his satisfaction at the arrival of his breakfast or at the successful perpetration of some piece of mischief. He is for ever playing and doing gymnastics and as long as he was permitted he took a special delight in upsetting the fruit and water dishes. As each dislodged vessel spun to the ground he would eye it quizzically and then shout 'Ha! Ha! Ha!! Haaa!!! Hooh!' at the top of his voice. He greatly objects to being driven into the aviary shelter at night, disputing every inch of the way and giving all the trouble he can. When the slide at last goes down he raps on it with his beak as a last defiance.

'At first I had great difficulty in accustoming the two Parrots to each other's society. Amazons seldom make friends easily and on this occasion matters were made worse by the couple having but one sound eye between them.

'However in the end they became very good friends, though the cock loves teasing his nervous and short-sighted wife, rushing at her and pretending to bite her for the fun of making her squawk, when he says 'Polly! Polly! Polly!' in a deprecating tone as though shocked by the language she has used. At times the two birds examine a nest barrel together and I have little doubt that they would breed were the hen a perfect specimen.' (The Marquess of Tavistock, 38.)

## ST LUCIA AMAZON PARROT *(A.versicolor)*

*Synonyms:* Blue-masked Amazon, Versicoloured Amazon.

*Description:* The forehead, crown and the sides of the head are blue, the throat being paler and merging into green; the forehead, lores and cheeks have a purple tinge. Some red feathers decorate the upper breast, which with the base of the neck is olive tinged vinous. The larger feathers of the head, also those of the back of the neck and the mantle, are green edged with black. The wing speculum is scarlet and the primaries are blue and black. The lower breast is golden-olive tinged with vinous. The upper and under tail-coverts are yellow-green and there is a broad yellow-green band at the tip of the tail; the central tail feathers are green, except at the tip, the lateral feathers being blue at the base of the inner webs. The beak is blackish with a horn-coloured spot at the base and orange is the colour of the iris. Length: 16in to 17in.

*Distribution:* The island of St Lucia in the Lesser Antilles. In 1930 Sydney Porter wrote that 20 years previously this parrot had been on the verge of extinction but it was then increasing fairly rapidly, due to the very rigid protection afforded it by the government of the island. So successful had the authorities been in this direction that due to the severe penalties the natives were terrified of killing, or even owning, a bird of this species.

In 1959 Keith Frost reported (AM vol. 65, 85) that *A.versicolor* was not as rare as was usually thought, and that five years previously he could have bought one in a market place in St Lucia for the equivalent of £1! In the wild it is now restricted to the central part of the island.

*Remarks:* Due to the admirable way in which this bird is protected in its native island, it is never again likely to be available to aviculture, in which it was known only by a few specimens. Among these was an aged specimen belonging to the Duke of Bedford which had been in the possession of Canon Dutton. When he received the Amazon he was dismayed to find that her breathing was poor, she was shaky on her legs and her feet seemed to be losing the power to grip. He therefore decided to give her a chance at liberty. 'I never for a moment expected success; she was too weak to climb and it seemed highly improbable that she could fly, but it was the only hope and I opened the top of the aviary. Jaco walked slowly out and surveyed the trees around her with growing interest. She began to call and get restless, raised her wings, and finally launched herself into the air. She got on remarkably well, and her first flight landed her half way up a tall elm. Subsequent flights took her to the top of the highest trees in the garden, and there she remained. For three days she flew to and fro without showing exhaustion from hunger; then she descended to the gardener's shoulder and was carried to the feeding tray, which she afterwards visited of her own accord. Then the rain came, 48 hours of it and very cold. Jaco began to look rather miserable, and I carried her into an aviary shelter. However she walked out at once and flew away. Another 24 hours' rain followed, and I expected to have to take her into hospital with a chill, but she was looking better than the day before; and marvellous to relate she has never ceased to improve, and all the frosts and deluges of this inclement summer have failed to harm her!'

She soon made friends with a crippled African Ringnecked Parrakeet which she preferred to a King Parrakeet. 'Soon after sunrise each day her raucous voice heralds her approach, and she passes my window slightly preceded by the king, whose graceful swinging flight is more rapid than hers. She looks very imposing, the dark blue and scarlet of her wings showing to great advantage, but she is no songbird; her cries with few exceptions are loud, dismal and discordant, and at times she is very loquacious!'

During Sydney Porter's stay in Dominica, he was shown a tame pair which lived at complete liberty. Strangely enough, the hen, which had been flying free for 16 years, had forsaken her mate for a Blue and Yellow Macaw, also at liberty.

IMPERIAL AMAZON PARROT *(A.imperialis)*
*Synonyms:* August Amazon, Dominican Amazon
*Description:* This magnificent parrot is the largest of the Amazons and regal, almost eagle-like, in its demeanour. The Duke of Bedford described it as 'truly the emperor of all true Parrots'. It has the head, neck, breast and abdomen dark purple-blue with black edges to the feathers, except those of the crown and the back of the head, which are edged with dark green. The breast is dark purple or mingled with vinous and the back, rump, upper and under tail-coverts, also the sides, flanks and thighs are green, edged with blackish and blue. The mantle is dark green, some of the feathers faintly edged with black and the wings are green with the speculum crimson. The primaries and secondaries are dull purple, green and dull blue. The tail is reddish-brown with a vinous tip, the central feathers tinged with green and the outer ones entirely reddish-brown. The bill is a dark horn colour with a pale mark at the base, and the iris is orange. Length: about 19in. The hen is said to be considerably larger than the cock.

Those fortunate enough to have seen this species alive invariably remark on its beauty. Casey A. Wood described (AM Fourth Series, vol. 11, 58) an Imperial in the possession of a family in Dominica: 'He looked as if he wore an iridescent, puce-coloured hood, pierced for his brilliant yellow eyes; but it might be more correct to say that his head, neck and under parts were of a dark purplish-blue that varied in shade as he moved.' Vigors described the first specimen brought alive to the London Zoo (Proc. Zool. Soc, 1836, 80) and remarked on the brilliant glossy purple sheen of the head, nape and breast. According to Sydney Porter: 'The sight of this bird walking with ruff erect and fierce flashing eyes would impress anyone. A Parrot usually waddles but *A.imperialis* walked with the dignity usually assigned to a queen.'
*Distribution:* The island of Dominica in the Lesser Antilles. This is, perhaps, the rarest parrot in the world and just survives in the high mountain forest of Dominica. In 1970 Neil Macleod reported seeing this species during a year spent in the island, and in 1959 Keith D. Frost stated (AM, vol. 65, 84) that it is 'very rare but it is *not* extinct. On my last visit to Dominica I did see one, and only last week news came to me from that island that a friend of mine there

had discovered a pair nesting very high up in a very high tree'.

In 1929 Sydney Porter explained the reason for the continued existence of this bird: 'Of course, the Imperial Parrot is rightly protected by law, but as a gentleman in the Administration said to me, it is absolutely impossible to enforce the law in such a district. The only laws known are the laws of Nature. But the bird is protected by Nature in such a way as no other creature in the world is, for I know of no living bird whose numbers are as small as those of *A.imperialis* and yet has managed to maintain itself as this bird has. Its home is the most remote, the most inaccessible, and the approach the most dangerous that I know of.'

In 1929 Porter travelled to Dominica to investigate the report that this species was extinct. A guide took him to the part of the island where they had been known to live. 'The way lay for the most part up and down perpendicular cliffs of about 1,000ft high, and these were covered with the densest tropical vegetation. . . . At last the guide informed me that we were in the district and sure enough in a few minutes we heard the ringing cries of *A.imperialis* and two birds flew out of a huge forest tree, circling round with almost motionless wings, looking very much like small eagles and very dark in colour when silhouetted against the sky. A little later we came upon another pair feeding upon a great fruit-bearing forest tree . . .

'The cock of the pair fed on the fruit, continually letting fall half-eaten ones which somewhat resembled a very dark purplish pomegranate. This fruit had a vile taste when eaten in the unripe state in which the birds appear to like it; even if only touched with the tongue it leaves a horribly bitter and astringent taste in the mouth for a long time afterwards.' (AM Fifth Series, vol. VII, 244). 'Though I tried the bird which I later on secured with it, and also the Bouquet's Parrot, they all refused to touch it. This was exceedingly strange as it forms the main food of both birds in the wild state.'

While on the island a native told Porter that just after the hurricane which occurred in 1928, causing great damage, a flock of these birds numbering between one and two hundred appeared in the valley seeking food. This flock probably represented the entire population of this species. It stayed for a short time and then separated into small parties and dispersed in various directions, but not before 10 had been shot and eaten. Porter collected information which accounted for over 38 Imperials killed and captured during the last three months of 1928 and the first two months of 1929.

*Remarks:* The number of Imperial Amazons known to have left Dominica during the last 100 years is very small indeed. The London Zoo first owned this species in 1865 and obtained another in 1901. Canon Dutton, Lady Thompson, New York Zoo and the Duke of Bedford also possessed single specimens. Porter lent the Duke of Bedford his bird to make up a pair. In 1961, an Imperial Amazon was loaned to London Zoo by the Governor of the West Indies. This is almost certainly the last one which will ever be seen in Europe and was probably the last since 1937.

The following two genera have no affinity with the Amazons – or with any other true parrot.

## Genus: *Deroptyus*

### HAWK-HEADED PARROT (*D.accipitrinus accipitrinus*)

*Description:* This is an exceptionally beautiful bird and one of the most unusual of all parrots in its feathering. It has an erectile ruff which is unique among parrots. In some birds the forehead and crown are dusky white, while in others the entire head, except the ruff, is brown, each feather having a shaft-streak of pale buff. The ruff consists of the feathers from the middle of the crown and the sides of the head; they are rich maroon, broadly edged with blue, and are so long that they cover the back of the head, from which no contour feathers grow, only down. When the ruff is erected it frames the head like an immense fan. It is interesting to view the bird from behind while its ruff is erected; the white shafts of the back of the feathers being reminiscent of the rear view of a displaying peacock. The colour scheme of the ruff is repeated throughout the entire lower parts but, in the area of the vent, the feathers are less prominently edged with blue. The upper and under tail-coverts are green and the underside of the tail and the inner webs of the tail feathers are black. The bill is black and the iris is brown or yellow. Length: 12in.

The four immature birds in my care at present have a varying degree of green on the crown; each bird has the iris brownish-white.

Several theories have been presented regarding sexing this species. Salvadori stated that males, but not females, have a red patch at the base of the inner webs of the lateral tail feathers. He also commented, however, that birds from Ecuador and 'Maranham' (presumably Maranhão) were without the red in the tail.

According to Ralph Small, there is no difference in the colouring of the two Hawk-heads at Chicago Zoo, which have bred on several occasions. On the other hand, Mrs N. Howard has a believed hen which shows no red in the tail, which fought any bird placed with it, until one was found with red in the tail; it was immediately accepted. However, I am inclined to believe that variation in colouring is geographical and not sexual.

*Distribution:* The Guianas and Venezuela, through Colombia, east of the Andes, to Ecuador, Peru and northern Brazil. Most observers of this species have found it less abundant than the typical parrots and usually in pairs, sometimes in small groups. In 1863 H. W. Bates recorded that although it was found in all the lowlands throughout the Amazon region it was not common anywhere. His companion shot an 'anacá' (its native name) at a wild-fruit tree. Haverschmidt described the display of five Hawk-heads as being reminiscent of that of certain pigeons: they flew upwards with rapid wing-beats, glided down, then ascended again. He stated that they roost *singly* in holes in trees; I should have thought it more likely that pairs or small family groups roost together.

The observations of E. McLaughlin while in Guyana (*Foreign Birds*, vol. 36, 212) are interesting. He found this species in a sandbelt forest. 'I watched a pair of these birds in a tall tree a couple of months prior to the breeding season preening and resting. Their voice sounds were a little like Amazons but weaker and when they flew away one made a chack-chack-chack cry reminiscent of a magpie.

'I learned from Mr Langenberg that this pair had nested for several years in a large dead tree not far from where I had seen them.

'A couple of months later we visited the nest tree. We discovered it had recently fallen. As it had been standing about a month previously Mr Langenberg searched the vicinity and found a pair in a new nest a hundred yards or so from the first.' Whereas the nesting cavity in the fallen tree was situated about 40ft above the ground, the new nest was at a height of about 70ft, just below the tip of a limb of a dead tree a foot or less in diameter. When the tree was struck one of the pair, believed to be the male, flew silently to a nearby tree. The spread tail of this species in flight easily identifies it from other parrots. The nest holes used by the pair were thought to be old woodpecker holes. An Amerindian told Mr McLaughlin that Hawk-heads feed on the fruits of inga and two species of black palm, also guavas.

*Remarks:* Only rarely imported and now very expensive to obtain but there are several pairs in private collections in Britain. In 1953 when Alan Lendon visited many of the zoos of the world, he saw this species only at London, Edinburgh, Antwerp and Wassenaar.

The behaviour of this most interesting bird resembles that of conures rather than true parrots. Its appearance, too, is reminiscent of a giant *Pyrrhura* conure – the broad bands of colour which edge the feathers of the neck and upper breast (also the lower breast) and the shaft-streaking to the head feathers, found in a couple of species of *Pyrrhuras* and no other neo-tropical parrot that I know of. Its shape, long-tail and general appearance is undeniably conure-like.

They further resemble *Pyrrhuras* in their addiction to roosting in holes which is not a characteristic of the true parrots. The four young birds in my care, housed indoors, all packed themselves into a hole in the wall containing a blocked-up air vent from the very first night. They go to roost at an extraordinarily early hour. At 6pm they are all together in their hole, although the sun might not set until 9pm!

In their choice of foods they show none of the conservative attitude of Amazons, for example, but like *Pyrrhuras*, sample everything offered. They take sunflower, peanuts, nectar, nectar and sponge-cake, fruit – preferably cherries – millet sprays, boiled maize, spinach beet and grass with the roots attached.

Everyone who has kept Hawk-heads has commented on their great intelligence, tameness and charm. They are altogether most appealing birds but, unfortunately, have one serious fault – their piercing shrieks and screams, which are almost deafening when emitted by two or three birds simultaneously. Like Queen of Bavaria's Conures and certain Amazons, they cannot be recommended for aviculturists in built-up areas. Young birds, at least, also have some attractive conversational notes which they make when one talks to them, so that I should imagine that they might be quite easy to teach to talk.

When alarmed, annoyed or threatening another bird, they erect the fan, which produces a bizarre yet lovely effect. This is truly one of the most engaging of new world parrots with a personality that matches its beauty. Miss Diekmann, secretary of the former Moscicki Collection, described this species as '. . . one of, if not *the*, most intelligent species of Parrot. It is quick-witted, affectionate, and playful. Those in our Collection, although as wild as Hawks when first imported, became tractable within a month, and began to show every indication of friendliness soon afterwards . . .

'We have, however, a particularly tame cock Hawk-head in our possession at the moment. He is everything one could wish for in a pet; companionable, amusing, sociable, and an excellent talker. He recognises all our regular attendants, and calls them by name, never once addressing them incorrectly.'

She observed that the cock was 'inclined to be an overbearing spouse, with no consideration for his better-half, and always ready and anxious to show off. On the other hand, he is prepared to defend her from any real or imaginary danger, and claims her individual attention at all times.

'. . . Of course, in keeping with character, the cock Hawk-head indulges in a great deal of mock heroics. Usually, however, aggressiveness is only an excuse for display and intimidation. The birds, when excited or angry, erect the curious ruff of red feathers around the neck, and emit a ferocious hissing noise. They sidle, swaying gently across the branches, until within striking distance, and, after a last ruffle of feathers retreat – only to begin the performance all over again.' (*Foreign Birds*, vol. 25, 63-4.)

Young birds appear to be very easy to tame. I caged one of the four in my care, allowing him a month in which to settle down, during which time I made no attempt to handle him. At the end of this period he was confident and playful, frequently hanging upside down from his perch and erecting his fan or indulging in mock battles with the twigs provided for his destruction. He allowed me to scratch his head with a twig and in two days the twig was dispensed with.

Soon he began to eye the door of his cage with interest and would climb out if the door was left open. He seemed to have a phobia about perching on my hand, but it was a simple matter to persuade him to climb on to a stick. Only a week after he first came out of his cage he would sit contentedly in my lap and as yet exhibits none of the wilfulness of character of Amazons and Caiques. Unlike many parrots, he allows one to stroke his body and under his wings. Altogether he is a most gentle bird and never attempts to bite.

*Breeding records:* The only successful recorded breeding of the Hawk-headed Parrot appears to be that of the pair at Chicago Zoo.* They were received as young birds in 1961 and placed in a small compartment 5ft square and 7ft high. A nest-box measuring 11in high, 12in wide and 24in long was hung at an angle of 30°. The

* At the time of going to press, the pair owned by Mrs N. Howard is rearing one chick.

birds were seen attempting to mate in November 1964. On March 13 of the following year one young Hawk-head fledged. It was removed to another cage during the middle of June and the parents nested on two more occasions that year, resulting in single chicks fledging on August 5 and November 23. While the chicks were in the nest the parents consumed large quantities of roasted peanuts and fruit, also raw carrot and raw heart. They seemed to crave for meat.

In 1967 the nest-box was removed for alterations to be made to the cage and was found to contain a chick between three and seven days old and one infertile egg. The chick was hand-reared on a mixture of the following items after they had been placed in a blender: two parts each of sunflower seed, white millet and peanuts; one part each of dog chow, rabbit pellets, mynah pellets and pablum cereal; half parts of a mineral supplement and calcium. The resulting powder was mixed with hot water and made into a porridge. Using this formula, a feed lasted as long as eight hours. The young bird opened one eye at 14 days, the other at 16 days old. At 30 days it was seen preening for the first time and at 54 days it flew.

Three Hawk-headeds were bred at Chicago Zoo in 1970, bringing the total to 13.

In 1969 a pair belonging to Paul Schneider of California hatched a chick but it lived only seven days.

BRAZILIAN HAWK-HEADED PARROT *(D.a.fuscifrons)*
*Description:* According to Hellmayr (19a) it differs from the nominate race in having the 'whole forehead and crown uniform dusky or only slightly mottled with brownish-white', and in lacking the red at the base of the tail. Some young birds have red at the base of the tail and also have green on the crown.
*Distribution:* The south bank of the lower Amazon from the Tapajóz to Pará (city) and to Maranhão.

## Genus: *Triclaria*

The single representative of this genus in no way resembles any other neo-tropical parrot.

PURPLE-BELLIED PARROT *(T.malachitacea)*
*Synonym:* Violet-bellied Parrot
*Description:* In appearance this must surely be the least typical of all South American parrots. Its colour scheme is simple, yet extremely

beautiful. The plumage is a most attractive shade of glossy, dark green. The male has the abdomen and part of the lower breast violet; in the female this area is green. The primaries are dark blue on the outer webs; the greater under wing-coverts and the inner webs of the primaries below are verditer blue. The tail is green, tipped and edged with blue; the underside is verditer blue. The iris is dark brown and the bill is horn-white. Length: 12in, of which almost 5in is accounted for by the comparatively long, broad tail. Immature cocks have less violet on the abdomen.

*Distribution:* South-eastern Brazil from Espirito Santo to Santa Catharina. This species prefers the darkest forests, either those situated on the plains or those on the slopes of the mountains. It is said to live in pairs, feeding on berries and succulents, sometimes raiding the maize plantations nearest to the forest edge, but it is very timid and disappears into the trees at the first sign of danger.

According to João Moojen (28), its Indian name 'Sabia-cica' means a kind of thrush or robin, on account of its 'melodious, soft thrush-like song. Natives of the coastal forest region in Brazil, where the bird is found from Bahia down to Rio Grande do Sul, frequently keep them in cages as pets.

'Blue-bellied Parrots easily learn to sing new songs or to imitate the human voice, like most parrots.'

*Remarks:* This is an extremely rare parrot which has reached Britain on very, very few occasions. Probably the first was the single bird received by Hubert Astley about 1905 from Hagenbeck; a few years later one was acquired by Berlin Zoo. I can trace no other importation until the pair received by R. W. Drury of Essex about 1961. Herbert Murray imported five in about 1965, three of which are still alive and may be the only ones in Europe. A male from this importation has been in my possession for over two years.

When these birds were received by Mr Murray they were reluctant to accept the usual foods. He discovered that they relished leaves and bark, therefore every week he cut 8ft or 10ft saplings for them. They also peck at anything growing on bark and, in a large aviary will hawk flies with the circular flight of a Spotted Flycatcher. Fairly soon they accepted a normal, if somewhat limited, diet of seed, peanuts and nectar. Fruit was never touched if placed in a food dish but was occasionally eaten when hung from a perch. Hawthorn berries, elderberries and grapes were sampled.

It is interesting to note that Mr Drury's pair showed a liking for all types of fruit, including pear, apple, banana, orange and grapes.

They also acquired a taste for bread and milk sprinkled with sugar, or bread soaked in nectar; their choice of foods was certainly most catholic in comparison with that of my bird. He eats daily, in order of preference, cherries if available, pips from grapes, buds or bark from trees, and spray millet. Sunflower seed, canary seed, peanuts and nectar containing a multi-vitamin supplement are also taken. I cannot persuade him to sample any other foods, with the exception of grass roots.

I concur with Mr Murray's observation that these birds eat leaves and bark in a 'frantic' manner; anyone fortunate enough to acquire this species should ensure that plenty of branches from fruit trees are provided. My bird was for some time housed in an aviary which contained a growing plum sucker; he helped himself to the buds and leaves.

This bird dislikes sunshine intensely and always sits in the shade. This, apparently, is not an idiosyncracy of this particular bird, for Mr Drury recorded that his pair showed signs of distress if the temperature in the birdroom in which they were housed rose above 65°F. I have never owned a parrot which so obviously enjoys cold, frosty weather, as this one does – but then he can express his enjoyment in a unique manner. He sings.

His song is clear and thrush-like and consists of a few notes repeated quite loudly; he can also whistle very quietly. His voice is mellifluous indeed in comparison with other South American parrots! He sings more often in winter, especially on cold mornings.

In character he is a most delightful bird; I find him utterly fascinating and one of the favourites of my collection. He is unafraid, rather than tame, and will display when I talk to him. He fans his tail, ruffles his rather short head feathers, dilates the pupils of his large brown eyes and walks with deliberate tread along the perch, bowing low until his beak almost touches the perch. When he reaches the end of the branch he flies off and returns immediately to repeat the performance.

Most neo-tropical parrots have rather heavy bodies, but the Purple-bellied is slim and graceful and shows great manoeuvrability in flight; ideally I should like to house mine in a 40ft flight, for it is one of the few parrots which would justify an enclosure of that size.

H. Murray wrote of this species in *Cage and Aviary Birds*: 'My examples possess certain characteristics that I have never experienced in birds other than Lorikeets. This applies in particular to their playfulness.

'Several of them will get together and play, usually by finding the lowest twig which hangs from the branches that I have given them. Then, holding on to the twig with one foot, and gripping another bird with the other, they revolve very rapidly and apparently to their great enjoyment, for they flap their wings and call loudly.'

*Breeding records:* This species has yet to breed successfully in confinement. H. Murray's pair first went to nest in 1968. In February they selected a nest-box in the 8ft x 17ft shelter of an aviary 48ft x 17ft. A young bird was heard after an incubation period of about three weeks. A week later the sound ceased although the cock continued to visit the box. When the nest was inspected about six weeks later it was found to contain a chick which had died at the age of about one week.

In 1969 the pair were successful in hatching another chick in April but the nest was deserted when the aviary was broken into. At the time the cock was taking a more varied diet than normal, including grapes, spinach, chickweed and buds. The pair had to be housed on their own as they had proved very aggressive towards other birds while breeding.

They went to nest again in April 1971, again without success.

APPENDIX I

# PHOTOGRAPHING PARROTS

BEST results in photographing parrots and other aviary birds are obtained by constructing a box especially for the purpose. This has two immediate advantages. Firstly, the single perch is positioned in such a way that the subject cannot be out of focus and, secondly, the background is exactly as required, thus removing one of the main problems of photographing birds in aviaries.

Photographs 16, 19, 25, 29, 31, 33 were taken in the photographic box described here (and many of the other photographs were taken in a similar box). It was constructed from hardboard and 1in batten – but the use of plywood would be preferable. The box measures 46in long, 24in deep and 24in wide to allow the use of large subjects such as Amazon Parrots; for small birds, however, it could be half that size.

To enable the sections to fit into the boot of a car and to be quickly and easily reassembled these were screwed together and not permanently fixed. The inside was painted white, with the exception of one end and part of the sides. This can be any colour desired, to give the best effect with the bird to be photographed.

Opposite the end wall a hole was drilled to take the camera lens. The position of the hole must be carefully chosen to ensure that the subject will be completely framed by the end wall. Below this hole a shelf was fixed to take the camera; a tripod can, of course, be used if preferred.

A 60 watt bulb fixed about 12in above the lens of the camera provides the lighting. A clip above the lens hole holds the flash unit and another small hole immediately behind the flash unit takes the lead which attaches it to the camera.

To persuade the bird to leave the cage after it has been photographed is not always easy. Theoretically, when the bulb is switched off, the bird should be attracted by the light from the opened door (position immaterial), which coincides with the door of a small cage.

APPENDIX II

# MUTATIONS AND ABNORMAL COLORATION

COMPARATIVELY few mutations have been recorded in neo-tropical parrots and to the best of my knowledge only one of these has been established. The blue Quaker holds a somewhat tenuous position in aviculture but I believe that it will be bred in increasing numbers, possibly with other mutations of this parrakeet.

The mutations of which I have records are listed below; undoubtedly more exist.

| | *Mutation* | *Text reference Page* |
|---|---|---|
| Blue and Yellow Macaw | blue and white | 47 |
| *Aratinga (finschi?)* | lutino (A colour plate depicting two of these birds appears in *Living Birds of the World* by E. T. Gilliard, plate 85) | |
| Quaker Parrakeet | blue | 130 |
| | yellow | 130 |
| Lineolated Parrakeet | cinnamon | 143 |
| Celestial Parrotlet | blue | 157 |
| All Green Parrakeet | blue | 161-162 |
| Tovi Parrakeet | blue | 167 |
| Caique | lutino | |
| Bouquet's Amazon | lutino | 234 |
| Orange-winged Amazon | lutino or yellow | 242 |

| | | |
|---|---|---|
| Blue-fronted Amazon | lutino | 239 |
| | dilute (A colour plate of this bird appears in Bates and Busenbark (2)) | 239 |
| Yellow-fronted Amazon | lutino | 243 |
| Panama Yellow-fronted Amazon | blue | 246 |

Birds with scattered yellow feathers in their plumage are not uncommon. The cause, however, is not genetical but dietary, or due to age or even to shock; sometimes the reason is not evident. A Red-bellied Conure which has been in my possession for several years is, at the time of writing, moulting out with a number of scattered yellow feathers; its tail is almost completely yellow.

On two occasions I obtained birds which were quite heavily mottled with yellow. One, the cock Purple-bellied Parrot, which had been in an aviary for about three years in normal plumage, had almost pure yellow primaries. At the next moult its plumage regained its normal coloration. Another bird, a newly imported Salvin's Amazon, lost all the yellow feathers after the second moult.

# BIBLIOGRAPHY


AM = *Avicultural Magazine,* journal of the Avicultural Society
*Foreign Birds,* journal of the Foreign Bird League
*Ibis,* journal of the British Ornithological Union

| | | |
|---|---|---|
| 1 | Allen, William (1967) | *Halfmoons and Dwarf Parrots* T.F.H. Publications, Inc. |
| 2 | Bates, Henry J. and Busenbark, Robert L. (1959) | *Parrots and Related Birds* T.F.H. Publications, Inc. |
| 3 | Bates, H. W. (1863) | *A Naturalist on the Amazons* Everyman |
| 4 | Beebe, C. W. | *Two Bird Lovers in Mexico* |
| 5 | Blake, R. E. (1965) | *The Birds of Mexico* University of Chicago Press |
| 6 | Bond, James (1960) | *Birds of the West Indies* Collins |
| 7 | Bond, J. and de Schauensee, R. M. (1940) | *Proc. of the Academy of Natural Sciences of Philadelphia* |
| 8a | Boosey, E. J. | *Foreign Bird Keeping* Cage Birds |
| 8b | Boosey, E. J. (1956) | *Parrots, Cockatoos and Macaws* Barrie and Rockliff |
| 9 | Butler, Arthur G. (1910) | *Foreign Birds for Cage and Aviary,* Part II |
| 10a | Chapman, Frank M. (1917) | *Bull. American Museum of Natural History,* vol. XXXVI |
| 10b | Chapman, Frank M. (1926) | vol. LV |
| 11 | Friedmann, H. F. and Smith Foster, D., Jnr (1950) | *Proc. of National Museum* |
| 12 | Fry, Hilary C. (1970) | *Birds of the World,* part 8, vol. 4 IPC Magazines Ltd |
| 13 | Gedney, C. W. (1879) | *Foreign Cage Birds,* vol. 1 |
| 14 | Gosse, P. H. (c. 1850) | *Birds of Jamaica* |
| 15a | Gyldenstolpe, N. (1945) | *Vet. Handl.* 22, no. 3 |
| 15b | Gyldenstolpe, N. (1951) | *Arkiv för Zoolog.* Bd. 2, no. 1 |

| | | |
|---|---|---|
| 16 | Haffer, Jurgen (1970) | J. Orn., 111 |
| 17 | Hartert, E. and Venturi, S. (1909) | Novitate Zoologicae, vol. XVI |
| 18 | Haverschmidt, François (1968) | *Birds of Surinam* Oliver & Boyd |
| 19a | Hellmayr, Charles E. (1905) | Nov. Zool. vol. XII |
| 19b | Hellmayr, Charles E. (1907) | Nov. Zool. vol. XIV |
| 19c | Hellmayr, Charles E. (1910) | Nov. Zool. vol. XVII |
| 19d | Hellmayr, Charles E. (1929) | Field Museum of Nat. History and Zoology, vol. XII |
| 20 | Herklots, G. A. C. (1961) | *The Birds of Trinidad and Tobago* Collins |
| 21 | Hudson, W. H. | *Argentine Ornithology*, vol. ii |
| 22 | Immelmann, Dr Klaus (1968) | *Australian Parakeets* A.O.B. |
| 23 | Johnson, A. W. (1967) | *The Birds of Chile*, vol. ii Platt Establecimentos Gráficos, S.A. |
| 24 | Koepcke, Maria (translation 1970) | *The Birds of the Department of Lima, Peru* Livingston Publishing Co., Pa., USA |
| 25 | Land, Hugh C. (1970) | *Birds of Guatemala* Livingston Publishing Co. |
| 26 | Luke, L. P. | *Lovebirds and Parrotlets* Cage Birds |
| 27 | Monroe, B. L. and Howell, T. R. (1966) | *Occasional Papers of the Museum of Zoology*, Louisiana, no. 34 |
| 28 | Moojen, Dr João (1960) | *Pageantry of Tropical Birds* A. Zwemmer Ltd |
| 29 | Peters, J. L. (1937) | *Check-List of Birds of the World*, vol. III Harvard University Press Reprinted by Museum of Comparative Zoology, 1961 |
| 30a | Power, D. M. (1966) | *Condor* vol. 68: 562-581 |
| 30b | Power, D. M. (1967) | *Condor* vol. 69: 28-41 |
| 31 | Prestwich, A. A. (1950-54) | *Records of Parrots bred in Captivity*, A. A. Prestwich |

| | | |
|---|---|---|
| 32 | Salvadori, Count T. (1891) | *Catalogue of Birds in the British Museum*<br>British Museum, Natural History |
| 33a | Schauensee, R. Meyer de (1964) | *The Birds of Colombia*<br>Academy of Natural Sciences of Philadelphia |
| 33b | Schauensee, R. Meyer de (1966) | *The Species of Birds of South America and their Distribution* |
| 33c | Schauensee, R. Meyer de (1970) | *The Birds of South America*<br>Livingston Publishing Co. |
| 34 | Seth-Smith, David (1903) | *Parrakeets* R. H. Porter |
| 35 | Slud, Paul (1966) | *The Birds of Costa Rica*<br>Bulletin of the American Museum of Natural History |
| 36 | Snyder, Dorothy E. (1966) | *The Birds of Guyana*<br>Salem, Peabody Museum |
| 37 | Taczanowski, L. (1884-6) | Ornithologie du Pérou, vols. ii and iii |
| 38 | Tavistock, The Marquess of | *Parrots and Parrot-like Birds in Aviculture* F. V. White & Co. |
| 39a | Todd, W. E. Clyde (1925) | *Proc. Biol. Soc. Washington*, vol. 38 |
| 39b | Todd, W. E. Clyde (1947) | *Annals of Carnegie Museum*, vol. XXX |
| 40 | Traylor, M. A., Junior (1958) | *Fieldiana, Zool.*, vol. 35 |
| 41 | Vane, E. N. T. (1958) | *Guide to Lovebirds and Parrotlets*<br>Cage Birds |
| 42 | Voous, K. H. (1957) | *Studies of the Fauna of Curaçao and other Caribbean Islands*<br>vol. VII |
| 43a | Wetmore, Alexander | *Bulletin US Natural History Museum* 133: 193 |
| 43b | Wetmore, Alexander (1968) | *Birds of the Republic of Panama* part 2<br>Smithsonian Miscellaneous Collections |
| 43c | Wetmore, Alexander (1972) | *Scientific Survey of Puerto Rico and the Virgin Islands*<br>New York Academy of Sciences, vol. IX, part 4 |

## Guide to the identification of Amazons

| Species | Forehead | Lores | Cheeks | Crown |
|---|---|---|---|---|
| *collaria* | white | white | pink | slaty blue |
| *l.leucocephala* | white | rose-red | rose-red | edged black |
| *l.bahamensis* | Differs from above in brighter colouring and lacking red on breast | | | |
| *ventralis* | white | white | blue | blue |
| *(a) xantholora* | white | yellow | partly red | white and blue |
| *a.albifrons nana* | white | red | partly red | white and bluish-green |
| *agilis* | | very rich green | very rich green | |
| *v.vittata* | dark red | | | Feathers heavily edged |
| *p.pretrei* | dark red | | | Feathers heavily edged |
| *p.tucumana* | | Differs in having green instead of red at bend of wing | | |
| *a.viridigenalis* | scarlet | scarlet | bright green | scarlet and mauve |
| *a.autumnalis* | scarlet | scarlet | scarlet | edged lilac |
| *a.salvini* | scarlet | scarlet | | edged lilac |
| *a.lilacina* | scarlet | scarlet | yellowish lime-green | edged lilac and reddish |
| *a.diademata* | Differs in having cere covered with red feathers | | | green |
| *d.dufresniana* | orange | orange | mauve | Yellowish green or green |
| *d.rhodocorytha* | scarlet and yellow | yellow | skyblue to mauvish blue | edged dark red |
| *brasiliensis* | pinkish-red | pinkish-red | dull greyish-blue | pinkish-red |
| *arausiaca* | violet-blue | violet-blue | violet-blue | |
| *f.festiva* | maroon | maroon | | green or bluish |
| *f.bodini* | red | red | bluish-green or blue | |
| *xanthops* | yellow | yellow | | yellow |
| *barbadensis* | white | yellow | yellow and bluish | partly yellow |
| *a.aestiva* | blue | yellow and blue | yellow or green | |
| *a.amazonica* | blue | yellow and blue | yellow | partly yellow |
| *o.ochrocephala* | green | yellow and green | | partly yellow |
| *o.panamensis* | yellow | (principal difference) | | |
| *o.oratrix* | yellow | yellow | yellow | yellow |
| *o.auropalliata* | | | | sometimes some yellow |
| *m.mercenaria* | | | | |
| *f.farinosa* | | | | yellow |
| *f.inornata* | Differs principally in lacking yellow on crown | | | |
| *f.guatemalae* | blue | | | blue |
| *vinacea* | red | red and green | | |
| *guildingii* | white | white | blue | white and yellow |
| *versicolor* | blue | blue | bluish | bluish |
| *imperialis* | purple-blue | purple-blue | | dark green |

see text for other

| Nape feathers | Ear-coverts | Wing Speculum (red) | Red in tail | Length in ins | Other features |
|---|---|---|---|---|---|
| edged black | dark bluish-green | No | Yes | 11½ | |
| edged black | dark grey | No | Yes | 13 | upper breast Rose-red |
| edged black | black | No | Yes | 12 | red patch on abdomen |
| edged black | black | Male only | Yes | 10 | |
| edged black | green | Male only | Yes | 9½-10 | |
| | black | Yes | Yes | 10½ | |
| black | | No | Yes | 12 | |
| black | | No | Yes | 13 | |
| edged black | bright green | Yes | No | 13 | |
| | orange | Yes | No | 13½ | |
| | | Yes | No | 14 | |
| edged black | | Yes | No | 13 | Beak black |
| | | orange or yellow | Yes | 14 | |
| | | Yes | Yes | 14 | |
| | | No | No | 14 | bands of yellow and red on tip of tail |
| | | Yes | Yes | 16 | upper breast red |
| | | No | No | 14 | rump crimson |
| | | No | No | 14 | rump crimson |
| | yellow | No | Yes | 10½ | abdomen yellow |
| | bluish | Yes | Yes | 13 | |
| edged black | | Yes | Yes | 14 | |
| edged black | | Orange | Yes | 13 | |
| edged black | | Yes | Yes | 14-15 | |
| yellow | yellow | Yes | Yes | 15 | |
| yellow | | Yes | Yes | 14 | |
| feathers edged black | | Yes | Yes | 13 | outer webs tail feathers deep purple |
| greyish edged black | | Yes | No | 15 | |
| edged black | | Yes | Faintly apparent in some specimens | 15 | |
| green blue-grey and black | | Yes | Yes | 14 | purplish vinous breast |
| | | bright yellow | | | general plumage tawny brown |
| edged black | | Yes | Yes | 16-17 | red below throat most feathers heavily edged black |
| purple edged black | | Yes | No | 19 | breast purple, most feathers edged black |

sub-species

## INDEX

Main text reference is given in italics. Numbers in bold type refer to coloured illustrations.

MAPS Vegetation and Land use 63 South America 129

# INDEX TO SCIENTIFIC NAMES

Main text reference only